LOS ALAMOS

A WHISTLEBLOWER'S DIARY

LOS ALAMOS

A WHISTLEBLOWER'S DIARY

_____

CHUCK MONTANO

DESERT TORTOISE PUBLISHING, LLC

Desert Tortoise Publishing, LLC

ISBN-13: 978-0-9904212-9-0
LCCN: 2015903794

Book Design by BC

Printed in the United States of America

Since we first met in 1974, my wife, Elaine, has kept me afloat in rough seas, shined light where I needed it, and stood at my side through it all. A partner in life, soul mate for eternity; to her I dedicate this book.

CONTENTS

prologue // xi

acknowledgments // xvii

chapter 1: coming of age // 1

chapter 2: becoming a labee // 7

chapter 3: enduring // 13

chapter 4: awakening // 17

chapter 5: topper man // 21

chapter 6: death of reason // 25

chapter 7: contradictions // 33

chapter 8: time to organize // 39

chapter 9: politics and justice // 45

chapter 10: unmasking demons // 53

chapter 11: culture // 61

chapter 12: ambition // 67

chapter 13: vindication // 79

chapter 14: collateral damage // 85

chapter 15: winds of change // 93

chapter 16: monopoly money // 97

chapter 17: swamp admiral // 105

chapter 18: conjuring // 115

chapter 19: hidden dangers // 121

chapter 20: lepers and lies // 131

chapter 21: broken promises // 143

chapter 22: deceit // 149

chapter 23: outrage // 153

chapter 24: failed trust // 169

chapter 25: gagging // 175

chapter 26: becoming dilbert // 185

chapter 27: principle // 191

chapter 28: influence // 199

chapter 29: collapse // 205

chapter 30: similarities // 209

chapter 31: whistling // 225

chapter 32: "mourning" after // 231

chapter 33: musical chairs // 237

chapter 34: shell games // 247

chapter 35: stacking the deck // 257

chapter 36: cat and mouse // 265

chapter 37: smoke and mirrors // 277

chapter 38: cover-up // 283

chapter 39: buried secrets // 301

chapter 40: truth, justice, and the american way // 315

CONTENTS

chapter 41: nature of things // 319

chapter 42: legacy // 331

chapter 43: in the beginning // 337

epilogue // 347

about the author // 351

PROLOGUE

DECEMBER 31, 2010, MARKED the conclusion of my thirty-two years in Los Alamos, and it was hard to believe that for half of that time I'd been walking around with a bull's-eye pinned to my back. Now, instead of a going-away gift and slice of retirement cake, I had a legal document in hand putting to rest six wasteful years of litigation. I was to leave the Los Alamos National Laboratory (LANL) for good, quietly . . . just disappear. One day in my work cubicle, the next day gone. No one could talk about it, or at least not yet.

I'd managed to remain in the lab's good graces for more than a decade and a half, but whistleblowing wasn't tolerated. And those who dared to were destined to be driven out of the institution, litigated into bankruptcy, or worse. Official resistance to resolving my complaint lasted years. It hadn't mattered how much my torment had cost taxpayers in terms of legal expenses, so long as the University of California (UC), the lab's parent, was spared any liability.

The university provided a facade of academic legitimacy that the military-industrial complex used to its own advantage.

Because of this role, protecting UC was akin to preserving the status quo. That was job number one. And as for the US Department of Energy (DOE), which was supposed to be administering the federal contract that enabled UC to "manage" LANL, it was the toothless guard dog of taxpayer interests. The department hardly ever barked, much less bit, when it came to the university or the federal labs under its watch.

My whistleblower complaint, filed in 2005, had exposed significant shortcomings in LANL leadership, including managerial malfeasance that enabled fraud, waste, and abuse to occur. A related revelation was the mysterious death of the deputy director—the laboratory's second-in-command, and whether he might be posthumously implicated in a procurement fraud that two internal sleuths—Glenn Walp and Steve Doran—were investigating in 2002. Both were seasoned law enforcement professionals, hired by LANL in response to a congressional mandate. But within the year they'd been fired for refusing to ignore problems they'd uncovered at the lab.

It had been six years since I'd filed my whistleblower retaliation complaint and now, all of a sudden, institutional leadership's determination to make an example of me had softened. A private investigator's report was the reason, for within days after it was introduced into evidence my claims were being resolved. Settling had shielded officials from having to testify in court regarding the subject of the investigation—circumstances surrounding the mysterious death of the deputy director.

"Dysfunctional and politically untouchable" was how Senator Pete Domenici, our senior US senator from New Mexico, described LANL in a July 25, 2004, *Los Angeles Times* article. It wasn't the institution I'd envisioned growing up in Northern New Mexico.

Los Alamos is on the east side of the Jemez mountain range overlooking the fertile Española Valley and New Mexico's largest river—the Rio Grande (big river). For time immemorial the Pajarito (little bird) watershed, upon which Los Alamos is perched, has sustained the river's flow. For thousands of years Native American communities have relied on it; for centuries thereafter so have descendants of Juan de Oñate's 1598 Spanish expedition into New Mexico. Now, thirsty farms and cities situated along its entire length rely on it as well.

The pine- and aspen-decorated Jemez mountain range, along with the pinion and juniper tree-covered Pajarito Plateau, were the result of ancient volcanic eruptions, the most recent one occurring perhaps 50,000–60,000 years earlier. A telling reminder of this violent past is evident in the twelve-mile-wide Valles Caldera—a volcanic depression located about ten miles west of town. In 1990, while watching the 10:00 p.m. news, I was reminded that related geologic forces were still in play. I heard what sounded and felt like a sonic boom on steroids, followed seconds later by another window-rattling event. The source of the commotion was a quake measuring 4.2 on the Richter scale.

At night, a half hour drive south of Los Alamos, the flickering lights of Santa Fe, the state's capital, can be seen. Sixty miles farther is the state's largest city, Albuquerque. A mere fifty miles north of Los Alamos, as the crow flies, is the tourist destination of Taos, home to the historic Taos Pueblo. In fact, nearly all of the state's nineteen Indian pueblos are located within a hundred-mile radius of the lab's forty-square-mile nuclear reservation, parts still considered sacred by Native Americans.

Much of the land needed to establish Los Alamos, which was founded in 1943 and subsequently populated with the finest minds in physical science and engineering, was obtained by force. Thirty-three homesteading families were displaced in the process. Nearby Pueblo lands were taken as well. The secret wartime effort code-named the Manhattan Project, followed by the fifty-year Cold War with the Soviet Union, enabled such abuses to occur in the name of national security.

The Manhattan Project gave birth to the atomic bomb and to the world's first scientific community—Los Alamos, the quintessential company town. Until 1957 guard towers, fences, and armed soldiers kept Los Alamos isolated from the world. But there were other ways to keep people apart too—barriers imposed by economics, privilege, social standing, and politics. Los Alamos received federal subsidies for such things as housing, roads, fire protection, security, energy, water, and other public services normally funded with local revenue bonds and property taxes. And while surrounding school districts were perpetually burdened with needs far outpacing available resources, the Los Alamos schools easily invested twice the New Mexico average per student, with the aid of a multi-million-dollar federal subsidy they received.

Over the course of the lab's seventy-year history, virtually all the educational and economic advantages associated with LANL remained centered in Los Alamos, referred to by many from nearby communities as "the Hill." Household incomes were three times the state average. By the '90s Los Alamos was being touted in national publications as having the most millionaires per capita in the country. Yet surrounding towns were among the poorest. In 2013, the Annie E. Casey Foundation, an organization dedicated to helping build better futures for children, ranked New Mexico as the worst state for a child's well-being.

I grew up in Santa Fe, and was fortunate to have had both parents with me through my childhood. My father was a workaholic, rarely getting a day to rest, and when I wasn't in school I was at his side . . . working. So I never had much time to get into trouble while growing up, plus my mother was intolerant of dishonesty, once forcing me, as a young boy, to return an apple I'd taken from a neighbor's tree without permission. My wife, raised fifteen minutes farther east, came from similar rootstock.

I grew up as the Cuban Missile Crisis and other Cold War dramas unfolded before my eyes. It was a time of citizen alerts and bomb shelter hysteria. The nation had been conditioned to believe the Soviet Union was itching to drop "the bomb" on us, and we, in turn, were forever poised to return the favor. Mutually assured destruction (MAD) was the strategy, which essentially meant pointing guns at each other's heads as a deterrent to anyone actually squeezing the trigger. This was the nightmare scenario that invaded my thoughts as a child, a world Los Alamos played the lead role in creating.

In 1971, while employed by the US Comptroller of the Currency auditing federal banks in Wyoming, I received my first security designation. In 1978, a move to Los Alamos to begin working at the lab meant providing our son and daughter access to one of the best public school systems in the state. This was the main reason for us settling and residing on the Hill for the next twenty years. Our children went on to earn college degrees, perhaps proof that the decision to raise them there was a smart one. But cancer rates were extraordinarily high in Los Alamos, so only the passage of time would determine whether we'd been right in deciding to stay.

December 31, 2010, was my last day as a LANL employee. The following day, my fifty-ninth birthday, marked the start of the rest of my life without a laboratory badge or security clearance. As I was nearing what I'd always envisioned would be my final decade of employment, I was now unemployed and facing the worst economy since the Great Depression. A job search for anyone, much less someone my age, would be daunting. Besides, what employer would ever want to hire a whistleblower?

Maybe I'd been unrealistic believing I could make a difference, perhaps too idealistic for my own good. Regardless, after four decades of continuous employment it felt weird no longer being tethered to an 8:00 to 5:00 job . . . or to the Los Alamos National Laboratory.

[Chuck] Montaño sued for retaliation in 2005 and settled with the lab about a year ago. The terms of the settlement are that he can't disclose the terms—ever—unless subpoenaed by a congressional committee or ordered to do so by a court of law. (Carol Clark, "Whistleblower Tells His Story," *Los Alamos Monitor*, January 18, 2012)

ACKNOWLEDGMENTS

IT'S DIFFICULT TO IMAGINE completing this book without the many who've offered me their kind advice, encouragement, and editing assistance from beginning to end, and the sacrifices of whistleblowers like Dr. Glenn Walp, who stand out as shining examples of what is still promising and good in people. In addition I want to thank Joanna Reiff, Joni Arends, Chris Mechels, Joe Gutierrez, Jay Coghlan, Bob Ortiz, Stephanie Hiller, and my attorney Lynne Bernabei. Lynne never wavered in her courage, focus, and determination to achieve justice, or hesitate in her willingness to confront the challenges that others considered insurmountable.

I also wish to acknowledge the important work of government whistleblower advocacy groups like the Project on Government Oversight (POGO) and the Government Accountability Project (GAP), plus the valuable contributions of journalists and columnists whose reporting makes it possible for whistleblowers to survive under very difficult circumstances, and among them being: New Mexico's Kathleen Parker, Adam Rankin, Keith Easthouse, David Roybal, Carol Clark, John Fleck, Jose Armas,

Wren Abbot, Ian Hoffman, Roger Snodgrass, Barbara Ferry, Doug McClellan, nationally syndicated columnist Jack Anderson, Pulitzer Prize winner Glenn Greenwald, *Democracy Now* "real news" host Amy Goodman, and network TV investigative reporter extraordinaire Sharyl Attkisson.

In today's world, which is increasingly dominated by those with a vested interest in keeping people misinformed and under perpetual surveillance, whistleblowers and journalists represent the last line of defense in the epic and ongoing struggle to preserve the democracy our forefathers intended for each and every one of us, and for future generations . . . a gift we can no longer take for granted, or assume will always be.

1

COMING OF AGE

On Friday, the nuclear weapons facility agreed to pay
$2.8 million—the largest settlement involving a labor
dispute in the lab's history. . . . "We consider this not only
a clear victory, but a CLER victory," said Chuck Montaño, president of Citizens for LANL Employee Rights
[CLER]. (Ray Rivera, "In Newest Settlement, Laid-Off
LANL Workers Will Get $2.8 Million," *Santa Fe New
Mexican*, May 16, 1998)

"JOHN, I DIDN'T GROW up wanting to be an activist or intent
on biting the hand that feeds my family . . . The lab made me
who I am." I'd said this in a meeting with then–LANL director
John Browne. We were discussing my advocating for laboratory
workers who'd been unjustly laid off.

Citizens for LANL Employee Rights (CLER) had been
established in 1995 by workers slated for termination in a
controversial layoff. I was not among those targeted, but
assisted in their organizing; plus I was voted by the group to be

their spokesperson and leader in the grassroots movement that ensued. And in the three years leading up to our settlement, I'd lost my lifelong reputation for being unassuming and compliant. Among those reporting our historic achievement was the *Albuquerque Journal North*:

> The lab will pay $625,000 to employees to settle. . . . [T]he lab also agreed to rehire a fourth of the workers, retrain others, and pay nearly $2.8 million to end a second suit brought by the same workers. . . . A Labor Department official stressed something that's worth repeating: "With its billion-dollar budget and high visibility, LANL should be a paragon of fairness in hiring, setting the example for both other government agencies and private business." . . . It's a sorry chapter in the history of LANL and Northern New Mexico. (Editorial: "Settlements a New Beginning?" *Albuquerque Journal North*, May 24, 1998)

I'd grown up quiet and, according to some, was somewhat of an introvert. But as an adult, being in the public eye had become an unavoidable consequence of my idealism. I cared about people, not about politicians and their politics. Nor did I crave the media attention that came with advocacy. But that's where I'd ended up.

My first introduction to Los Alamos came through my father, a dozen years before I moved my family there in 1978. His struggle on earth, and fear that I might follow in his footsteps, ultimately brought me back.

Like most men of his generation, my dad enlisted in the military, serving during the Korean War. Afterward, he settled into a life working in the construction trades. During the week he worked as a mason for home builders in the newly established Los Alamos bedroom community of White Rock, which was being built for LANL. On weekends I came along to help him tack chicken wire to exterior walls of houses slated to be plastered the following week. It was hard work for a boy, harder still for a man who knew this was what he'd be doing the rest of his life. My father's limited education reduced his options and would ultimately shorten his life. Later on, my father was diagnosed with scleroderma, a disease of the connective tissues that was associated with prolonged exposure to the outdoors. His fight for survival ended before his sixtieth birthday.

All of White Rock's streets were new—freshly paved, unlike the washboard dirt roads common in nearby villages. Homes in different phases of construction could be seen sprouting up in all directions. Completed homes, with brick facades facing front yards newly landscaped with lawns and trees, had families moving in within days of completion.

For decades, living within one's means had been the norm for most rural Americans, including Northern New Mexicans. Yet by the late 1950s, television was leading the charge to change those old-fashioned habits of thrift and planning. Living rooms in homes across America were being saturated with images of perfect families living perfect lives in perfect homes built-in perfect communities, with commercials forever selling new and improved products promising to make life better for everyone. Of course, easy financing would make it all possible.

I learned early on that people on the Hill, including those residing in the lab's bedroom community of White Rock, were highly educated, and I sensed that working at the laboratory had something to do with their lifestyle. Outside of Los Alamos, I'd never been in a completed home, nor had I seen any home that wasn't at least partially, if not entirely, made from adobe (mud brick). Plus the notion of an enclosed space for a car was foreign to me. Compared with the dry, earth-toned landscapes common to the region, Los Alamos was different. It was cradled within tree-covered mountains, and felt cooler and appeared greener than anywhere I'd been. While nearby towns were centuries old, the growing community on the hill was the newest in the state.

By the late '60s the antiwar and civil rights movements were firmly established in universities across the nation, including my small college campus, which was located about an hour's drive northeast of Santa Fe. The GI Bill gave Vietnam veterans access to higher learning, and they were among those leading the charge for societal change. It was an amazing time . . . a learning experience that went far beyond classroom teaching, and when I first heard the phrase "military-industrial complex."

Many of the returning servicemen had emotional and physical injuries, including my first-year college roommate, a gentle soul from New York State who'd survived a mine explosion while in 'Nam. He'd kept his limbs, but extensive shrapnel burns on his arms and back justified the nightmares that made him talk and sweat profusely in his sleep. He got little rest, had difficulty concentrating because of it, and didn't return after winter break.

I met Mike through his freshman year roommate. His roomie was an acquaintance of mine from high school—a nice guy, but lacking in focus to do well in college. Because of it he lasted only one semester. Mike, on the other hand, was determined to succeed. He, like me, was the first in his family to attempt university learning. We shared a blue-collar heritage, and were in need of second-year roommates, so we became roomies our sophomore year.

At first glance Mike was carefree. Two of his most endearing qualities were his sense of humor and ready smile. He grew up a couple of hours away, in the "hidden science community" on the Hill. Whenever he spoke about it, he'd turn uncharacteristically solemn. His parents had moved him and his two siblings to Los

Alamos after his father gained steady employment at the lab. With the new job came hope for a better life. It was a typical story for the times—Northern New Mexicans were frequently recruited from nearby villages and towns to provide maintenance and construction labor for the laboratory, as well as cooking and housekeeping help for the growing number of educated professionals recruited from everywhere else.

Mike's family settled in a part of the community known as the Denver Steel subdivision, where small modular homes were trucked in for quick assembly on small lots. They weren't anything like the houses I'd seen constructed in White Rock, which was just a few miles away. None came with garages. As a result, the streets in Mike's neighborhood were perpetually lined with cars.

Status, according to Mike, meant everything in Los Alamos, and what you lived in said something about your place in the community . . . and the lab. I didn't want to believe him at the time, but years later I learned this for myself while being introduced to a Los Alamos church congregation. There were three new families being shepherded in that day, mine being one. Each family had a church member as a sponsor, and each sponsor proceeded to introduce family members in terms of professional credentials, universities they attended, LANL titles, and related job duties. Mike was right.

Even before Los Alamos became an open community—no longer closed to those not cleared for entry—housing was a government-issued perk linked to status. Those with greater perceived value to the laboratory were given better housing. Theoretical physicists were at the top of the pyramid, chemists and engineers were near the middle, and everyone else moved into a Denver Steel unit or commuted from nearby communities to work at LANL. Thus, from the beginning, lab duties and rank had been a litmus test in the community, and Northern New

Mexicans, as a general rule, never measured up in the minds of those doing the measuring. Such preconceived notions and judgments can leave people scarred, and this was the world Mike had grown up in. What he described was a strain between people and cultures, a tension existing since the laboratory's founding. But when he reminisced about friends he'd made in Los Alamos, his cheerful demeanor would return. All across the nation the gulf that separated people by background and upbringing was narrowing, and attitudes toward others were being reshaped by a younger, more open-minded generation. This was happening on the Hill as well, albeit at a much slower pace due to its unique demographics, history, extreme isolation, and privilege.

After graduating from college, Mike moved to California. When he returned to New Mexico for a visit, we'd reconnect. It appeared he'd found his niche, far away from the difficult times he'd had growing up. He seemed happy, so much so that I was shocked one day to learn that he'd moved back to Los Alamos. As we sat in the car listening to music, he explained his return. It was about his family, and about making more money working at the laboratory than he was making in California. On top of that, his cost of living was negligible since he lived with his parents. He planned to remain there until he could save enough to buy his own place . . . a plan rooted in necessity and practicality. Suddenly a tune playing on the radio grabbed his attention. "That's my favorite song," he blurted out. Our conversation stopped, and we both listened. It was "Baker Street" by Gerry Rafferty—a ballad about a town he characterized as "cold" and as having "no soul." Rafferty lamented that he'd been wrong thinking it "held everything," perhaps happiness as well. The lyrics were painful, saying something about Mike that I failed to grasp at that moment, and that would haunt me for the rest of my life.

2

BECOMING A LABEE

MIKE AND I STOPPED hanging out once I got married, but now and again we'd still touch base. When he called in early 1978, it had been a while since I'd heard from him. There was an entry-level opening in the laboratory unit where he worked, and according to him it was right up my alley. I'd graduated with honors from college, my undergraduate focus being accounting and math, and had worked for Peat, Marwick, Mitchell & Co., the world's largest public accounting firm at the time, as well as for the US Comptroller of the Currency as a federal bank auditor. All this, in Mike's view, would put me at the front of the line for the position in question.

The job was in the Special Nuclear Material (SNM) Safeguards Group. I'd be accounting for grams of material instead of dollars and cents, tracking the movement of items containing SNM and conducting physical inventories to ensure everything was where it was supposed to be. The Manhattan Project era was still fresh in people's minds, and I knew there was an associated prestige with being a LANL employee. To be tied to that history, and the mystique surrounding atomic science and nuclear technology, was enticing. I submitted my job application with hopes of at least being granted an interview.

Many weeks went by before Mike called to tell me the interview process had begun. "Have you been contacted?" he asked.

"No," I responded. "What should I do?"

"You should call the lab's Equal Employment Office (EEO)," he said. His experience growing up on the Hill had made him wary. LANL managers there were known for playing favorites with friends and relatives.

In 1978, one the most important cases on the United States Supreme Court's docket was the *Regents of the University of California v. Bakke.* Allan Bakke, an engineer in his early thirties, had twice been denied admission to the UC medical school. This led him to challenge the university's practice of setting aside openings for qualified applicants from underrepresented groups. He characterized it as creating "quotas" for others who may be "less qualified," arguing that this violated the Equal Protection Clause of the Fourteenth Amendment of the Constitution. The high court ruled in his favor, thus establishing "reverse discrimination" as a valid claim.

Affirmative steps could no longer be taken to adjust for the lasting effects of centuries of past discrimination. Good-faith effort had become the standard; tangible results, more or less, were optional. The death knell for equal opportunity enforcement was sounding, but I'd managed to get in under the wire. I was finally granted an interview, which was all I wanted . . . a chance to present myself and my abilities to the hiring manager for consideration.

The interview went well, and my official start date as a lab employee ("labee") was June 5, 1978. My new boss was in his mid-fifties, wore thick glasses, and was always nursing a cup of coffee or lit cigarette with ash dangling precariously from its tip. His first name was Munson, but everyone called him Whitey due to his albino-like complexion and hair. He, like virtually all in charge at LANL, had been recruited to New Mexico from elsewhere. Yet he seemed to fit in well, and not just with those of a similar background, but with everyone.

Whitey commanded respect by giving it . . . and through example, as opposed to his title and rank. He was a special kind of leader; a chemist by training who somewhere along the line got involved with plutonium (Pu), and was now in charge of the lab's Special Nuclear Material Safeguards Group. Since the group's function was to ensure all items containing SNM were properly accounted for, this included Pu, which was held in processing streams designed to concentrate the plutonium, extract it from liquid, refine it into metal, and then fabricate into precise cannonball shapes called "pits." At each step in a process samples of the material were taken for chemical assessment and nondestructive assay. The objective was to maintain quality control, and to avoid conditions that could lead to a critical event—a sudden and intense burst of radiation.

Along each step in the process or experiment, plutonium and other SNM got left behind. It was hidden in pipes, equipment, walls, vents, and ductwork; or it was captured in filters, chemical sludge, oil, gloves, rags, tools, and other materials that were used. The difference between what went in a process and what came out the other end, and could not be found in waste, was called MUF—Material Unaccounted For. The bulk of MUF was associated with holdup, the stuff left behind somewhere. But some also ended up in the environment, and in those working with these materials.

Before I began my new job my body had to be evaluated. Lying on a gurney in a lead-lined vault, which was in a basement situated next door to the community hospital, I was instructed to relax and lie still for about an hour. Radiation detectors were strategically positioned all around me. The lights were turned off and soft music began playing. The evaluation was something every labee who might come into contact with radioactive material was required to undergo. The objective was to obtain a baseline reading of how much of the stuff was already in the individual's body, perhaps from aboveground nuclear weapons tests or some other source. When an employee left the lab, or at least stopped working in areas where SNM was in use, a similar evaluation would show whether there was any measureable increase. If so, at that point, the labee was a walking, talking repository of MUF.

For those working with radioactive material on a more sustained basis, additional monitoring was needed. Those employees, including myself, were required to wear detection badges throughout the day that contained materials used to measure exposure to different types of radiation. The badges were turned in monthly for analysis and replacement. On a monthly or quarterly cycle, we were required to provide urine for evaluation as well, while those working most closely with SNM also provided stool samples every so often.

Six months after starting my employment, I was sitting in the office Mike and I shared. With Christmas just days away, the holiday mood was in full swing. Even though I'd been at work for over an hour that morning, Mike still hadn't arrived. Perhaps he wasn't coming in, but normally he'd call to let someone know. The roads were icy; traffic was backed up around town. Suddenly Whitey walked in, appearing flushed, with tears welling up in his eyes. "It's Mike," he said, pulling off his glasses to wipe his eyes. "He's dead."

A week later my fellow pallbearers and I laid my former college roommate to rest for eternity. The cemetery was situated atop a hill in La Madera, New Mexico. Off in the distance I could see the snow-covered Jemez Mountains, where Los Alamos lay hidden in the trees. While walking back to the car, tears began clouding my vision. I was struggling to understand what had happened, and why.

Mike was on his way to work the morning of his death. The streets were packed with snow, and while driving he'd slid off the road. In the middle of the morning rush a police officer had requested that Mike walk a straight line, singling him out for a sobriety test. Everyone knew everyone else in the community, and it was likely that Mike had been spotted, in broad daylight, on the side of the road that morning, perhaps by people he'd grown up with, or maybe by a colleague from work. Rumor and judgment would surely follow—nothing unusual for a small company town like Los Alamos. But Mike had spent his childhood battling the preconceived notions of others, and now this. Instead of continuing to work, he returned home. When authorities found him, he had his hunting rifle at his side.

Mike was a dear friend.

3

ENDURING

IT WAS DIFFICULT TO keep coming into work each day after what had happened to Mike. But Whitey was patient, truly caring about all his employees. Thus, when news of his condition broke a couple of years later, I was devastated.

For a large part of his career, Whitey had worked with radioactive material. He was a heavy smoker and voracious coffee drinker as well; surely that didn't help. But he wasn't elderly, so it came as a shock to learn he'd been diagnosed with an aggressive form of cancer. Where it started was in question, but before it completed its deadly mission it was discovered throughout his entire body. Cancer is a horrible way to leave this world, beginning as it does by ravaging a person's body into submission, and ending by consuming that person's will to live.

A few of us in the office volunteered to take Whitey to his chemo sessions ninety miles away in Albuquerque, using personal vacation time and sick leave for that purpose. At first there was a glimmer of hope, as there always is. In the beginning, it's about maintaining a positive attitude in the face of insurmountable odds, and the prospect of a miracle. But as time passes and bad turns to worse, hope begins to fade. That, too, is part of the process.

One day, toward the end, I was driving Whitey back from therapy when he broke down in tears, confessing that he knew his life was at its end. His loved ones and their welfare were his only concerns at that point. In his day of reckoning, I understood that our lives are measured not by our titles or possessions, but by the effect we have on others.

Whitey, too, was a dear friend.

His successor was a transplant from Lawrence Livermore National Laboratory (LLNL) in Livermore, California. He was morbidly obese, and had the habit of lowering his head to peer over his glasses at the person sitting across from him. One day, as some of my colleagues and I sat in his office, he announced that inspectors from the US Department of Energy were slated to visit. Our job, as he saw it, was to "run interference." Run interference?

A few weeks later we were doing our annual physical inventory of special nuclear material (SNM). This entailed visiting every LANL site storing or working with SNM (i.e., plutonium, uranium, and any other exotic variety of atoms federal law required accounting for). Every mesa and canyon seemed to have a site utilizing special nuclear materials. Because of this, chemical and radiological contamination was a plague throughout the Pajarito Plateau, plus a corresponding threat to the watershed that supplied the state's largest river at its base.

Area G is a laboratory waste disposal site, situated on the lab's southwestern boundary, on one of the many Pajarito Plateau finger mesas formed after eons of volcanic eruptions. Bounded on the south by the community of White Rock and on the east by San Ildefonso Pueblo land, this is where SNM-contaminated waste is sent to be packaged for storage, or for transport elsewhere. And, when appropriate, for disposal.

LANL was required to do both an assessment to establish the quantity of regulated material recoverable from the waste, and a related analysis to determine the cost benefit of initiating recovery. What wasn't worthy of recovering was tossed into unlined dirt pits, shafts, and trenches in Area G. A private citizen could be fined for dumping used motor oil on the ground, but it seemed okay for LANL to dispose of radioactive waste into the soil—waste that could remain hazardous for thousands of years. It made no sense, except for the fact that it was cheaper to do this . . . at least in the short run.

As I stood surveying one of the waste disposal sites with an SNM custodian at my side, I noticed a barely used piece of equipment sticking out of the rubble. "What's that all about?" I asked. It was a huge forklift contaminated with plutonium. Someone had decided it was more cost effective to get rid of it than to clean it up. Plus a new federal mandate was about to require the laboratory to account for everything ending up in Area G, meaning that a paper trail would have to be maintained for whatever was being disposed of there, and why. According to the site custodian, a LANL-wide directive was issued, instructing managers to get rid of things before the new law went into effect. It was easier and cheaper to discard the contaminated stuff now; plus the rationale for trashing things was less likely to be questioned without a permanent record someone could evaluate later.

I stood there stunned by what I'd just learned. There was enough contaminated trash buried in Area G to fill up the Empire State Building, literally, and the community of White Rock was a short five miles away as the dust flies. Unlined and uncapped holes in the ground were being used to get rid of radioactive waste, and without reliable records nothing could be proved. If sidestepping accountability was the desired end, then perhaps "running interference" was a logical means for doing so, but it wasn't right.

4

AWAKENING

I LEFT THE SNM Safeguards Group in 1982 to join the laboratory's financial accounting organization, and a couple of years later received an unplanned $1,400-per-year salary increase. A group called the American GI Forum had filed a complaint years earlier with the Office of Federal Contract Compliance Programs (OFCCP) of the US Department of Labor, alleging systemic bias in LANL employment practices. Judging others by ancestry or by physical characteristics that have nothing to do with their ability is the essence of discrimination, yet the OFCCP investigation produced evidence that something along these lines was going on. It was a concern I'd heard others discuss in hushed tones, including those who'd been with LANL much longer than me. Perhaps the unanticipated pay raise, at this point, signaled an institutional commitment to equitable treatment and, if so, an enlightened leadership capable of embracing it. That was my hope.

My job in the mid-1980s was to bring the laboratory's financial accounting systems up to date. After a few years of doing this, the chance to join the University of California's Los Alamos internal audit team presented itself. But by 1992 the university was no longer in charge of the laboratory's audit effort, and in 1994 a new position called a cost accounting team lead appeared in LANL's job listings. With sixteen years of seniority under my belt, and a recently earned professional certification that deemed me a "subject matter expert" in cost accounting, I thought it was a perfect opportunity for me.

When the rejection came I was disappointed, but not surprised. This wasn't the first time I'd been passed over for a promotion; there was always someone "better qualified" for the job. From the start of my LANL career, I'd been told by human resources personnel, and individuals in lab management, that without advanced education it would be difficult to get ahead. In response I enrolled at the University of New Mexico, earning a graduate degree in the process. But then I was told it wasn't enough, that I needed to be professionally certified as well to be competitive. So I studied and took tests for years, and eventually garnered four professional designations. But after earning all these credentials my bids for advancement were still being rejected, and I wasn't even being granted the courtesy of an interview. To make matters worse, those chosen over me often possessed much less in terms of education, seniority, or experience. It had taken me nearly two decades to reach this point—to finally accept what Mike had warned me about from the start. Credentials, he said, *did* matter, but what really counted at the lab was being a friend or relative of someone in charge. According to him, officials doing the hiring favored the acquaintances of other managers, the expectation being that the "courtesy" of extending their friends and relatives preferential treatment would be returned in the future. This, in essence, was the underlying reason for the OFCCP's adverse determination against LANL in the early '80s.

The person chosen over me this time had been with the laboratory less than a year; prior to that he was a manager at a hamburger franchise. As was so often the case in Los Alamos, he was a friend of a friend—which, in turn, made him the candidate of choice. This was the last straw, after sixteen years of my hoping things would improve on their own. It was time to complain.

The Human Resources (HR) Division was responsible for responding to employee complaints, but it worked closely with the LANL legal office for one reason—to protect the institution from being sued. This resulted in an investigative process heavily weighted toward gathering information for use in the lab's defense, versus getting to the truth. It took months to get a determination, but HR eventually ruled in my favor, despite pressure from the lab legal. HR concluded that "what looked and sounded like a duck" must, therefore, be a duck, meaning that the evidence of favoritism and bias was overwhelming. But one final hurdle still remained—Siegfried (Sig) Hecker, the LANL director. Hecker, according to the human resources department, needed to concur with determinations that favored employees, but not so for rulings that went against them. It was a bizarre process, likely insisted upon by lawyers.

Sig Hecker was a widely recognized plutonium researcher before becoming the Los Alamos director. He was of Austrian descent and his father, it was rumored, had been an unwilling accomplice of the Nazis during WWII. Because of that history Hecker, like few others, should have known what it was like to be at the mercy of tyrannical authority. I was hopeful, but upon receiving his decision was sorely disappointed. He seemed to reject outright the notion that someone less qualified could be chosen for advancement in Los Alamos, thus ignoring entirely HR's determination of facts. It was appalling, that the results of a thorough investigation could be wiped away by the whims of a single individual, but this was Los Alamos, and the rules that applied elsewhere didn't necessarily apply at LANL.

In the early '80s the OFCCP determined that laboratory employment practices were deeply flawed, but more than a decade later and the ruling had done little to effect change in the attitudes or behavior of those in charge. Hecker's focus had been to maintain deniability for the institution, despite the human resources department's findings or recommendations. This was a management strategy mapped out for lab leaders by institutional attorneys, rooted in the fact that taxpayers will be required to finance it no matter what, and in the reality that the US Department of Energy will make certain of it.

5

TOPPER MAN

EVER SINCE ARRIVING IN Los Alamos, I'd been a community volunteer. I'd wanted to avoid the stereotyping Mike had seen while growing up there, where people assume things simply because they don't know you. But the town was a reflection of the lab—the same attitudes that governed LANL were mirrored in the community.

In 1994, at about the time the laboratory director rejected the HR determination in my favor, I was serving on the high school governing board when a parent approached me with a concern. It had to do with a mural painted on the school's gymnasium wall. It was an image of Topper Man, the school mascot. The glaring giant stood on a mountain, both arms extended as though simultaneously laying claim and blocking access to the secretive community on the hill. But on closer scrutiny the parent noticed something—the two middle fingers on the right hand were pressed tightly together, and the two outer fingers were spread noticeably apart. It looked like the letter *W*. This, according to the parent, signified "white power." It was a shocking interpretation, but I needed to convince myself it had validity. When my daughter arrived home from school that evening, I asked if she'd ever heard anything unusual about the mural in question.

"Oh," she said. "Are you talking about the white power thing?"

"What?" I responded. "Do you mean to tell me you know about that?"

"Everyone does," my daughter answered, revealing that she and a group of her classmates had visited with the principal at the start of the year about the matter, but nothing had come of it. I'd first met the principal while serving as one of two parent volunteers on the middle school governing council. Having worked with her for years, I was surprised she hadn't taken the concern seriously.

When my son arrived a few minutes later, I asked the same question—had he heard anything unusual about the mural?

"You mean the white power symbol?" he said.

"Why didn't you ever tell me about this?" I asked.

"I don't pay attention to it," he countered.

It seemed that young minds were being conditioned, by the image of Topper Man, to view discrimination as an inevitable part of life. Was this the Los Alamos school system of Mike's youth? Was this the world we still lived in? I needed more confirmation. My wife, who was the nurse in charge of the gastroenterology lab at the hospital, had an assistant who'd graduated from the local school system years earlier. I was curious about what she thought, and within a couple of days I found out. Not only did she share the same interpretation of the mural; it had been viewed that way, within the community, for the past dozen years.

My meeting with the principal was cordial, but she immediately downplayed the issue, even after I insisted that the problem was real, given the effect it was having on students and parents. She offered to discuss the matter with the district superintendent, to see what his take was. It took a couple of weeks to receive the final word, and it wasn't what I'd hoped. The mural, she explained, wasn't intended to be divisive, and the superintendent agreed with that view. Thus, nothing needed to be done. But intent wasn't the issue, I countered. Perception was, and the fix, I suggested, was simple—repaint the two middle fingers so they wouldn't be pressed so tightly together.

Schools across the country were banning professional football team attire from campus. Even religious symbols on T-shirts were being prohibited because of perceived gang associations. I reminded the principal of this, but she remained steadfast in her refusal to do anything. It was the same message and attitude I'd received from the director at the lab, and it had nothing to do with fairness. It was all about dominance—what Mike experienced growing up in Los Alamos. It was a controlling mind-set among those in authority, and now my own children were being subjected to it.

6

DEATH OF REASON

THE BERLIN WALL BEGAN crumbling in June 1990. By
December 1991 the Soviet Union had collapsed, and a national
debate had begun regarding the need to dramatically reduce US
defense commitments and expenditures in the aftermath. And
so with the end of the Cold War officials were left scrambling
to find a new mandate for the Los Alamos National Laboratory,
one that could sustain its funding for decades to come. By 1994
public meetings were being held by the Department of Energy
to solicit community input on the matter and, at the same time,
to stir up public support for keeping the lab's funding intact. A
few weeks earlier, I'd been sitting in the high school principal's
office appealing for her to address the concerns parents and students alike had with the Topper Man mural. Now I was standing
before the public and the DOE in one of those hearings.

I took a photo of the Los Alamos High School mascot and
placed it on view foil—a transparent film used to display images
on a screen or, in this case, a wall. A few members of the audience
gasped, apparently aware of the hidden meaning. I explained
the problem with the mural, equating the image to the mind-

set of some in lab leadership, and the related problems workers were having because of that attitude. A few people approached me afterward, thanking me for what I'd done. A couple of news reporters came over as well. Standing near the building's exit, apparently waiting to intercept me as I left, was a Department of Energy official. He introduced himself and asked where, precisely, the mural was located. I answered him, clarifying as well that I was not just speaking for myself, but that I was one of two parent-representatives on the high school governing council. I explained that the matter had been brought to my attention by another parent, and had been confirmed by students. He shook his head, clearly bothered by it all.

According to local news reports the next day, someone from the DOE phoned the high school principal that night, got her out of bed, and insisted the mural be fixed within twenty-four hours. Otherwise, the Los Alamos schools would lose the nearly $10 million in annual subsidies provided by the DOE. What I failed to accomplish through years of community service and two meetings with the principal, the Energy Department did with one phone call.

By the time reporters arrived the next morning, the change was made. What they found was a giant poised atop a mountain, still glaring down at the world, but with two middle fingers missing.

"I thank the DOE for what they did. I thank them very dearly," said [local resident Dora] Warwick. . . . When her family moved here a year ago, they were shocked by the hand signal—a gesture interpreted as the letter W made in a mural of the Los Alamos mascot Topper Man, she said. She has seen white supremacists make the gesture on television, she said. (Kathleen Parker, "Topper Man and the Message," *Santa Fe New Mexican*, January 3, 1995)

It didn't take long for retaliation to begin at the laboratory. Audits I'd been working on were suddenly put in limbo and then, after weeks of being kept idle, I received a new assignment. I was to "reengineer" the audit effort, essentially reinvent the audit wheel. Reengineering—the latest corporate craze—was a concept rooted in manufacturing. The idea was that if there was a better way of doing things, those working on the production line were best suited to determine where and how to change things—hence, the importance of involving them in the decision.

With respect to auditing, the rules—namely the standards— were mandated by professional groups like the Association of Certified Public Accountants, the Institute of Internal Auditors, and the Association of Certified Fraud Examiners. Thus, the reengineering task was a diversion as the lab figured out how to permanently sever my connection to the internal audit function. The career derailment came in the form of an official notice:

> The AA-3 audit group must move towards the optimum versatility possible within the group to be able to shift resources where needed. . . . My intent is to have a fully cross-trained staff that can competently perform both internal and contract auditing functions and can move between those functions as workloads require. . . . I am assigning you to the contract audit function . . . (Lab Memorandum from R. Rodriguez to C. Montaño, April 2, 1996)

This was how LANL ended someone's career—a carefully worded memo mandating a unilateral reassignment, potentially even a career opportunity. The lab legal office was helpful in wording such notices.

After being transferred out of the internal audit arena, the Financial Management Information System (FMIS) audit, which I was doing, was discontinued. The FMIS audit was the backbone of the general ledger—the primary accounting and financial reporting database for the institution. I discovered serious problems in this area, systemic failures in managing dozens of key accounts, including monthly bank reconciliations not being done. Much later, during the course of a 2010 deposition of University of California lab oversight official Robert (Bob) Van Ness, I realized the audit had been stopped to prevent these deficiencies from being disclosed:

(Questioning of Robert Van Ness, UC manager for lab operations, by Lynne Bernabei, Esq.)

Q: Now, do you recall that in that time period of 1999, you wrote an e-mail regarding certain problems with completing of reconciliation for fiscal year 1999?

A: Do you have something you want to show me about that?

Q: Yeah. Do you recall the memo—

A: Well, not the way you've described it, but maybe—

Q: What do you recall about any issues you've had with the reconciliation with—

A: Bank account reconciliations?

Q: Right.

A: I don't know if that was the right year or not, but there was an issue.

Q: And what was the issue, as you understood it?

A: Well, the bank accounts hadn't been reconciled for a number of years.

Q: Did you perceive that to be a serious problem?

A: Yes, I did.

Q: And why is that?

A: Well, it leaves a lot of possibilities for things that could happen.

Q: Like fraud?

A: Like fraud.

Q: And if you know, how did you find out about that?

A: I don't remember.

Q: Were there any other issues with any other account reconciliation problems?

A: I don't remember.

. . .

BY MS. BERNABEI:

Q: Mr. Van Ness, look at what's been marked Van Ness Exhibit 4. Is this an e-mail you sent on or about August 30, 1999, to a number of people at Los Alamos and at the University of California?

MR. BOHNHOFF [Mr. Van Ness's legal representation during the deposition]: Counsel, there's a number of markings on this document. Is this your markings or your client's, or is this how it was obtained from the files of the lab?

BY MS. BERNABEI:

Q: This is how we received the document. These are not our markings. Now, Mr. Van Ness, is this an e-mail that you sent at that time?

A: It appears to be.

Q: And you say that the subject matter of this is a draft bank reconciliation memo; is that correct?

A: Yes.

Q: And in this memo that you write to Los Alamos saying you haven't gone far enough, you write, do you not, in sentence two of paragraph two, with respect to the report, "While this is a much improved draft, it evidences a lack of understanding and/or appreciation of the responsibilities of the financial organization and raises serious questions in the areas of hiring, training, supervision, process integrities, judgment competence, and overall management," right?

A: Yes.

Q: And then you go on to say at the bottom, the second bullet point, "When a series of controls break down, it is a strong indication that management is flawed." That's what you write, right?

A: Yes.

Q: And then you go on later in that same paragraph, "A series of team and group leaders failed to perform and misrepresented facts. This raises questions of ineffective hiring, training, and supervision as well as an appropriate working environment in general." Is that correct?

A: Yes.

Q: And is that what you believed when you wrote this memo?

A: Yes.

Q: Now, what action did the University of California take in terms of your conclusion? What did it do as corrective action after you came to the conclusion that there was a strong indication that management at Los Alamos was flawed, that led to this problem? What did you do?

A: We required them to come up with actions and processes that were going to correct the circumstances that led to this situation.

Q: And what were those actions and processes?

A: Well, I don't recall.

Q: Did you fire anybody? You say management is flawed. Did you fire anybody over this problem?

A: We did not fire anybody.

(Deposition transcript, Robert Van Ness, June 17, 2010, p. 62)

Derailing audits and investigations midstream is a responsibility-avoidance ploy. Such tactics, coupled with the passage of time, serve only to protect the status quo. By removing me from the audit function the FMIS audit was halted. And this, in turn, had prevented the serious deficiencies I'd found from being reported in a timely fashion.

7

CONTRADICTIONS

IN THE EARLY '90S I was evaluating automated processes at the laboratory, after being hired on by the University of California Office of the President (UCOP) to do these types of audits. One area I looked into was classified data handling. Two critical concerns surfaced in connection with that audit: scientists were downloading classified files to their personal computers, and a computer drive containing highly classified data wasn't in secured storage, where it was supposed to be.

A few years later, the laboratory's failure to resolve either concern resulted in allegations of espionage and losses of secret information.

By downloading classified files to their personal computers, scientists could transport the data off-site if they were so inclined. I knew that in their minds they were doing it for a good reason, doubting as they did the LANL Central Computing Facility's (CCF) ability to convert electronic files, or recover them if necessary, whenever computer hardware, operating systems, or software routines changed. For these scientists, relying entirely on CCF meant risking years of research effort.

When I worked as a federal bank auditor, it took two people to open a financial institution's vault—"dual control" was the term used. There were dual locking mechanisms, and a second person always had to be present; cameras, strategically positioned, made certain of it. A two-person entry log served to keep track of who entered, and for what purpose. This level of control was required for money, but apparently not for national security information, as was noted in a *New York Times* article from 2000:

> A pair of computer hard drives believed to contain nuclear secrets that had been missing from the Los Alamos National Laboratory were found this afternoon behind a copying machine. . . . Officials say that a total of 86 people had access to the vault where the hard drives were stored and that among them were *26 scientists who could enter without escorts* [my italics] and remove material without logging it in or out. (James Risen, "Missing Nuclear Data Found Behind a Los Alamos Copier," *New York Times*, June 17, 2000)

Laboratory managers routinely ignored what auditors reported. Because of this, serious security and financial lapses occurred that could have otherwise been averted. This disregard for independent and objective assessments of lab operations, despite the common sense preventive, protective, and detective measures that these audits advocate, ended up costing taxpayers lots of money. Labees paid as well with their reputations, careers, and health, while managers typically escaped accountability. As for those who reported these kinds of problems, aka "non–team players," they weren't likely to remain employed at LANL very long.

The focus of internal auditing was on activities *internal* to the lab. But with the function being under laboratory management's control, internal auditors were required to rely on the self-serving assertions of managers without verifying their claims. "Faith-based auditing" is what I characterized it as, and it had nothing to do with audit standards or the profession. For vendors, however, it was different—their assertions required validation.

My new assignment, the contract audit effort, entailed reviewing procurement proposals and contracts, essentially looking outside LANL for problems rather than within. The focus was on verifying the numbers associated with lab purchases—establishing the reasonableness and permissibility of related vendor billings, ensuring pricing was correct and supportable. The US code of Federal Acquisition Regulations (the FAR) is the set of rules governing the acquisition of goods and services for the federal government. It's the applicable authority, as well, for all LANL purchasing activity.

Upon joining the contract audit team, I learned that LANL was exempt from many of the rules mandated for vendors. Under the FAR, contractors weren't allowed to include lobbying expenditures in their pricing of goods and services. My job was to determine if such costs were being passed on to the government and, if so, eliminate them from the contractor's billing. (Yet the Los Alamos lab was being reimbursed by the DOE for the very same activity.) There were two functions involved—the Government Relations Office and Community Relations Office. LANL attorneys characterized them as educational resources—"educating" elected officials, government agencies, and community leaders, as opposed to "lobbying." And the DOE, as was typically the case, assisted by agreeing with the lab's view. The effect was to morph what the FAR defined as unallowable or questionable into an exception for Los Alamos.

Similar logic was applied with respect to the lab's Public Affairs Office (PA). Under the Federal Acquisition Regulations, costs associated with staff recruitment and related advertising were allowable, but costs incurred for image enhancement and self-promotion were not. PA was about the latter—presenting the institution in a favorable light. Vendors weren't reimbursed for such expenditures, but if LANL characterized those costs as "educating" the media and general public, as opposed to promoting the lab's image, the DOE was fine with it.

A similar threading of the needle was done for gifts and contributions, aka donations. These weren't allowed under the FAR and, thus, were not billable to the taxpayer. But LANL was doing something called outreach—attending dinners and galas . . . contributing tens of thousands of dollars to be a corporate sponsor of such events. These expenditures served to gain favor with local communities, influential groups, and politicians. And because it was termed "outreach," the DOE, again, went along.

Each time I questioned contradictions in what LANL was able to recover from the US taxpayer directly, versus what laboratory vendors were allowed to recoup, I was instructed to do my job and stop asking so many questions. My job was to enforce the FAR with respect to those providing goods and services to the laboratory but ignore the fact that LANL was thumbing its nose at the very same requirements, and pretend I didn't notice.

The individual who granted Los Alamos exceptions with respect to the FAR was the Department of Energy contract administrator (CA). The CA was responsible for administering the contracts the Energy Department had with its prime contractors, such as the one it had with the University of California for managing Los Alamos. This was the DOE representative who lab and university officials lobbied for exemptions—the person who stood to gain the most in terms of career opportunities by minimizing UC's exposure to liability, and by sparing it from having to reimburse taxpayers for questionable and unallowable costs reported by auditors.

To question things was to be a non–team player at LANL, and auditors were among the worst when it came to that. It was their professional responsibility to ask, to validate, to establish the veracity of what they were being told, and to report accurately. Just not in Los Alamos.

8

TIME TO ORGANIZE

THE PAY ADJUSTMENT I received in the early '80s, in connection with the class-action complaint filed against LANL by the American GI Forum in the late '70s, was an eye-opener. The complaint alleged discriminatory employment practices in Los Alamos, and was eventually settled for 10 million dollars, plus millions more in attorneys' fees. The investigation into the complaint had gone on for years. Tactics used to delay the investigation included moving documents from New Mexico to California to deny access:

> An unusual amount of controversy surrounds what should have been a sixty (60)-day compliance review of LANL begun on July 7, 1980, and finally conciliated on July 1, 1985, five (5) years later under abnormal conditions. . . . Lack of cooperation on the part of the lab made it difficult if not impossible to complete the review. . . . The National Office settled for far less than it should have in conciliation negotiations with the laboratory and in so

doing, created the appearance of political interference.
(OFCCP Investigation. "The Los Alamos Case: A Study
in Under-Enforcement," US House of Representatives,
Committee on Education and Labor, May 22, 1987)

The laboratory's willingness to defy anyone, *including the federal government*, meant it was willing to drag out the resolution
of any issue for as long as necessary, so long as the University
of California didn't incur any of the cost. As it turns out, the
OFCCP investigation of the early '80s was a harbinger of things
to come. By 1994, planning for a lab-wide culling of the workforce
was under way. As the '95 holiday season approached, contract
and regular employees across the institution were contemplating receipt of an at-risk notice, which would mean they'd been
targeted for termination.

Politicians, businesspeople, clergy, educators, officials and
other people from Espanola Valley got the word from Los
Alamos officials on Tuesday: Cutbacks are coming and
they are going to hurt a great deal more in the Valley than
they are on the hill. Approximately 1,000 workers will lose
their jobs within a month, with another 500 losing their
jobs next year . . . (Walter Howerton, "LANL Readies for
Cutbacks," *Rio Grande Sun*, August 24, 1995)

The layoffs were being touted within the halls of LANL as a
golden opportunity for managers to get rid of those they didn't
like. The intent, as formally announced, was to execute three
rounds of layoffs. The first would occur in '95, followed by rounds
two and three in '96 and '97.

Labees were feeling increasingly insecure about what was
happening; more and more began attending informal gatherings

convened off-site by a handful of fellow workers. The meetings were held monthly in a small conference room at a local church, with the hope being to someday establish an independent employee association within the lab. Nothing like it existed in Los Alamos, or at least nothing that wasn't under the influence of laboratory management. It was an admirable goal, and I'd become a regular participant as well.

Lab leadership had decided to terminate people at will and across the board. To openly express concern about this was dangerous, and could increase the likelihood of being targeted. Speaking up in church was, perhaps, less risky, but not by much. Los Alamos, after all, was still a company town.

The monthly meetings became weekly, and the growing crowd made it necessary to meet in the chapel where Sunday services were held. Still, people ended up standing along walls and in the lobby, straining to hear. We needed more room and Jake Villarreal, governor of the nearby Pojoaque Pueblo, came to the rescue. He said the group could use a larger venue at his casino, and for free.

The weekly meetings became two-hour-long Saturday morning sessions in Pojoaque, New Mexico—twenty miles from LANL— with labees and family members attending, along with friends and community leaders. Open discussions were held with everyone in the room, while strategy sessions typically convened in private.

Because of the way the layoff was structured, labees residing in surrounding hamlets and towns were the ones most likely to be chosen for termination. This meant the lion's share of the adverse economic impact would fall on nearby communities. Lab officials typically resided in Los Alamos, hence their bias toward preserving their own quality of life and economic interests on the Hill. Few had ties to Northern New Mexico; fewer still had much empathy for the concerns of those outside the management ranks of LANL and the university.

The "at-risk notice" was the official notification of potential for termination. It didn't mean the recipient would actually lose his or her job, but the clock was ticking, and if spared in the first round of the layoff trilogy, rounds two and three were still ahead.

The at-risk employee had sixty days to find another job within the institution. Seniority or past performance had no bearing. The longer you'd been at the lab, the more likely you were to be on somebody's "don't like" list, which was the only criterion that seemed to matter. The odds of at-risk employees finding other placement weren't good. Yet in the midst of this growing tempest, a privileged few received a generous raise:

> The University of California has seen fit to give the top brass of Los Alamos National Laboratory a comforting round of raises, raises averaging 5.6 percent for 25 blessed high-level executives. The highest jumped by 11.8 percent. Lab employees had been waiting anxiously for a thaw in the yearlong pay freeze enacted by the Clinton administration, and what a thaw it has been. But for Los Alamos, the champagne must be flowing in only a few quarters. The Energy Department is girding the mesa for at least 500 layoffs in the coming months, and 1995 is supposed to be the good year. Just wait until '96. (Jonathan Weisman, "Some Salaries Up, Some Employees Out," *New Mexico Business Magazine*, May 1995)

Lab leaders had free rein to pick whomever they chose to eliminate, and for whatever reason. Seniority, performance evaluations, and military service weren't relevant; meaning anyone who'd raised a safety concern, complained of retaliation, questioned an unfair decision, or rebuffed a supervisor's sexual advances could be targeted for termination. Workers who'd fallen ill were also fair game, older workers in particular.

When labees received their at-risk notices, they were marched into closed meetings with supervisors and told their selection was based on an assessment of skills relative to organizational needs. Victims didn't know what that meant, or which skill sets were taken into account. For them, the injustice was painfully obvious. Their value had been established through a process exempt from scrutiny, question, challenge, or review. To add to the sense of insult, years of service meant nothing, and accomplishments meant even less.

Those providing support efforts were the focus of the layoff, and this meant women and minorities were intended to bear the brunt of the firings. Scientists and engineers were supposed to be exempt (this too had been announced), but yet some still ended up getting at-risk notices. That's because the overriding objective was to clean house—to get rid of those whom managers didn't want, for whatever the reason and regardless of job duties.

Engaging elected officials in the struggle that lay ahead was crucial, but labees didn't have a labor organization to assist them, or a public affairs office to spin events in their favor, or the endless lobbying resources of the laboratory to "educate" politicians and community leaders to submission. A "David and Goliath" struggle was about to commence. The giant on the hill was armed and ready for battle, while his opposition—those slated to become unemployed—didn't even have a rock.

9

POLITICS AND JUSTICE

PETE DOMENICI, FORMER SENIOR Republican senator from New Mexico, was born to an undocumented immigrant mother seeking a better life for herself. Domenici's long tenure in the US Senate placed him in the position of ranking member on the powerful Energy and Natural Resources Committee, and on the Appropriations Subcommittee on Energy and Water Development. Because of these assignments, his leverage over the US Department of Energy's budget was significant, which is why his moniker at LANL was Saint Pete. Jeff Bingaman was the Democratic leg of the New Mexico US Senate duo, and together they were formidable when it came to protecting Los Alamos.

Section 3161 of the Fiscal Year 1993 National Defense Authorization Act was the legislation that financed the federal mandate for the Department of Energy to downsize itself. Endorsed by both US Senators from New Mexico, Act 3161 stemmed from the collapse of the Soviet Union and related anticipated reductions in the nuclear weapons arsenal, plus provided financial relief for constituents in the event they lost their jobs because of it. We'd won the Cold War, but in the process we'd almost gone bankrupt, and now we had an environmental mess to clean up. For many, the envisioned reduction in Cold War expenditures meant the nation might now, finally, be able to invest in environmental restoration, and in vital domestic needs such as infrastructure repair and in alternative pathways to avert the devastating effects of global climate change. But the "peace dividend," as it was called, wasn't to be. The military-industrial complex had other ideas, conjuring up new threats for the nation and new missions for the weapons labs.

Terrorism became the new fear, and ensuring the safety and reliability of nuclear weapons without detonation testing became the new mandate. And in the midst of this post–Cold War shakeout, laboratory leaders embraced Act 3161 as an opportunity. Funding for the act would be obtained by downsizing facilities involved in the production and maintenance of nuclear weapons. Reducing the size of the stockpile meant corresponding reductions in staffing levels and budgets. And this, in turn, provided money for related severance packages. This meant LANL could get rid of people without impacting its own operating budget. But the lab wasn't a production site for the DOE complex; it was a research and development facility. Because of this, it was about to receive a funding windfall, compliments of what was called the stockpile stewardship program:

> Last week, congressional negotiators approved $1.2 billion for the DOE's "stockpile stewardship" program, an effort to ensure the country's nuclear arsenal remains accident-proof and performance-ready. . . . A top DOE official said more money will be needed in the future . . . $3 billion to $4 billion per year. (Keith Easthouse, "Lab, DOE Get More Money for Stewardship," *Santa Fe New Mexican*, November 1, 1995)

46

The stockpile stewardship initiative was intended to replace nuclear weapons detonation testing with dramatically improved diagnostic and computer modeling capabilities, utilizing new multimillion-dollar state-of-the-art facilities. Also being envisioned for Los Alamos, though not yet formally announced, was the expansion of the lab's plutonium processing and warhead fabrication capabilities. This alone would provide a significant funding stream for decades to come.

Previously, whenever a layoff was required, it was based on funding shortages for a specific programmatic effort, and only those employed in that area were subject to termination. They, in turn, were given preferential hiring treatment within the laboratory, and most ended up finding placement elsewhere within the institution because of it. This time, however, things would be different. Regardless of funding, people were going to get fired.

LANL officials initially asserted that the layoff was based on a projected budget shortfall, claiming funding reductions would be occurring in coming years. If the targeted-for-termination workers could prove otherwise, perhaps jobs could be saved. That was the strategy for the first meeting with our senior senator from New Mexico. The chilling winds of late September 1995 provided an appropriate backdrop for the meeting in Senator Pete Domenici's Santa Fe office. He listened intently to our claim that the LANL Institutional Plan, which projected a funding windfall in Los Alamos for years to come, proved that the budget concerns being touted by those in charge, as the basis for the layoffs, were unfounded.

The laboratory's knee-jerk reaction, after the media reported our meeting, was to question the accuracy and reliability of related projections. But if the document was wrong, LANL's own planning effort was in question. Furthermore, Senators Bingaman and Domenici worked hard to secure the lab's funding, thus objecting to institutional insinuations to the contrary. Lab leaders had painted themselves into a corner, and now needed a new excuse for terminating people.

The next gambit was called the "workforce restructuring initiative," which entailed identifying skill sets no longer needed, or thought to be in excess supply. Managers would be making the determination, with labees having no idea which skills were being valued, and no opportunity to showcase past accomplishments for consideration. The entire process was kept hidden from those affected; managerial meetings were held behind closed doors and were immune to challenge. Regardless of need, LANL director Siegfried Hecker and his leadership team seemed intent on getting rid of people. Contracted personnel were the first to go:

> Most of the legal proceedings and media attention have focused on the lab employees that were laid off. But more than 500 workers for contractors also lost their jobs . . . [including] an industrial hygiene engineer, [who] claimed he was unfairly selected for the layoff. . . . He also contends he was laid off in retaliation for advocating safety measures for employees. (Doug McClellan, "Laid-Off Workers Get Lab Extension," *Albuquerque Journal North*, December 16, 1995)

Act 3161 provided $20,000 in severance pay per terminated regular full-time labee, plus $10,000 to each for retraining and twelve months' worth of subsidized health-care coverage. But the laboratory director was only inclined to authorize severance pay, and wouldn't allow anyone to volunteer to leave LANL in exchange, meaning you were eligible for the payment, but only if you were fired. Senator Domenici shook his head in frustration as we informed him of Hecker's stand. Allowing people to leave on their own made sense since older workers, typically more costly to the institution, were also the ones most likely to volunteer. The senator agreed.

Following our meeting with Senator Domenici, the lab director suddenly changed his mind, deciding to allow people to volunteer to leave after all, and receive severance pay. The elation of the moment, however, was short-lived, because over 500 labees had expressed interest in leaving but Hecker would accept no more than 250 volunteers. It was an arbitrary number, but a statement nonetheless as to who was still in charge. The University of California's refusal to intervene sent a message as well, its poor regard for the plight of Northern New Mexicans making for bad public relations. The DOE, at that point, attempted to distance itself:

> The federal government would have shouldered all costs of extended low-cost health insurance benefits to laid-off Los Alamos National Laboratory employees, an official says. The University of California, which manages the lab for the US Department of Energy, refused to extend the benefits. "We would have reimbursed (the university) so it would not have cost them anything," said Barbara Wetherell, a DOE spokeswoman. . . . Robert DeGrasse Jr., director of the DOE's Office of Worker and Community Transition, said Tuesday the DOE could not force the university to offer benefits because it wasn't allowed for in the current management contract. (Associated Press, "DOE Would Have Paid for Insurance," *Los Alamos Monitor*, January 25, 1996)

Political pressure, triggered by bad press, once again changed minds. LANL would, after all, give employees targeted for termination all the benefits they were due. The layoff was delayed and the number of planned firings reduced, but forced terminations were still going to occur. The only option left for those still in the director's crosshairs was legal action, but the laboratory had every major law firm in New Mexico on retainer.

Lawyers practice law, politicians run for office, and judges do both. Justices with lifetime appointments are nominated, their good fortune being confirmed by politicians who are beholden to key donors, and among the most generous contributors are members of the military-industrial complex. Senator Pete Domenici was a key ally and beneficiary to this group. His decades in office made him a powerful force, and those failing to recognize this did so at their own peril:

> Former US Attorney David Iglesias was fired after Sen. Pete Domenici, who had been unhappy with Iglesias for some time, made a personal appeal to the White House, the Journal has learned. . . . At some point after the election last Nov. 6, Domenici called Bush's senior political adviser, Karl Rove, and told him he wanted Iglesias out and asked Rove to take his request directly to the president. (Mike Gallagher, "Domenici Sought Iglesias Ouster," *Albuquerque Journal*, April 15, 2007)

On the eve of an election, Iglesias, the US attorney for New Mexico, had been asked to participate in a scheme to sway voters by expediting the filing of charges against political adversaries of the senator. Iglesias's reluctance to play politics with legal indictments cost him his job. Senator Domenici wasn't the only official implicated in the scandal, but we labees were challenging the one New Mexico interest he made no apologies about going to the mat for—the Los Alamos National Laboratory. Workers had reason to be concerned.

In a last-ditch effort to save jobs, targeted employees filed for a court-imposed injunction. The hearing was held November 10, 1995, before the Honorable Judge Jim Hall, and lasted two days. LANL retained the services of the Rodey law firm, the state's largest, which occupied three floors of the Hyatt Regency in downtown Albuquerque, with a satellite office in Santa Fe. Rodey had a reputation for usually getting its well-heeled clients what they wanted.

Judge Hall listened intently to the targeted labees' attorneys—Carol Oppenheimer and Morty Simon—appeal for an injunction to stop the firings. Their argument was that workers had been chosen for termination in a manner that violated basic labor protections and lab policy, hence the need to stop the layoff. The following evening, the at-risk employees and their families congregated in the offices of the Simon & Oppenheimer law firm, waiting for the judge's decision. Media crowded into the lobby area, with cameras and lights strategically positioned to catch the moment. It was getting dark when the decision arrived by fax—the layoff, at least for now, was on hold.

The evidence showed that the lab failed to adhere to its own policies, the related assumption being that firing people under such circumstances could result in "irreparable harm." Common sense would suggest as much—if you're unable to pay your mortgage, you lose your home. Wasn't this the essence of irreparable harm? The labees who were queued for termination were lucky, for in a world of legal hairsplitting and political tap dancing, common sense doesn't always prevail. This is particularly true in judicial proceedings involving powerful interests, as in the case of the Los Alamos National Laboratory, the University of California, and the US Department of Energy combined.

Days later, the joy and celebration over Judge Hall's ruling turned to heartbreak and disbelief, as institutional lawyers wasted no time appealing to the New Mexico Supreme Court. The high court convened quickly. The unraveling of people's lives could proceed as planned:

> Last week, the New Mexico Supreme Court overturned Hall's injunction, ruling that while the employees have a right to seek damages at a trial, the lower court did not have a right to interfere with the lab's efforts to streamline its operations. (Keith Easthouse, "Bitter End for Laid-Off Workers . . . Last Day at LANL," *Santa Fe New Mexican*, December 1, 1995)

It was a cruel eleventh-hour judicial intervention on the lab's behalf, coming just days after the district court's compassionate ruling and hours from our national day of Thanksgiving. It was the soon-to-be-laid-off labees' Pearl Harbor moment. Their holiday season was going to be bleak.

10

UNMASKING DEMONS

THE GOOD NEWS WAS that not all labees receiving at-risk notices were forcibly discharged. Some left under the voluntary separation program, and a handful found other placements inside the lab. Our lobbying efforts effectively saved at least 250 from being forced out, but now we were entering a new phase. It was time to give our worker protection movement a name.

"What should we call ourselves?" someone asked during one of the informal gatherings of labees who'd received at-risk notices.

"We need a name with an acronym that's easy to remember," I responded.

"We probably should incorporate as a nonprofit," someone else suggested, "just in case we need to do fundraising."

"We're a family now," chimed in another. "Our friends and families are with us."

"True," I said, "we're all concerned citizens. How about calling ourselves Citizens for LANL Employee Rights?"

The acronym would be easy to remember—CLER—pronounced "clear." After a quick show of hands, LANL's first independent labor association came into being. With a second vote I became its founding president, and four others assumed the role of CLER's governing board. Nearly 200 former labees and family members were part of the organization.

Legendary female activist and anthropologist Margaret Mead once said, "Never doubt that a group of thoughtful, committed citizens can change the world; indeed, it's the only thing that ever has." We now had a citizen movement, and committed was what we were.

On the eve of the 1995 holiday season, the terminated labees were escorted off the laboratory premises by armed guards. One labee, a fifty-year-old electrical engineer, shared his feelings with a local newspaper. "It was like being punched in the gut," he said. A few days afterward, salt was poured on the wound. In the press, a lab official described the former employees as "low-hanging fruit"—easy pickings, in other words. The derogatory reference enraged the fired workers into action, effectively becoming their rallying cry.

The layoff was unnecessary and, above all, executed unfairly. The average age of the fired worker was forty-five, and the average term of service was fifteen years. Some were scientists and engineers; two were even nuclear weapons designers. Yet all had one thing in common: a manager who didn't like them.

Instilling fear was an intended by-product of the terminations, as confirmed in an e-mail from the head of the human resources department, sent in confidence to laboratory leadership. Intimidation meant there'd be less likelihood LANL decisions would be challenged in any significant way. But for some the message was more primal—a statement of dominance, with local news outlets reporting a handful of surviving labees strutting around wearing T-shirts displaying the phrase "Ethnic Cleansing." Women had been disproportionately targeted for termination, and the proportion of laid-off Hispanics was twice their representation in the LANL workforce. Laboratory statisticians calculated that the odds of this occurring, without bias factoring into the decision, were about one in three million. For the US Department of Labor, and because of CLER's lobbying for it to initiate an investigation, the stench emanating from the layoff's aftermath was hard to ignore:

> The US Department of Labor will conduct an investigation into the way layoffs last fall of several hundred Los Alamos National Laboratory workers was carried out. (Keith Easthouse, "US Labor Department Will Probe Layoffs," *Santa Fe New Mexican*, February 10, 1996)

Workers had been fired willy-nilly, but their responsibilities didn't go away. In the aftermath, highly paid lab officials were tasked to do the "menial" labor of those they'd just terminated. Local newspapers exposed the absurdity, including the fact that mail delivery came to a standstill because too many clerks were let go. Photos of mailbags stacked to the ceilings appeared in news clips, while managers earning over $100K a year were called upon to sort and deliver mail.

> Jury selection is to begin Monday on a lawsuit alleging that some Los Alamos National Laboratory managers used layoffs as a pretext to rid the lab of older and minority workers, whistleblowers, and employee-rights advocates. . . . Plaintiffs are seeking lost pay and other compensatory damages on their claims of breach of contract, violations of a California records law, and destruction of evidence. . . . They also contend the managers covered up evidence on the lack of objectivity

by shredding preliminary paperwork used in ranking employees for the layoffs [my italics]. (Associated Press, "Trial to Begin Today in Layoff Suit against Lab," March 3, 1997)

To be hiding documents, as UC had done a decade earlier with the OFCCP investigation of LANL employment practices, was unseemly. But shredding evidence in connection with a lawsuit? The true nature of what occurred, and why, was captured on the face of an internal memorandum that the laboratory's legal office sent to managers after the unnecessary firings. Underlined and in large bold capital letters was the memo's concern: "**ADVERSE IMPACT WAS FOUND** at the division level for total minorities." The legal office then followed up with a confidential memo, advising laboratory leadership not to allow individual divisions to release statistics on the ethnic makeup of terminated employees.

At the first CLER meeting following the layoff, my primary order of business had been to reveal the nature of the challenge that lay ahead . . .

"Fairness has nothing to do with it," I said. "Truth, justice, and the 'American way' is only in the *Superman* comic books. Now we're dealing with reality, folks, and the truth is we're in for a long, difficult battle."

I continued. "We'll need leverage to win. The lab has millions of dollars to litigate with, and an army of lawyers, along with government relations and public affairs people. We have ourselves and our story, and if the media is willing to report truthfully, we might build community support. If the public is on our side, we can leverage politicians to act, and with the public and a few politicians on our side, maybe we can achieve justice . . . maybe."

The meeting was difficult. The fear in people's eyes had turned to pain. The common sentiment among those who'd lost their jobs was that it wasn't fair—both how they'd been targeted, despite years of service, and the fact that there was no recourse. As the meeting hall quieted down, a man stood up to share his own anguish. "My little boy asked me last night what I did wrong to get fired," he said, his eyes welling up with tears. "What do I tell him?" The room went silent. Others began sharing their own sense of betrayal and loss. Soon many were sobbing openly. The need to grieve was apparent.

I knew that if we were to have any chance of succeeding, we needed to win public support, bring the lab's motives into question, and frame issues to CLER's advantage. In order to derail the LANL locomotive, we needed to be strategic, not stand on the tracks as the train rushed forward. So we introduced ourselves to journalists, news program directors, editors, and editorial boards. We held press conferences, staged demonstrations, and assembled media releases with information packets to help reporters understand key points we wanted to make. And when meetings were held with politicians, we structured them so that they had to take an action or decide on something; afterward, we encouraged news outlets to follow up with them to see if they would. It was the grassroots way of getting elected officials to act, lacking as we did the enormous lobbying muscle of LANL, or its legal, political, and public affairs resources.

The best thing we could have going for us, organizationally, was to be underestimated by everyone, including the lab and its supporters. LANL had never lost a labor dispute in its history, and there was no reason to believe that might ever change. CLER was the proverbial tortoise; the laboratory was the hare. If the "rabbit" was certain of its invincibility, perhaps we could win the "race" by surprise.

One day, as the layoff dispute was heating up, my doorbell rang. Standing there at the threshold of our home was our neighbor, a manager in the laboratory's Public Affairs Office.

My daughter occasionally babysat his younger children, so my immediate thought was that he needed a babysitter. He handed me a freshly baked pie and said, "Let's not let the layoff ruin our friendship." Maybe it was a sympathetic gesture, akin to a condemned man's last meal, but nice nonetheless. Perhaps it said something about what he thought the inevitable outcome would be—a colossal defeat for CLER and me.

As the designated spokesperson for the terminated labees my task was to lead the charge, so to speak, but I was an amateur general and my army was exhausted, demoralized, and unpaid. My neighbor was just the opposite, as one of many laboratory officials positioned, trained, and organized to do battle in support of LANL. It wasn't going to be pretty, or much of a contest at that. The struggle had just begun but, apparently, at least for some, the lab had already won. If institutional leadership was thinking this way, then maybe CLER—the tortoise in the race—had a chance, and as events unfolded it became increasingly apparent that it did. When there was a rally, CLER members showed up in force, chanting and carrying signs. If there was a press conference, they'd be there as well, making themselves known. Most were middle-aged individuals who'd never advocated or demonstrated for anything in their lives. They were no longer labees but were still citizens and, as such, bound and determined to exercise their constitutional rights. LANL officials, however, didn't quite see it that way:

> Hockey has the penalty box. Now, Los Alamos National Laboratory has the protest box. Lab officials have told a group of dissident lab employees they may picket in front of public areas—but only if they confine their soapboxes to one of three 10-foot-square boxes on the sidewalk

... (Doug McClellan, "LANL Seeks to Box In Protesters,"
Albuquerque Journal North, April 16, 1996)

It was ironic that an institution founded in the midst of a world war against tyranny now seemed committed to undermine the rights of a democracy. It wasn't as though the fired labees were "fanatics," or a threat to national security. On the contrary, until recently they'd been full-fledged laboratory workers, having undergone an extensive security background check when they were hired, which was updated every five years thereafter. To treat them, at this point, as though they might be radical "outside agitators" was, if anything, an indictment of the nuclear complex's security clearance process. A couple of news sound bites later, institutional leadership did a quick about-face, maneuvering itself out of the corner it had, once again, painted itself into. Labees could now step outside the confines of the jail-cell-sized box LANL officials had initially intended for them.

CLER members like Rose Stevens, Larry Gibbons, Jerry Leyba, Ken Van Riper, Archie Velarde, Hal Frost, Bill Parras, Henry Atwater, Eloy Maestas, Larkin Garcia, and others were the heroes of battle, never giving up and forever ready to confront the next challenge. Eloy and Larkin were retired veterans; the latter had served five combat tours of duty as a navy commander. Their military service, as was the case with seniority and past performance, hadn't meant a thing to those deciding whom to fire.

In February 1998, CLER became a force to be reckoned with when—by a stroke of luck and good timing—President William Jefferson Clinton and Federico Peña, DOE secretary at the time, happened to drop in on Los Alamos. When the president arrived at the Los Alamos airport in his Marine One helicopter, unemployed workers and family members were standing nearby carrying signs in one hand, waving with the other.

CLER members spotted President Clinton peering back at them through the thick tinted glass of the presidential limo; he even managed to return a wave or two before being hurriedly whisked away. Later, the president asked LANL officials about what he'd seen, and reportedly expressed hopes for a quick resolution to the labor dispute.

Only twice before in the laboratory's history had a sitting US President visited Los Alamos. Perhaps it was a good omen—President Clinton's surprise visit. But his plea for a speedy end to the suffering landed on deaf ears. The LANL director was unyielding, similar to Pharaoh in the biblical story of Moses. His heart, it appeared, was hardened by his refusal to admit his mistake, and by those advising him never to concede.

11

CULTURE

THE WAR OVER THE layoff had begun and I, along with
CLER board members Tom Granich, Theresa Connaughton,
and Lyda Martinez were on the way to meet with our congressional delegation in Washington, DC. We were also scheduled
to meet DOE secretary Hazel O'Leary and Bob DeGrasse, her
designee overseeing the department's post–Cold War restructuring effort. We left for Washington on March 6, 1996, and a
crew from the University of New Mexico's Oral History Program
was there to photograph our departure from the airport. Later,
a photo from that day appeared in the January 1997 issue of the
New Mexico Historical Review. We were making history—workers attempting to hold LANL officials accountable for the first
time ever. We'd managed to schedule appointments, in advance,
with everyone we needed to meet while we were in DC, except of
one—Congressman Bill Richardson.

Richardson had been voted into office in 1982 to represent
New Mexico's newly created third district. We were his constituents, along with the hundreds who'd been involuntarily let
go in the lab layoff. But, according to him, he was going to be

outside the Capital Beltway while we were in town, meaning he couldn't meet.

Our first stop was with Senator Jeff Bingaman, followed by an afternoon meeting with Senator Pete Domenici. During our visit with Domenici, his secretary interrupted to announce that his next appointment had arrived. The senator requested we continue our discussion after he met with the new arrival, so we exited to the waiting area. There, standing in the doorway, was our missing-in-action congressman. "Fighter for New Mexico" was his campaign slogan back home; now we knew the truth. Richardson was as surprised as we were because there'd been no miscommunication, misunderstanding, or change in schedule. Like someone caught in the act of deception, he snickered, drew himself up, and asked, "What are you doing here?"

"Well," I responded, "I guess we're here to see you." He shook his head and proceeded past us.

The congressman had been maintaining an arm's-length relationship with the fired labees for months; now we knew why. Since he was angling for a presidential appointment, sidestepping complications associated with supporting fired workers in his district made sense. He'd need Senator Domenici's goodwill to line up Republican support, and the senator abhorred controversy when it came to Los Alamos. And so the former labees, in desperate need of their representative's help, would have to proceed without it.

In 1997, less than a year later, Richardson became US ambassador to the United Nations. Within months he garnered a second appointment in the Clinton administration, this time to a cabinet-level position as DOE secretary. Both times he was confirmed without a hitch, having played his political hand masterfully. His New Mexico constituents were abandoned for the sake of his political ambitions. But years later, President Clinton would be sacrificed as well.

> Richardson backed Obama despite his ties to [Hillary]
> Clinton and her husband, the former president. Richard-
> son served as ambassador to the UN and as secretary
> of the Energy Department during the Clinton adminis-
> tration. (AP report, "New Mexico's Richardson Endorses
> Obama," *NBC News*, March 21, 2008)

After our meetings with Senators Bingaman and Domenici, we were scheduled to visit with DOE secretary Hazel O'Leary. At the last minute she was summoned to a hearing, so we met with her deputy, Charles Curtis, instead. His office was on the upper level of the DOE's Forrestal Building, which was named after the first secretary of defense, James Forrestal. It overlooked the grandeur of the Washington Mall, with a spectacular view of the Smithsonian "Castle." Curtis pulled his executive chair out from behind his desk to sit knee-to-knee with us. Our discussion focused on how to effect change in Los Alamos.

"The lab's corporate culture is the problem," I said.

"What would you propose we do about that?" Curtis responded.

There were three things that had to occur, and all were needed for the plan to work. The first bulleted item on our single-page handout was, *"Inject appropriate terms and conditions into the prime contract."* The agreement between the university and the Department of Energy for the management of LANL was the prime contract. Specific terms injected into the contract could hold management accountable for desired outcomes and behaviors. For example, if lapses in safety and security were the concern, the contract could require that the University of California absorb costs and penalties associated with related failures, conceivably improving workplace safety in the process, plus enhancing protection over classified information.

The next item dealt with the search for a new LANL director, which was in the process at the time. "The next director," I said, "shouldn't come from the ranks of LANL or UC." The objective was to avoid choosing someone beholden to the existing culture.

Our third recommended action was to put the LANL contract out for competitive bid, which had never been done before. The process would require the university to reconsider its way of doing business in Los Alamos, plus invite others to contribute ideas as to how best to achieve the lab's mission.

At the conclusion Curtis asked, "How would you respond to those who say now is not the right time to be changing management in Los Alamos?"

"Now, with the Soviet Union no longer in existence, is precisely the right time," I responded.

Our CLER contingent left DC that evening feeling we'd done our best. The trip was useful, especially our meeting with Senator Domenici. He'd given us critical assurance regarding our request that the layoff be investigated by the US Department of Labor Office of Federal Contract Compliance (OFCCP). We'd asked if he'd assist with a letter of support, and his response was unequivocal—no, for he wasn't about to do anything that conflicted with his overriding mission of preserving the lab's funding. But when I asked if he'd agree not to oppose our efforts, again he was unhesitant. He wouldn't help, but he also wouldn't interfere, which was the assurance we needed. Without his backing, getting the OFCCP to engage would be difficult. But if he didn't actively oppose us, at least there was a chance.

Our meetings within the Beltway demonstrated just how difficult it is to be taken seriously, by those whose hands are on the levers of governance, without the money and backing of influential allies. The UC-managed labs were cash cows for the military-industrial fraternity, and the complex carried plenty of influence through its campaign contributions. Because of this, the status quo at LANL wasn't likely to change. As for agency bureaucrats, they didn't lengthen their stay in government by giving credence to concerned citizens advocating for the public good, or by protecting taxpayer resources without first getting the political green light to do so. On the contrary, they were obligated to the same overwhelming force politicians were beholden to—corporate interests.

The philosophical discussion with the DOE deputy secretary was a feel-good moment, but not by much. Goliath—the giant on the hill—was protected by powerful allies. David—the laid-off workers who thought their "Fighter for New Mexico" would rise to their cause—still stood alone.

12

AMBITION

IN THE SUMMER OF 1998, my wife and I were in a hotel room in Madrid, Spain, when we first heard the name of the protagonist in LANL's latest scandal. We were on our first trip beyond the western hemisphere, and were hoping we'd left the LANL layoff turmoil behind for a while. From the Old World I watched in amazement as the story unfolded on Spanish TV—suspected espionage in Los Alamos. The reporter said the alleged spy's name was Wen Ho Lee, and that he was suspected of divulging secrets to the People's Republic of China concerning the design of the W88, an extremely compact thermonuclear warhead developed in Los Alamos twenty years earlier for the US Navy. It was a relatively old design, yet still very sophisticated.

Multiple W88s can be crammed into the tip of a single Trident missile, with each delivery system costing upward of $70 million. At least five US Trident-carrying submarines are deployed at any given moment, with as many as forty-eight independently targetable warheads per ship. This makes the W88 one of the most lethal designs in the nuclear arsenal. If the Chinese had figured out how to make one, Lee's alleged leak could have indeed been a threat to US military superiority. A legitimate question was whether the Chinese were figuring things out on their own or getting an unauthorized assist. Someone in authority seemed to believe it was the latter.

Dr. Wen Ho Lee was an employee of the Los Alamos National Laboratory, and had developed computer code, some of which was used in nuclear detonation modeling by weapons designers, including those working on the W88. But Wen Ho was *not* among them, meaning he was never directly involved in that effort. The news report may have mentioned he was only under investigation or just a suspect, but people tend to assume the worst. The *New York Times* broke the story; a "reliable source" had leaked it—an unnamed party from within the US Department of Energy.

Lee was Chinese, but he'd grown up in Taiwan, which meant he was Taiwanese, not a citizen of the People's Republic—an important distinction given that Taiwan was the last stronghold of resistance against the 1949 Communist takeover of the mainland. Taiwan had remained, more or less, a sovereign nation ever since. Plus Wen Ho, who was a child during the Japanese occupation of Taiwan, was witness to the brutality of that moment, and was among those who celebrated when the United States and its allies freed the island of the tyranny of its occupiers. And even then, for the average citizen, the Taiwanese regime was harsh as well, especially for those who weren't members of the power elite, which Lee's parents were not—they were extremely poor. So Lee, as much as anyone from similar circumstances, had reason to embrace the United States as his home.

A mentor-like acquaintance of mine had once warned me about mob behavior, which is what I feared was happening in Wen Ho's case.

"People are like chickens in a chicken coop," he said.

"How's that?" I asked.

"Well," he explained, "when a chicken breaks a feather and starts to bleed, others keep chasing it, pecking at the wound, and making it bleed even more. If the injured bird can't escape, it's eventually pecked to death." As a child I'd spent many memorable days in Taos, New Mexico, on my grandparents' farm, so I'd observed the behavior of this particular type of fowl on many occasions. With respect to Dr. Lee, I sensed something along these lines was about to occur.

Back in present-day Los Alamos, the regularly scheduled Saturday morning meeting of Citizens for LANL Employee Rights (CLER) had begun. The room was full, and Spain was now a distant memory. We were discussing the latest developments in the ongoing layoff dispute. A memo someone had discovered was being circulated. It was a message from the director of the lab's human resources department—a PhD-holding psychologist by trade—to others in management. It was a strategy communiqué, pointing out that the involuntary terminations of labees would improve the lab's overall work ethic by getting survivors to put their collective "nose to the grindstone." Plus fear meant people were less inclined to exercise their rights.

The adverse economic impact associated with another layoff would probably cause community and state leaders to think twice about opposing LANL activities that would potentially put communities and workers at greater risk—expanded plutonium processing, for example. The first massive layoff had proven the lab's willingness to shift programmatic efforts, terminate people at will, and, if necessary, redirect procurement spending that benefits area businesses and politicians beholden to them. The insecurity associated with another lab-wide layoff would surely keep Northern New Mexico in check.

As the CLER meeting continued, the discussion shifted to Wen Ho Lee. CLER members Cathy and Bob Clark were close friends of the Lee family, and believed Dr. Lee was innocent. The families were neighbors in the LANL bedroom community of White Rock. Bob was a scientist, a PhD whose forte was Monte Carlo simulation, a class of computational algorithms using risk, uncertainty, probabilities, and repeated random variable sampling. Despite the uniqueness of his expertise, he was among the hundreds who'd lost their jobs in the targeted terminations.

Another Wen Ho Lee supporter was Chris Mechels, whose expertise was supercomputers. He'd left LANL on his own, but remained concerned about abuses he'd witnessed while there. His view was also that Dr. Lee was being unfairly targeted. After a while everyone at the CLER gathering seemed to concur—Lee was a convenient scapegoat for alleged spying that probably didn't even exist, and the "unnamed" news source in this regard was a key reason for being skeptical. The suspected leaker was DOE secretary Bill Richardson, our former US congressman.

The secretary had been raised in other parts of the world but chose New Mexico for his political base when a new congressional district was established for the northern region. While growing up he'd been surrounded by privilege and wealth, thus possessing not only ambition, but the backing of powerful interests to run for higher office. Richardson was fluent in Spanish, and with a large Spanish-speaking population in the newly formed district, that would come in handy. The problem was that he wasn't from the area, or the same economic stratum as 99 percent of those living there. Yet surrounding himself with swarms of homegrown political gadflies looking to latch on for a ride made it appear he was a native son in spirit, if not fact. And once the endorsement of "locals" was secured, he used the draw of high-profile personalities to expand his appeal. Richardson provided tax breaks to the entertainment and film industry, and arranged social gatherings for celebrities in town, inviting the "movers and shakers" of New Mexico society to attend. These included key members of the legislative and judicial branches of government, plus owners and editors of strategically important news outlets.

From the start, Richardson had skillfully managed his political rise, which meant he'd garnered the freedom to govern with minimal oversight. Thus, from a legislative standpoint, he managed to get everything he wanted; media-wise, he escaped much of the healthy skepticism someone in his position should have gotten. Without effective checks and balances, it was inevitable the public interest would suffer.

Dr. Wen Ho Lee had been peripheral to the W88 warhead development. His expertise was examining material dynamics under high pressure and stress. He'd developed computer code to model these effects—routines that had greater practical value for the design of industrial processes than bombs. He'd given unclassified talks related to this aspect of his work, including presentations in the People's Republic of China, which was not unusual. It is, in fact, required of researchers—talks and publications saying something about the relevancy and importance of their work; hence their worth to the funding source and institution receiving those resources. When visiting colleagues came to LANL, Dr. Lee, like any hosting official from the lab would do, invited them to his home for cocktails and dinner. This was a common courtesy among those doing collaborative research or sponsoring speaker engagements in Los Alamos, and it didn't matter if the visitor came from England, Timbuktu, or China.

Leading up to the 2000 US presidential campaign, the People's Republic of China (PRC) had made financial contributions to the Democratic National Committee (DNC). The reality was that both political parties—Republican and Democratic—routinely received donations from other countries hoping to influence American policy. But Republicans, in this instance, had managed to portray the PRC donation as evidence that an Al Gore presidency would be soft on the PRC. It was in the midst of this developing brouhaha that a staffer working for then–DOE secretary Bill Richardson became convinced that a Chinese spy had taken refuge in Los Alamos. At that point the secretary was a frontrunner in the contest to become Gore's running mate. And if he could get credit for nailing a PRC spy, it would undermine the Republican campaign to discredit the DNC, bolster his chances for VP, and possibly reap career benefits for the staffer involved.

As a discussion about Lee unfolded during our CLER meeting, I learned that he'd once received an "at-risk" notice, but avoided being terminated by finding another assignment within the laboratory. I also learned that he, like so many others doing research at the lab, had copied his own computer code to protect it. When the lab's Central Computing Facility replaced a computer or software, routines that researchers had painstakingly developed could be compromised, vital computer files could be lost or misplaced, and months, if not years, of research might be jeopardized.

Dr. Lee had spent enormous amounts of time and effort developing, testing, and fine-tuning computer models for his research projects. Thus by making copies of his own work, he was hoping to prevent a catastrophe. But for Wen Ho to be copying anything, at that point, was another nail in the spy coffin that had already been built for him.

Lee's critical mistake, years earlier, was making a onetime phone call to a Lawrence Livermore National Lab scientist who, at the time, was under FBI surveillance. He hadn't said anything incriminating during the conversation, but guilt by association seemed to be in order. That, coupled with the downloading of his computer code, his trips to China, and associations with visiting Chinese scientists, might be considered suspicious. But was he a spy? Bob and Cathy Clark—his close friends and neighbors—didn't think so. They viewed him as someone innocent enough to get into trouble without knowing he'd done anything wrong, much less illegal. Wen Ho Lee was from a different culture, time, and place. And now, after being raised in abject poverty in Taiwan, he was a US citizen caught in a tangled web of international intrigue and political gamesmanship—the ultimate nightmare for anyone, especially for someone so naive.

> The FBI and Energy Department probably doomed the nuclear-espionage investigation of LANL scientist Wen Ho Lee with a series of errors, poor judgments, and delays, a Senate committee said Thursday. . . . The bipartisan report by the Senate Committee on Government Affairs says the investigators failed to look into other suspects, fought among themselves over a search warrant to a computer, and made other "compound missteps.". . . Some authorities think that if Lee is prosecuted at all it might be on the far less serious charges of violating lab security procedures . . . (Wire services, "Senators: Lee Case Full of Flaws," *Santa Fe New Mexican*, August 6, 1999)

Wen Ho had copied his own work, which, contrary to initial news reports, was not designated secret or confidential at the time of his copying. But federal officials lobbied for and obtained the designation they wanted from the lab, albeit after the fact.

Dr. Paul Robinson, director of the Sandia National Laboratories, characterized the files Wen Ho downloaded as having the potential to "change the world's strategic balance." But Dr. Harold Agnew, former LANL director and, at the time, CEO of General Atomics of San Diego, characterized the data as dated and incomplete. Scientists who were much more expert and current in their knowledge of such matters also concluded there was nothing particularly worthy of all the fuss being made. Lee, in other words, was being railroaded.

By the end of the ordeal, federal judge James Parker, who was nominated by President Ronald Reagan in 1987 to serve in the United States District Court for the District of New Mexico, had seen enough, and felt compelled to apologize for the injustice committed against Dr. Lee and his family. He said, addressing Dr. Lee in front of a courtroom full of stunned onlookers:

> "The executive branch has enormous power, the abuse of which can be devastating to our citizens . . . The top decision-makers in the executive branch, especially the Department of Justice and the Department of Energy and locally . . . have caused embarrassment by the way this case began and was handled. They did not embarrass me alone. They have embarrassed our entire nation and each of us who is a citizen of it. . . . I am sad for you and your family because of the way in which you were kept in custody while you were presumed under the law to be innocent of charges the executive branch brought against you. . . . I might say that I am also sad and troubled because I do not know the real reasons why the executive branch has done all of this. We will not learn why, because the plea agreement shields the executive branch from disclosing a lot of information that it was under order to produce that might have supplied the answer. . . . I sincerely apologize to you, Dr. Lee, for the unfair manner you were held in custody by the executive branch."
> (Wen Ho Lee with Helen Zia, *My Country Versus Me*. Hyperion. 2001.

And years later we'd learn more:

> [New Mexico] Gov. Bill Richardson appears to fig-
> ure prominently in what one First Amendment expert
> describes as a "rather monumental clash between the
> press and government." . . . Richardson, who was secre-
> tary of energy, and several others were again identified
> in a recent federal appeals court ruling as likely sources
> of leaks in 1999 that identified Lee as a suspect in an
> FBI investigation into espionage and the loss of nuclear
> secrets to China. (Adam Rankin, "Gov. May Figure in Lee
> Lawsuit; Richardson Named as Likely Source of Leak,"
> *Albuquerque Journal North*, July 10, 2005)

Nearly ten years after leaving the national political stage in dis-
grace for his failures as DOE secretary, Richardson was once
more embroiled in controversy:

> According to Public Policy Polling's blog, a recent poll
> shows that Bill Richardson, once one of the most popu-
> lar politicians New Mexico has ever known, has become
> "one of the least popular governors in the country." . . .
> Richardson's disapproval number is 63 percent. (Steve
> Terrell, "Richardson Poll Numbers Crash," *Roundhouse
> Roundup*, February 23, 2010)

Richardson, as a politician, had been charismatic to a fault. And
like so many others, I'd been persuaded to vote for him over the
course of many election cycles. I regret now having done so, for
as he exited the New Mexican political stage he left swirling in
his wake several pay-to-play schemes, a state payroll stacked

with 500 political appointees, scandalous amounts spent on huge-ticket items, including a commuter rail, a national spaceport, a state jet designed for crisscrossing the nation, and more:

> Bill Richardson, the former governor of New Mexico who ran for president in 2008, is being investigated by a federal grand jury for possible violations of campaign finance laws. . . . One of the accusations is that Mr. Richardson raised $250,000 from supporters to quiet a woman who had threatened to file a sexual harassment suit. (Marc Lacy and Dan Frosch, "Ex-Governor Is Said to Be Focal Point of Inquiry," *New York Times*, December 1, 2011)

Bill Richardson had been within a hair's width of becoming Al Gore's presidential running mate, but his controversial tenure as DOE secretary, including misplaced and lost secrets at LANL, undercut his bid. Years later, as baseball Hall of Famer Yogi Berra might say, it was déjà vu all over again:

> New Mexico Gov. Bill Richardson has kicked himself out of Barack Obama's cabinet—the first major self-inflicted gash for the president-elect's team. Richardson officially withdrew his nomination as commerce secretary on Sunday afternoon. (Richard Sisk, "Scandal Hits Obama Administration as New Mexico Gov. Bill Richardson Withdraws as Commerce Secretary," *New York Daily News*, January 4, 2009)

For Dr. Lee, at last there'd be some vindication:

> Wen Ho Lee, the former Los Alamos nuclear physicist,
> finally may be vindicated. . . . [T]he federal government and
> five media companies have agreed to pay a settlement of
> $1.6 million, of which Lee will receive $750,000 . . . (Helen
> Zia, "Why Privacy Matters—the Wen Ho Lee Case," Open
> Forum: *San Francisco Chronicle*, June 6, 2006)

The term "collateral damage" lulls us into believing that the cost
to others is somehow unavoidable, perhaps even necessary. But
for the innocent casualty, there is no solace.

13

VINDICATION

After guiding Los Alamos National Laboratory for more than 10 tumultuous years, through the end of the Cold War and last fall's controversial layoff of some 800 workers, Director Sig Hecker announced his resignation Wednesday. . . . A high-level source said Wednesday that the controversy generated by the layoffs caused Hecker's standing to slip. . . . [The source stated] "The layoffs were his undoing." (Keith Easthouse, "Director of LANL to Quit," *Santa Fe New Mexican*, May 24, 1998)

The LANL director who'd insisted on the unnecessary layoff was now, himself, "involuntarily terminated" as lab director. The entire ordeal was, as the saying goes, "like making sausage." Everyone was "ground up" over the course of the three-year dispute, and in the process the layoff trilogy, planned for three consecutive years, ended with year one.

This blessing—the decision to halt further layoffs—was paid for with the tears of those who'd lost their jobs in '95. Some lost their homes as well in the wake of their terminations, others their marriages; two former employees even died from medical complications aggravated by related stress. The New Mexico Supreme Court's decision back then, which enabled the LANL director and his inner circle to proceed with the firings, had been unwarranted and cruel.

During the entire struggle I remained employed at the lab, working weekends and after hours to help move the CLER agenda forward. Central to our success was one seminal event—a legislative hearing that allowed the public to express its views on Los Alamos without having to sugarcoat anything, get preapproval, or be subjected to sixty-second time limits or topic constraints. It was arranged when the pro tem for the New Mexico State Senate, Manny Aragon, happened to bump into the California Senate majority leader, Richard Polanco, at a national conference. Aragon mentioned the LANL layoff dispute making news locally, plus UC's involvement in it. This piqued Polanco's interest, and he in turn committed to convene a public hearing to learn more about what was going on in Los Alamos.

Just last year, a handful of top California lawmakers learned they run a nuclear-weapons laboratory in New Mexico. And that New Mexican legislators are dismayed with its management by the University of California. Today, both states' legislators will hear more about Los Alamos National Laboratory as an odd creation of World War II—a once-secret California-run institution that sits on a New Mexico plateau and, critics say, is above key labor laws in both states. (Staff Report, "California Lawmakers to Hear about LANL," *Albuquerque Journal North*, May 8, 1998)

In 1998, on a beautiful spring day in early May, terminated laboratory workers, family members, community leaders, and others lined up, one after another, to give their statements at the first-ever joint California–New Mexico legislative forum on LANL. Many lashed out at the University of California for its absentee landlord-like oversight of the lab. One local legislator characterized the relationship between UC and LANL as being akin to a colonial occupation, while his California counterparts seemed genuinely surprised the university was even in Los Alamos. For decades, LANL and the university had managed to keep the Los Alamos lab off the radar screen of California lawmakers, which is why they were surprised to learn that the 7,000-plus UC employees residing in Northern New Mexico had no labor rights. The university had always asserted that labees were California employees, so New Mexico law lacked jurisdiction. But UC also claimed that since they lived in New Mexico, California law didn't apply either. It was a stunning catch-22 that no one had ever taken note of . . . until now:

> It's taken a half century, but workers at Los Alamos National Laboratory are on the verge of getting the same labor rights as their California colleagues. . . . Two Golden State legislators were incredulous on hearing that neither California nor New Mexico labor law covers LANL workers. . . . Until last year, many California legislators had no clue they ran a weapons laboratory in Northern New Mexico. (Ian Hoffman, "Lab Labor Practices Examined," *Albuquerque Journal North*, May 9, 1998)

In the early '90s, labees were forced to meet off-site in a community church because independent employee organizations weren't allowed on-site. It didn't matter that LANL belonged to the US taxpayer, or that labees themselves were taxpayers—lab leaders were simply used to doing as they pleased. It was a "taxation without representation" mind-set, and the university was responsible. On the eve of the new millennium, the governor of the State of California tried making amends:

> On New Year's Day, roughly 7,400 workers at Los Alamos National Laboratory will gain collective bargaining and other labor rights for the first time in lab history. California Gov. Gray Davis on Sunday night signed a bill giving an array of labor rights to all University of California employees at Los Alamos. (Ian Hoffman, "LANL Workers Get Labor Rights in 2000," *Albuquerque Journal North*, October 12, 1999)

An act signed into law in the '70s called the California Higher Education Employer-Employee Relations Act (HEERA) provided labor protections for all university employees "whose employment is principally within the state of California." These nine words served to exclude New Mexico–based UC employees from HEERA coverage, unlike their counterparts at the Lawrence Livermore and Berkeley federal laboratories in California. The discovery that UC employees stationed in Los Alamos had no state-imposed labor protection was made by Citizens for LANL Employee Rights member Chris Mechels, the organization's consummate researcher of UC policy and related rules and regulations.

Two people led the charge to eliminate the LANL exclusion in HEERA: the majority leader of the California State Senate and Denise Ducheny, the state's Budget Committee chairwoman for the Assembly (House of Representatives). Ducheny also held sway over the university's budget. Labees had, at last, found the right "stone." The giant was now reeling.

UC officials decided it was time to resolve the dispute over the '95 LANL-wide layoff, which at that point was nearing the three-year mark. This wouldn't have happened, though, had it not been for the selfless assistance of the California legislators, or the New Mexico Senate pro tem who brought them to New Mexico. They'd made the impossible possible, and, for once, LANL Public Affairs hadn't turned reality on its head. Nor was the truth restrained by lab attorneys or twisted into knots by hordes of Los Alamos government and community relations lobbyists. The settlement of this dispute was historic; the change in HEERA legislation represented a stellar moment for a handful of elected leaders truly committed to public service.

A week before the May 1998 joint California–New Mexico legislative hearing, I was asked by the then–acting deputy director of LANL administration to assist him on a special project. After sitting with him in his office and discussing the assignment he had in mind, he suddenly and unexpectedly asked, "So what're you planning to tell the committee?" He was referring to the hearing, and the fact that I'd been invited to testify.

"I haven't decided," I responded. At that moment, the old adage 'Keep your friends close but your enemies closer' came to mind. My new assignment had brought me "closer."

My task, under the acting deputy, was to validate accomplishments within his span of control, and to establish whether those reporting to him were achieving their performance goals. Among his direct-reports (managers answering to him) were those responsible for the laboratory's accounting, procurement, budgeting, and legal departments. It was a strange feeling, being in the same building and on the same floor as the director's inner circle. It was stranger still to attend the weekly staff meetings the deputy held with the heads of these organizations.

The acting deputy director believed in mentoring subordinates, and within this context advised me in late 1998, early into our relationship, that if I wanted to have a meaningful career I should leave the laboratory. He respected my advocacy for the labees terminated in 1995, but he also felt his colleagues in lab leadership weren't so inclined to forgive or forget—not that I felt I needed forgiving. But his frankness was refreshing, and it meant he wouldn't last long at the institution. By 1999 he was gone—another casualty of those too intolerant to respect differences, too entrenched to accept change, and too closed-minded to recognize that the wrong committed in the 1995 layoff had been righted.

14

COLLATERAL DAMAGE

"WHY DON'T YOU GO back to where you came from?" asked the woman, who was speaking to my wife, Elaine. The woman was a recovery room nurse at the Los Alamos Medical Center where my wife ran the gastroenterology unit for the hospital, and was upset that my advocacy on behalf of labees had resulted in a settlement. She'd made the nasty remark after first confirming, with Elaine, that she was, indeed, my spouse.

"This *is* where I'm from," Elaine responded. "I was born and raised here." "Here," for her, meant fifty miles away in a small Northern New Mexico village called Pecos.

Los Alamos is a company town, and so not everyone in the community was inclined to celebrate the exoneration of those unfairly terminated in the '95 layoff. The woman who lashed out was the spouse of a lab manager. The irony was that she and her husband had arrived in New Mexico only a few years earlier—a shared trait among many in laboratory leadership. But her statement echoed the sentiments of some in the community who viewed "locals" as not really being "from" Los Alamos, perhaps not even fully American. Stereotyping is rooted in such assumptions, typically motivated by someone's appearance, where that person is thought to be from, or maybe even just the unfamiliar sound of the individual's name.

When the Wen Ho Lee story broke in 1998, there were many in government, in the media, and in the general public whose rush to judgment was based entirely on Dr. Lee's ancestry, appearance, and name. Had they held off in their judgment, they might have learned that long before he surfaced in the news, related aspects of the W88 warhead design, which he was being falsely accused of revealing to the People's Republic of China, were discussed, dissected, and analyzed in many unclassified articles, talks, and websites. The Chinese, therefore, could have utilized these widely available venues, in conjunction with their own research, to glean the "classified" insights about the W88 they were now suspected of having. Plus there were dozens of other individuals, within the nuclear weapons establishment, who were in a much better position to divulge secrets about this particular warhead. Dr. Lee, in fact, had never been directly involved with either its development or design.

Stereotyping comes from the notion that different groups are somehow genetically predisposed to succeed or fail . . . or be spies. Women feel it too—the anguish of being judged, versus being valued for accomplishments and ability. My thoughts on this issue may be partly rooted in my own insecurities, but another slice of me recognizes prejudice is real. At an annual gala event, sponsored by the LANL Foundation, this reality once again reared its ugly head.

The gala was being held in Santa Fe, at the La Fonda Hotel in the historic Santa Fe Plaza. The man next to me, Bruce Darling, was the University of California's vice president for laboratory management. He was the highest-ranking UC official responsible for lab oversight. Speaker after speaker took to the podium, singing the praises of one grant recipient after another.

Suddenly Darling made an observation that caught me off guard: he stated how impressed he was with how well local Hispanics spoke English. I felt a need to respond, pointing out that many Northern New Mexicans were descendants of the colonizing efforts of Spain in 1598, which occurred more than twenty years before the pilgrims landed at Plymouth Rock. "We didn't cross the border," I continued, "the border crossed us."

Darling appeared flustered by my reaction, proceeding to explain that his father had been a US State Department official stationed in South America, and that our mastery of English in New Mexico was better than the people of that continent. His observation implied to me that Northern New Mexico was, in his mind, akin to a Third World state—essentially a colony of his employer, the University of California. Years later, in a legal deposition, Darling denied the incident, claiming it wasn't in his nature to have said something like that. But for me it was a lightbulb moment I couldn't have imagined, nor would I soon forget.

The LANL Foundation had been established in 1997 by the LANL acting deputy director—the same person who'd been my mentor. Such institutions were common in the corporate world he'd come from, helping as they did to build bridges and mend fences with local politicians and community leaders. Strategically directed grants—gifts of money—produce goodwill for difficult times, as in the wake of a bungled layoff.

> The Los Alamos National Laboratory Foundation has
> awarded nearly $800,000 in community and education
> outreach grants to 64 educational institutions and non-
> profit organizations serving several New Mexico coun-
> ties. Since 1998 the LANL Foundation has invested
> more than $16 million in 1,200 grants. (Staff Report,

"LANL Awards Nearly $800,000 in Grants," *Albuquerque Journal North*, January 2, 2005)

In time, criticism directed at LANL and related news coverage became noticeably less insightful and frequent. The giving away of greenbacks had apparently done its job—winning friends and influencing people, and communities.

At its founding, the LANL Foundation received a start-up grant from federal coffers to the tune of tens of millions of dollars, thanks to the laboratory's perennial patron saint, Senator Pete Domenici. The University of California chipped in a few million more, but then used its indirect (overhead) rate to recover its "contribution" from taxpayers. The overhead rate is basically a tax that vendors, including UC in this case, apply against federal contracts. Under the Federal Acquisition Regulations (the FAR), UC's actions were unallowable:

> The US Department of Energy's Office of Inspector General is investigating whether the University of California improperly charged the federal government $6 million to support a New Mexico foundation. . . . Accusations are contained in a draft audit. . . . The report says the Energy Department approved UC's proposal in 1997 to establish the nonprofit Los Alamos National Laboratory Foundation. . . . However, the audit says, the university charged an excessive share of its annual contributions to the foundation to the government . . . (Keay Davidson, "UC Probed Over Los Alamos Reimbursements," *San Francisco Chronicle*, November 19, 2005)

For those doing business with the government, the "overhead rate" is often used to mask what's occurring, which is billing taxpayers for unallowable costs. In accordance with the FAR, direct charges, such as labor and materials, need to be applied to specific jobs or programs. But there are other expenditures as well that benefit all efforts, such as executive salaries, administrative services, advertising and marketing, training, memberships, and depreciation for equipment and facilities. These are called "indirect costs," and because they indirectly support all programmatic efforts, they need to be allocated (shared) among them so that these costs, as well, are recouped from those who provide funding for these efforts. The overhead rate is how this is done, hence the importance of computing the correct rate, and why determining the allowability and necessity of expenditures included in the indirect cost pool is vital. Otherwise, taxpayers may end up reimbursing government vendors for costs that are unnecessary, unallowable, and provide no benefit to the pubic, as is the case with expenditures for liquor and contributions made to foundations that give away taxpayer money to buy influence or promote an image.

A West Coast vendor once tried to palm off, on the federal government, the cost of owning and maintaining a luxury yacht, which was used primarily for pleasure and served no legitimate business need. The vendor did this by including related depreciation figures and operating costs in its indirect calculation. In another case, I discovered an Albuquerque vendor doing the same with a twin-engine propeller plane. Such billing schemes—hiding unallowable, questionable, excessive, and unnecessary costs in indirect cost pools—is what causes taxpayers to pay $200 for a run-of-the-mill toilet seat and $150 for a standard Home Depot hammer.

Audit reports challenged these bilking practices, but the decision whether to do anything about them was made by the contract administrator for the entity procuring the goods or services, not the auditor. With respect to the foundation, it gave money away as grants, meaning there was nothing being procured or received in return, and so to the extent it was taxpayer money being utilized, gifts and contributions were unallowable under the FAR, which is why UC, in utilizing the overhead rate it applied to contracts with the federal government to recoup its donations to the Los Alamos Foundation, was in violation. But, as usual, the DOE contract administrator, responsible for administering the prime contract between the Department of Energy and the University of California, okayed it.

It was improper, as well, to expect or require subcontractors—vendors being awarded contracts directly, by UC and the laboratory, for the acquisition of goods and services—to make donations to the Los Alamos lab foundation. Who administers these contracts if not LANL and the university, and what is the likelihood either will reject a subcontractor's attempt to recoup from the public amounts they're "donating" if UC, itself, is doing the same? Besides, major suppliers contributed to the LANL Foundation for good reason—because they, as $10,000-per-foundation-event sponsors, were racking up points for when their contracts came up for renewal.

A few months before the LANL gala, I was with Dr. Reynal Guillen, a University of California–Los Angeles (UCLA) professor. He'd completed his PhD dissertation on the subject of scientific colonialism and invited me to address his class about the labor unrest in Los Alamos. As we strolled through campus, I noticed a bulletin board plastered with ads, among them the announcement of a talk sponsored by the UCLA Asian Ancestor Student Association. It was to be held that same evening, on campus, with Alberta Lee, the daughter of Wen Ho Lee, speaking. We decided to attend.

Alberta was working around the clock to counter the hyperbolic atmosphere surrounding her father's incarceration. It was taking a visible toll on her, but what surprised me was the hostility of some in the audience, perhaps stemming from the outrage people feel when one of their own does something that brings shame or suspicion upon the entire clan. I'd had similar feelings when individuals of Hispanic descent were in the news for some alleged indiscretion or other. I'd felt betrayed, because shared heritage is the book jacket we all wear, and many still render judgment based on what's on the surface, versus the content within.

Alberta began by providing background on her father's predicament. A few moments into her presentation she was fighting back tears, visibly exhausted by the ordeal her family was being put through. Suddenly a member of the audience interrupted with, "Why was he arrested if he wasn't doing anything wrong?" But before Alberta could respond, someone else interjected, "Why was he downloading secrets?" The questions were accusatory, sounding too much like the institutional propaganda that regularly appeared in the media. I stood up to confront what was happening, sensing a "chicken with the broken feather" situation was about to unfold. I implored the audience to keep an open mind, mentioning my association with LANL and my reasons for believing Alberta's father was being unfairly persecuted. I explained that he, as others before him had done, was downloading electronic data—his own—in order to protect it from clerical mishandling. The audience, largely of Asian descent, settled down and allowed Alberta to present her talk without further interruption. It ended up being an enlightening evening after all.

Wen Ho Lee spent nine months in solitary confinement in a Santa Fe jail before his release. He was allowed to leave his cell for exercise an hour each day, though he was forced to wear an orange prison jumpsuit and was always restrained in leg irons and handcuffs chained to his waist. He was under twenty-four-hour video surveillance the entire time, and was not allowed to speak with family or friends in private, or to converse in any language other than English. He'd been stripped of all rights and dignity, and yet, despite all the hoopla surrounding his arrest, not a single charge of espionage was ever brought against him. However, he still had to admit guilt to something . . . anything... or risk spending the rest of his life in fishbowl-like confinement. But as Julian Assange—editor-in-chief of the whistleblower website WikiLeaks—so adroitly points out, "The process *is* the punishment."

The plea deal gave smug prosecutors and the misguided officials who created the mess to begin with a way to save face. Wen Ho Lee pleaded guilty to one count of mishandling classified information in exchange for time served; to do otherwise would've been difficult for anyone. A jury would have probably found him innocent of everything, but the wrong jury could have just as easily put him away for life. The feds had failed to establish any basis to charge, much less prosecute for espionage, but with unlimited resources could keep Dr. Lee tied up in litigation for years. At the conclusion, upon the case being plea-bargained and settled, the federal judge in the matter—the Honorable Judge James Parker—apologized to Lee for the miscarriage of justice.

15

WINDS OF CHANGE

THE '80S WERE A time for imposing financial discipline on government. LANL was largely spared, but with the implosion of the Soviet Union in '91, the "Red threat" could no longer be used as an effective funding lever. And so by the end of the '90s, the talk around LANL was that the powers that be were looking to turn Los Alamos into a plutonium warhead production site.

The Strategic Defense Initiative (SDI), nicknamed Star Wars, was originally intended to protect the US from the Soviet Union. It had been proposed in the early '80s by Edward Teller, who, along with Ernest O. Lawrence, cofounded the UC-run Lawrence Livermore National Laboratory. Teller's idea was that lasers mounted on satellites could knock out incoming missiles, hence the nickname. In the early '80s, President Ronald Reagan embraced the initiative, which managed to keep money flowing into the national labs through the beginning of the '90s. In 1993, after years of research-related spending, President Bill Clinton renamed SDI the Ballistic Missile Defense System. The focus, at that point, shifted toward achieving the means to destroy incoming missiles with ground-launched projectiles, versus satellite lasers. But the money stream for this activity would be drying up sooner rather than later. A more sustainable source of funding was needed.

For many years lab and university officials, and their political allies, had promised they would never allow Los Alamos to become a production site for nuclear weapon cores, commonly known as "pits." LANL, they insisted, was for research; its primary mission was science. But when the Rocky Flats plutonium (Pu) factory on the outskirts of Denver, Colorado, was shut down in 1992 after a number of Pu fires, as well as incidents of widespread contamination, political pressures for a replacement site began ramping up and minds began to change.

LANL was where the initial R&D for Pu warheads occurred, and where related production processes were developed and refined for use at Rocky Flats. Los Alamos, therefore, possessed the needed expertise in plutonium physics, chemistry, metallurgy, engineering, and machining, and had a willing workforce already in place. What was lacking, in the mid-90s, was a secure long-term funding source. Star Wars monies were running out, and the stockpile stewardship program, intended to replace nuclear weapons detonations with state-of-the-art diagnostics and computer modeling capabilities, could only keep the laboratory going strong for another decade or so. Beyond that was the unknown.

Nowhere in the DOE complex, except for LANL, did plutonium-processing capability exist to the extent required for producing Pu warheads in large quantities. The only question was need, given that the estimated useful life of plutonium cores already in the nuclear weapons arsenal, including those in storage, was well over a hundred years. Perhaps the more pressing issue was the aging of the bomb-making workforce. As they retired, their expertise went out the door with them. To recreate it from scratch and stretch it decades into the future, or to build a new bomb-making facility in a less populated area with a younger workforce in place, would be a significant expense and political challenge. Besides, the powers that be in Los Alamos were always willing to accept extreme risk in exchange for substantial economic gain. The impact on the rest of Northern New Mexico was largely inconsequential.

> The Los Alamos National Laboratory may have contributed a greater percentage of plutonium contamination at the bottom of Cochiti Lake than once thought, according to new data gathered by lab scientists. . . . A recent core sample taken from the lake's bottom indicated that half the plutonium present came from laboratory operations . . . (Keith Easthouse, "Contamination at Cochiti Lake Traced to LANL," *Santa Fe New Mexican*, September 25, 1997)

And to the extent we ignore the voices of the past, we condemn ourselves to relive what they've experienced:

> Dick VanBuskirk has beryllium disease and chronic trouble breathing. He worries what will happen to his wife after the inevitable happens because the couple has no money. Alex Maestas, exposed to mercury, has two friends who lost their teeth and later died because of mercury poisoning. Darlene Ortiz says her entire family has health troubles ranging from pancreatitis to cancer. Lea Koska lives in constant pain but just isn't sure what's wrong with her. What they have in common is Los Alamos National Laboratory. (Kristen Davenport, "LANL Workers Sound Off about Illness," *Santa Fe New Mexican*, March 19, 2000)

The decision as to whether to turn Los Alamos into a Rocky Flats sequel would be made by politicians and others far removed from the people and communities adversely impacted, and for the benefit of a military-industrial complex that always stood to gain. Beyond these financial and political interests, nothing else mattered.

16

MONOPOLY MONEY

In May 1998, I'd accepted what was supposed to be a limited-term assignment with the acting deputy laboratory director for administration. Now, six months later, with the deputy gone, I was on "unassigned" status. Those who find themselves in this predicament are normally there because funding for their program has ended. If unable to find a new position within the lab, they're at the top of the list in the event of a layoff. The number one priority at this juncture is to flush out another assignment, and fast.

Y2K was fast approaching—the new millennium. For the first time since the invention of electronic data processing, the last two digits of the calendar year would be zeroes. Computer software hadn't been designed to take this into account, and the concern now was that automated processes might stop functioning as intended. No one knew for certain what the new millennium held in store, but the potential for an automation meltdown was too real and significant to ignore.

My undergraduate alma mater—New Mexico Highlands University (NMHU)—was running out of time in its Y2K race to finish converting all its business systems before the year 2000, and it was within this context that I was offered a temporary position supporting its technology group with the transition. Because of my background in computerized systems design, testing, and implementation, plus experience automating the laboratory's accounting processes, NMHU officials looked forward to having me assist with their revamping effort. It would get me out of Los Alamos for a few months, and since I wasn't being utilized at the lab, it was a godsend to be doing something useful for a change. For NMHU, it was a win as well, given that LANL agreed to pay 100 percent of my salary and benefits while on assignment to my alma mater. I was a "gift," compliments of the lab and US taxpayer. In a university setting, it was akin to a sabbatical. But at LANL it was called "professional development." Getting out of the lab's executive wing, where I still occupied office space following the departure of the former deputy director—my onetime mentor—was something laboratory officials wanted. And since I was just twiddling my time away, with nothing to do, escaping "unassigned" status for a while would give me time to find a more permanent role within the laboratory . . . hopefully. External assignments, where a labee was allowed to work at another institution for a while, were considered "perks," but could also be used to encourage people to leave Los Alamos for good. In either case, professional junkets like this required DOE approval and, needless to say, the lab had no problem getting it.

Toward the middle of my one-year assignment I received a phone call from the person who'd just replaced my former "mentor." His name was Joseph "Joe" Salgado, and he was a former Department of Energy deputy secretary, which at the time made him the most powerful executive in that agency after the DOE secretary. His responsibilities now, at LANL, in 1999, made him the lab's second-in-command.

During Salgado's call he assured me if I returned from my NMHU assignment early, I'd receive job duties worthy of my expertise and seniority. I was starving for the opportunity to do something meaningful at the lab, so returning prematurely wasn't a difficult choice to make. But, in return, I was being expected to settle an administrative ruling, rendered by the DOE Office of Inspector General (OIG), in 1998. The OIG had decided, after an exhaustive investigation lasting nearly a year, that in 1996 I'd been removed from the LANL audit arena in retaliation for having advocated for the workers laid off in 1995. Laboratory officials had refused to accept the OIG's conclusion and, as was typical of the DOE's stable of military-industrial contractors, preferred the matter be adjudicated in a court of law.

My case, when Salgado called, was just a few weeks away from going to trial, perhaps explaining the timing of his call. But since I had no desire to drag my employer to court, settling the matter informally, as he proposed, was an easy decision to make. I just wanted the retribution to stop, thus agreeing to return from my sabbatical six months early with the understanding that the retaliation I had been experiencing at LANL would end. The next week I was sitting in front of another LANL official discussing my new laboratory role—Project Lead for Internal Controls.

A few weeks after assuming my new duties in the accounting arena at the lab, a copy of a scathing e-mail landed on my desk. It was from a high-ranking UC official—Robert "Bob" Van Ness—and addressed to the laboratory controller, the person responsible for financial reporting and related administrative activities. In it, Van Ness harshly criticized LANL's failure to implement even the most basic internal control over its accounting processes. His criticism was evidence that the Financial Management Information System (FMIS) audit I was not allowed to complete in 1995 had been derailed on purpose. And because of it, the serious deficiencies I'd discovered then were never reported or resolved, which is why I'd been brought back, after several years, to fix them. Van Ness had somehow learned about these problems, which is what triggered his harsh e-mail critique. But in Van Ness's deposition, taken in 2010, he couldn't recall how he'd found out. On that day there was a lot, in fact, that he could no longer remember.

The laboratory was under pressure to do better at managing its finances. It began in the '80s, with President Ronald Reagan's crusade to rein in government spending. But the decades came and went without much improvement in Los Alamos:

Sen. Pete Domenici, R-NM, on Tuesday praised the way Sandia National Laboratory is being managed, but said the Los Alamos laboratory doesn't have enough control over its finances. (John Fleck, "Domenici Criticizes LANL's Fund Management," *Albuquerque Journal North*, August 30, 1995)

When Los Alamos National Laboratory scientists in 1988 first proposed building an enormous machine to take three-dimensional X-rays . . . they thought it would cost $30 million. Seventeen years and more than $300 million later, it still does not work . . . (John Fleck, "Nuke Programs Have 'Systemic Problems,'" Albuquerque Journal North, October 9, 2005)

By 2001 I was responsible for the General Accounting Team, a group of a dozen or so degreed accountants. Not long after assuming this new role questionable requests began arriving on my desk, demands that essentially placed my team at odds with not only accounting and audit professional standards, but the law.

At the end of each year, there was a rush to replace equipment—computers were the prime example. Another ploy was to use excess funds for training boondoggles at year's end; anything to commit funds so that virtually nothing was left to be returned to the primary funding source—the taxpayer. Politicians fighting the budget wars back in DC didn't like seeing money being left on the table. Emptying the plate today meant a bigger slice of the funding pie tomorrow.

Within LANL, the year-end spending spree was called the "silly season." And in the event money for a particular programmatic effort actually ran out, there were a few accounting tricks available. If necessary, incurred costs could be shifted to a different effort, or applied against other pots of money having little, if anything, to do with the program incurring the cost. Commitments could be underestimated; recording of accounting transactions could be delayed until the next fiscal year. The skill was in doing this type of manipulation without it being too obvious.

One of my audits, in the late '80s, was reviewing costs incurred by the laboratory's largest contractor, a five-year $500 million facilities construction and maintenance contract. I found that accrued liabilities were significantly understated. When a liability is underestimated, the recorded expense for that period is understated as well. This, in turn, is a financial misstatement and audit finding.

After the vendor and I went back and forth a few times trying to establish the reason for the understated liability, the truth finally came out. It was a cost passed on to the lab, and the contractor was directed to reduce its claim for the period so LANL could balance its own budget. The vendor was being required by lab officials to violate a fundamental accounting principle—matching costs to the accounting period they're incurred in. For any contractor under a similar circumstance, it would have been self-defeating *not* to comply.

The first inkling I had that things were going to be difficult in the General Accounting group came in the form of an employment separation check that was brought to me to sign. It was a disbursement check approaching $200,000, made out to a lab executive who was retiring. According to policy, no employees were entitled to severance pay if they left the laboratory on their own; plus it was a violation of Federal Acquisition Regulations to just be giving away taxpayer money. My boss, the Accounting Division leader, didn't appreciate my concern. "Shit rolls downhill," she said. "Just sign the damn thing." She wasn't an accountant by training, and at times appeared confused by the financial checks and balances normally associated with sound business practices. As a result, she once authorized a multimillion-dollar duplicate payment, failing to first determine whether the disbursement was already issued. But she was good at following orders from above, and in the final analysis that's what mattered most.

In the succeeding year, after becoming the general accounting team leader, I co-led the lab's year-end financial closing process, along with a colleague from the budgeting ranks. (Our fiscal year end was September 30.) The objective was to make certain that the amount of costs incurred equaled the amount of funding that was authorized, so as to ensure that, at year end, no money was left unobligated or unspent. Equally important was to avoid cost overruns. To accomplish this the institution's records were "closed" several times, each iteration being an attempt to zero out the difference between recorded expenditures and approved funding. To accomplish the year end balancing act, budget specialists initiated corrections after each closing cycle. These specialists moved costs from one funding source or programmatic effort to another. Work orders for such things as building repairs or space reconstruction, as well as procurement orders for goods and services, got released or held back. This was done in order to regulate the amount of funds committed (obligated) in the current fiscal year, as opposed to the next. With each closing iteration, different transaction types were "taxed" at different overhead rates to recover indirect costs from different funding sources. It was like trying to hit a moving target, with those involved working around the clock for days in order to finally get things right.

From an accounting principles standpoint, as well as a cost accounting perspective, where expenditures need to be matched with services rendered and related funding sources, the annual closing process was an open invitation for shenanigans. And it was in the midst of this year-end fray that an employee of mine was directed, by the Accounting Division leader, to apply costs against the wrong programmatic effort, and to correct the transaction in the following fiscal year once additional money arrived. But in this particular case it was illegal to do that—to spend more than was authorized. To purposely apply a cost overrun against the wrong funding source, and then pretend it was done in error, was essentially digging your own grave. My employee, for good reason, was concerned about what she'd been told to do.

The division leader didn't take kindly to employee push-back. Her background was budgeting and she'd gotten her education in India, where business practices were apparently quite different. Plus her knowledge and understanding of accounting rules and regulations was lacking. (She once demanded that I explain the formation of a *balance sheet*, the most basic of all financial reports—a listing of all assets, followed by liabilities, the difference being equity.) Nonetheless, she was in charge, and as such expected her dictates to be followed without question. Once again I was on the receiving end of her favorite refrain, "Shit rolls downhill."

The inappropriateness of what the accounting department leader wanted a member of my team to do didn't seem to matter to her, but it did to me. So I sent my employee an e-mail restating her concern, pointing out that I'd passed it on to the manager in question. I suggested that she save my e-mail for future reference—an insurance policy if you will, to protect her from being blamed for doing what she knew was wrong but was required to do.

Twenty-five years earlier I'd quit the lab's Nuclear Material Safeguards Group because I was told my job was to help "run interference." Now here I was in the Accounting Division, dealing with a similar mind-set. It was a way of thinking that kept stakeholders on edge, held taxpayers hostage, and exposed communities to unnecessary risk.

17

SWAMP ADMIRAL

I'D BEEN IN THE media quite a bit following the 1995 lab-wide layoff. By 1998, even those who had nothing to do with Los Alamos seemed to have some inkling of my existence. Occasionally I was approached in a Santa Fe restaurant or Albuquerque mall by a curious stranger, someone who'd heard about my LANL employee rights exploits on TV or in the newspapers. They often expressed support, were surprised to learn I wasn't among the laid-off labees, and were always curious as to why I'd become an advocate for workers' rights. My motivation stemmed from a disdain I'd always had for bullies—people deriving pleasure from creating havoc and instilling fear. Maybe that's why my hometown newspaper decided, in 1998, to honor me:

> What higher compliment can one say of a person than they made a difference? . . . The framed 11-by-13 inch photo [of the laid-off workers] is a reminder of when times were tough. [Montaño said] "This was the eve of the layoffs, September of 1995. . . . I wanted a picture

for posterity. . . . Los Alamos National Laboratory had
terminated 250 employees. . . . People didn't know what
they were going to do." (Monica Soto, "Making a Difference," *Santa Fe New Mexican*, July 26, 1998)

The terminated labees had begun their journey in a Los Alamos
church. A group photo captured what needed to be remembered
about that moment: the hurt, the fear, the pain, the uncertainty
of what lay ahead—all a reminder of what lab officials had done.
Behind each face was a family in need, and together they represented an entire Northern New Mexico community put on notice
by the military-industrial giant on the hill.

In 2003 the Joint California/New Mexico Legislative Committee on LANL Oversight was scheduled to meet in California's
capital, Sacramento. My past notoriety won me a free ride on a
private jet, to observe. While in flight I learned the joint committee was planning to endorse the University of California staying
in Los Alamos. The lobbying efforts of the university and the
lab had paid off, and I'd been invited along as a courtesy by a
legislator, who perhaps felt somewhat sheepish about this turn
of events. The next day, at the California State Capitol, an individual stood near me. I wasn't sure he knew me, but I recognized
him and a couple of others mingling close by from the laboratory's Government Relations Office. It was Pete Nanos, the new
LANL director, and UC's last best hope for keeping the Los Alamos contract for another sixty years. We were all congregated in
the men's room for the same reason, a last-minute pit stop and
a quick check of the "do" before the start of the day's big event.

We'd arrived the previous day in our loaner—the private
jet. Upon our arrival we were informed we'd be dining that evening at the home of the UC-Davis campus chancellor. The university had nine campuses distributed throughout the state,
and the head of each campus was known as the chancellor.

Each campus was as big as the largest university in the state of New Mexico, if not larger. In short, UC is the largest research university in the country, and its faculty among the most prestigious on the planet.

The chancellor's home was located along the Sacramento River. Living quarters were above the garage. The double-car structure had been built below street level, with garage doors at both ends. A narrow ramp with handrails, similar to a swinging bridge, went from street level to the second floor. The house had been designed this way to accommodate floodwaters from the adjacent river, the objective being to enable water to flow freely through the garage, while still allowing access to the living quarters above. It was an ingenious solution, not unlike the eccentricities built into some homes I'd seen in Los Alamos. At the time, we lived in such a home. The original occupant was a tall scientist who'd had kitchen and bathroom counters installed six inches above standard height. Because there were small children living in the house, he decided to forego placing electrical outlets in the bathrooms.

A nice meal and cocktails, particularly the day before a legislative hearing, could go a long way toward achieving understanding. "Information sharing" is what LANL called it. Apparently that meant "education" with a heavy dose of schmoozing mixed in for good measure.

During the pre-dinner social, Robert "Bob" Dynes, chancellor of the San Diego campus, drifted over to where I stood with Manny Trujillo, president of the University Professional and Technical Employee (UPTE) Local 1663. UPTE was a university-wide organization, a branch of which was established at LANL in the wake of the CLER movement. Manny was president of the Los Alamos chapter and slated to testify at the following day's hearing. Dynes introduced himself to us. He and his UC-Davis counterpart were planning to attend the legislative hearing the next day; exactly why was unclear to me. It seemed like a long way for Dynes to travel just to observe something that really didn't appear to have anything do with him or his campus. Suddenly he asked us how things were going in Los Alamos.

"Things could be better," I said, "if UC paid attention to what was happening there." I was referring to the labor unrest, but wasn't going to get the opportunity to clarify. Dynes smiled awkwardly and quickly moved on. I glanced at Manny, who was now grinning from ear to ear.

"I guess he didn't want to hear about problems," Manny said.

"Maybe not," I responded, "but *that's* the problem."

A few weeks later, a UC announcement came out clarifying why Dynes was there. We'd just met the next president of the University of California.

The hearing convened the following day in legislative chambers at the California State Capitol. It was a typically austere, courtroom-like setting with elevated seating for legislators in the front; an area facing them with a desk, microphones, and chairs for those testifying; and an audience seating area in the back.

The current UC president, Richard Atkinson, was the first to address the committee. Sitting next to him was the newly appointed LANL director, retired navy rear admiral Pete Nanos. Dynes sat in the spectator section close to where I was, along with members of the local media and others from the director's entourage. Atkinson's role was to provide the committee assurance that the university took seriously its responsibility for the three laboratories it oversaw for the federal government. Atkinson stressed that the university did so as a "service to the nation," and then introduced the new director for Los Alamos.

The service-to-the-nation mantra was something UC delivered regularly. When students or faculty questioned the university's association with Los Alamos, an institution whose primary mission is to develop, test, and maintain the nation's arsenal of nuclear weapons, the response was always the same—service to the nation. But in reality the university received nearly $100 million dollars a year in management fees, as well as royalties for patents and licenses associated with lab research. The fact that every LANL employee was required to sign a related agreement said volumes:

Patent Agreement

This agreement is made by me with The Regents of the University of California. . . . Any invention or discovery which I conceive or make while employed by the university shall be examined by the university to determine rights and equities. . . . In the event any such invention or discovery shall be deemed by the university to be patentable, and the university desires, pursuant to determination by the university as to its rights and equities therein, to seek patent protection thereon, I shall execute any documents and do all things necessary, at the university's expense, to assign to the university all rights, title, and interest therein and to assist the university in securing patent protection . . . (Signed by Charles Montaño, May 21, 1979)

UC's political capital was greatly bolstered as well by having three national laboratories at its beck and call—Berkeley, Livermore, and Los Alamos. University staff had access to research facilities and capabilities they might otherwise not have. Plus with control over three federal labs, the University of California held sway over tens of thousands of jobs and billions in procurement dollars. California business interests in particular benefited greatly from the arrangement. The evolution of the National Ignition Facility (NIF) at Lawrence Livermore National Laboratory, one of the three government facilities under the UC umbrella, was a case in point.

Lawrence Livermore National Laboratory (LLNL) had developed an approach for achieving sustainable laser fusion. Funding came through the stockpile stewardship program, whose objective was to support the maintenance of the country's nuclear weapons inventory. If successful, the laser fusion approach could also provide pathways for producing vast amounts of energy for commercial use. Though a competing approach developed elsewhere held greater promise, the California economy was in dire need of a stimulus. Plus questions were being raised on Capitol Hill as to whether, with the end of the Cold War, there was any valid reason to continue funding two nuclear weapons labs—Los Alamos and Livermore.

Business interests influence politicians with campaign contributions, and politicians, in turn, persuade those who determine how to divvy up the taxpayer funding pie. The decision over whether or not to keep the funding spigot open for the Livermore Laboratory and State of California boiled down to technical merit versus political mandate. Lab directors working for UC were tasked to decide. Unsurprisingly, the LLNL approach was chosen, even though the alternative appeared to be environmentally safer, plus more financially sound and technically feasible. NIF was the result, with taxpayers bearing the enormous cost of its eventual failure, and all of humanity now poised to pay for the undermining of a groundbreaking scientific endeavor that might have freed us from the planetary stranglehold that is oil dependency.

This June 2000 report from NRDC's [Natural Resources Defense Council] nuclear program details serious prob-

lems with the National Ignition Facility, a laser facil-
ity under construction by the Department of Energy at
Lawrence Livermore National Laboratory in California,
including enormous cost overruns as well as the likely
inability of the project to achieve its primary mission. (C.
E. Paine, M. McKinzie, and T. B. Cochran, "When Peer
Review Fails: The Roots of the National Ignition Facility
[NIF] Debacle," 2000)

NIF lacked technical merit, but the military-industrial complex,
based in California, needed the economic boost associated with
the project.

With the total tab for NIF now running to an estimated
$7 billion, the [Livermore] laboratory has been pulling
out all the stops to claim success is just around the corner. . . . But "next year" already is years behind schedule, and so far, as William Broad reported in the *New
York Times* last week, NIF simply "has not worked." (Bill
Sweet, "National Ignition Facility: Mother of All Boondoggles?," *IEEE Spectrum*, November 5, 2012)

By 2013 even California's own US senator, Dianne Feinstein,
could no longer defend it:

Feinstein is a member of the powerful Senate Appropriations Committee and chairs its subcommittee on energy
and water development. She rejected their [twenty-five
members of the House of Representatives'] request to
support NIF's request for $486.6 million for the coming
year, saying it "is hard to justify" as there is no "clear

path forward for achieving ignition." (David Perlman,
"Feinstein Declines to Halt NIF Budget Cuts," *San Francisco Chronicle*, May 16, 2013)

Back in Sacramento in 2003, the moment we'd been waiting
for finally arrived. The new lab director—a retired navy rear
admiral—had a penetrating stare as he addressed the legislative committee. He spoke clearly and directly but was seemingly
unable to smile easily. Even in staged photographs, the serious-
ness of his demeanor was undeniable. Perhaps he was the right
person for the job at this point in the laboratory's history. The
question was whether he'd be allowed to do it. For the moment,
at least, he had a plan—to drain the swamp.

Los Alamos National Laboratory interim director Pete
Nanos told University of California regents Wednesday
he would "drain the swamp" at LANL . . . (Adam Rankin,
"LANL Boss to Drain Swamp," *Albuquerque Journal
North*, January 16, 2003)

The admiral-director was committed to doing whatever was necessary to free the "ship" from the muck and put it back on course.
He'd received his orders—his mission was to crack the whip in
order to convince the US Congress that the university deserved
to remain in Los Alamos.

In his own testimony, Manny Trujillo, UPTE president for
LANL workers, built on the swamp analogy, pointing out that
progress was unlikely unless those inhabiting the swamp were
also controlled. Holding people responsible was his meaning, for
without accountability nothing would improve.

A few weeks later the newly designated LANL director was
ready to address his new command for the first time. It was

standing room only in the lab's main conference hall. The rest of the workforce was crammed into rooms across the laboratory, where they watched via cable net. Most had read or heard about the director's testimony in California, and his swamp analogy hadn't sat well with many.

Nanos stood tall and looked sternly at the audience. It was clear he'd been briefed, and what he'd learned didn't bode well for the troops. He paced back and forth, speaking about the lab mission, funding issues, future directions . . . the type of stuff directors routinely talked about during such presentations. When the topic of the university's contract with DOE to run Los Alamos finally came up, his voice became elevated as he warned labees that any more gaffes by them could cost UC the contract. It was everyone's responsibility, he said, to work hard at ensuring that didn't happen. He repeated what he'd said in Sacramento, regarding some lab employees being arrogant and defiant of authority, and emphasized that these individuals would either shape up or get shipped out, and he'd be the one doing the shipping.

Director Nanos had delivered a wake-up call in his first Los Alamos address. UC could lose the contract to run the laboratory, and in layman's terms that meant the pot of retirement gold at the end of the rainbow could slip away. He had a real challenge on his hands but wasn't necessarily stating his case effectively or focusing his wrath on the right people. Fixing systemic problems and maintaining internal control integrity was the responsibility of managers, not the lower-tier personnel normally saddled with the blame. And as for arrogance, that was a valid concern. But "the attitude" stemmed from advanced education, high pay, the notion that we simply knew better than everyone else, and the fact that no matter what, nobody in authority was ever held accountable. The LANL slogan—World's Greatest Science Protecting America—said it all.

18

CONJURING

I'D ENDED MY ADVOCACY for workers' rights in 1999, after the '95 layoff dispute was settled, hoping perhaps institutional leadership would turn a new leaf. I should have known better. Four years later it's 2003, and once again I'm sitting in a legislative committee room, this time in Santa Fe. An analysis I'd done a few months earlier, which proved that LANL female employees were severely underpaid compared with their male colleagues doing the same work, has prompted a meeting with various legislators. They've assembled to hear arguments related to a study LANL put out in response to my assessment, referred to as the Welch Study, named after the out-of-state statistician hired to do it.

The laboratory had spent $241,000 dollars to have someone with a PhD counter the free salary disparity evaluation I'd done over the course of a couple of days. The consultant presented to the committee a mathematical algorithm allegedly explaining away much of the pay inequity in different job classifications. My analysis, according to LANL leadership, was flawed, but in reality it wasn't. Officials weren't inclined to admit anything, so a class-action complaint would have to follow. Two separate lawsuits filed soon after sought declaratory and injunctive relief for violations of the Federal Equal Pay Act and the New Mexico Human Rights Act. Veronique Longmire and Laura Barber were representative plaintiffs in one, Gloria Bennett and four other women on the other. Both complaints were later combined into one and certified, by the court, for class-action status,

The Welch Study had been a taxpayer-funded shell game. But the consultant who did it was still a professional—an unwilling accomplice who was now inclined to admit not being able to explain, or justify, why certain factors were included in the algorithm he'd used. Under focused questioning by legislators, he admitted introducing the "mystery factors" on the lab's insistence. It was a stunning admission, and exposed the reality that the algorithm had been designed to artificially understate the disparity. A quarter million in taxpayer dollars was spent to perpetrate a hoax, and here's how it was done: If the algorithm was $A + B = C$ and C was not the result the laboratory wanted, another factor was added to achieve the intended outcome. The algorithm might now be $A + B + X = D$, with D being the desired result—a smaller salary disparity. The mystery X was what the consultant couldn't explain.

Had a scientist injected variables into a research effort and not been able to explain the purpose or impact, that individual would have been subjected to a severe tongue-lashing among colleagues. The peer review process requires professionals be able to explain their work so that if anyone wanted to, the effort could be replicated and the results verified. Nonetheless, even with the mysterious adjustments, the computed wage gap for women was still statistically significant, and the list of employees seeking redress got longer.

The related class-action suit dragged on, and after years of lab-induced delays, related motions for dismissal, and taxpayer-funded public relations campaigns dedicated to image bolstering, damage control, and denial, there was, at last, a settlement. But even after paying $16.4 million to end the case, LANL would still insist it did nothing wrong. And while the wage equity suit may have been settled in 2006, there was no provision in the resolution to actually eliminate disparity:

> Lab employee Veronique Longmire, one of two women who brought the lawsuit in December 2003, objected to the settlement . . . [because it] did not adjust salaries for female lab employees to fix what she believes are built-in inequities. Without that, she said, any discrimination that exists will continue with the law's blessing. (Associated Press, "Comment Sought on Proposed LANL Lawsuit Settlement," *Albuquerque Journal*, August 8, 2006)

And to add insult, the settlement was distributed among all members of the class, whether deserving or not, regardless of the person's salary, and despite the individual's role resisting those advocating for fairness in the workplace:

> It's been said you can judge a person's character not by what he says but by what he does. There are at least two lab attorneys (Castille and Prando) on the list of salary disparity class settlement recipients referenced here, plus two Level 4 Managers from Lab Legal (Chandler and Woitte). How many other highly paid managers took a share of the settlement for themselves? How about HR and other personnel whose primary mission it is to discredit employees complaining of workplace abuse? http://lanl-the-rest-of-the-story.blogspot.com/2008/09/

lanl-salary-disparity-settlement.html (Posted by Frank Young, "LANL Salary Disparity Settlement Beneficiaries,"*LANL: The Rest of the Story*, September 12, 2008)

The powers that be had effectively thumbed their noses at the victims and the taxpayers who ultimately get stuck with the tab. And as for Longmire's doubts regarding the laboratory's commitment to treat workers fairly, unfortunately she was right:

> A comparison of paychecks indicates that it's still a man's world. *On Numbers* looked at the median earnings of men and women in 942 metropolitan and micropolitan areas, using data from the US Census Bureau's 2010 American Community Survey. . . . Among medium-sized markets, the income disparity among genders is the greatest in Los Alamos. Men in the community that is home to Los Alamos National Laboratory earn a median of $81,712, while women earn $41,391. (Staff reporter, "Gender Income Disparity Greatest in Los Alamos," *New Mexico Business Weekly*, January 20, 2012)

The new LANL director had come to Los Alamos and prescribed the same medicine for everyone, technical and nontechnical staff alike. But he was dealing with an entrenched culture. It was inevitable that there'd be resistance:

> Scientists and engineers who design the nation's nuclear bombs are sporting an odd bumper sticker on their cars in the remote mountain community at Los Alamos National Laboratory: "Striving for a Work-Free Safe Zone.". . . Nanos, who took over the lab in early 2003

after the prior director resigned amid a series of financial and security scandals, has tried to make changes. But he has met strong resistance . . . (Ralph Vartabedian and Christine Hanley, "A Nuclear Lab's 'Cowboy Culture,'" *Los Angeles Times*, July 25, 2004)

Pete Nanos didn't have to wait long for the next major faux pas to occur:

Two years of security and safety-related scandals climaxed in July, when lab officials learned two computer disks containing secret data were missing. Nanos hit the roof and held several staff meetings during which he chewed out staff members, [and] called certain employees "butt-heads" and "cowboys" . . . (Keay Davidson, "Los Alamos Lab Chief Calls Worker Meeting," *San Francisco Chronicle*, October 19, 2004)

The clock was nearing midnight on the prime contract to run LANL. This was a long-standing arrangement that the University of California may now have to compete for. Also, the loss of two classified computer disks wasn't supposed to occur once Nanos took charge in Los Alamos, but it did. Desperate times now called for extreme measures, and if embracing the DOE's desire to turn LANL into a plutonium warhead plant was needed to keep UC's hold on Northern New Mexico, then so be it.

19

HIDDEN DANGERS

LOS ALAMOS, IT SEEMED, was a good place to raise a family. The school system was the best in the state, and because it was an affluent community, the streets felt safe. But apparently, in the air and water there were things no one knew about. According to a 1999 article in the *Santa Fe New Mexican*, Los Alamos County residents developed thyroid cancer at a rate four times higher than the nation's between 1987 and 1993.

Like so many others in the community, my wife developed thyroid cancer, which, thank goodness, we discovered in time. And yet nowhere in her family tree or work history could we find a cause, except for the fact that we lived in Los Alamos. She was never employed by LANL, but did run the gastroenterology laboratory for the local hospital and, in that capacity, found the incidence of colon and intestinal cancer among labees to be extraordinarily high. In short order, mandatory colonoscopies ceased being part of LANL's health plan—perhaps an attempt to avoid another health study that could establish a connection to the work being done at LANL. I'd often walked the trails around and through the community, observing remnants of experiments and stains of chemicals dumped into adjacent canyons. Over time, wind and water carried contaminants off the lab reservation, but laboratory leaders were always tight-lipped about such things, and, as a result, many who'd never worked at LANL would suffer for it.

In 1989 DOE secretary admiral James D. Watkins assembled "Tiger Teams" to assess Department of Energy contractor-run facilities for environmental contamination and cleanup in the aftermath of the Cold War. Related findings released in 1991 identified over 2,000 toxic sites in Los Alamos alone. And in 2003 the Centers for Disease Control and Prevention (CDC) began reconstructing radiation releases to establish the amounts of special nuclear materials that had actually, versus reportedly, escaped into the environment, and thus put people at risk, health-wise. But then, even for the CDC, there was the usual laboratory resistance to contend with:

> Federal health officials are criticizing Los Alamos National Laboratory once again, for denying or limiting access to documents requested as part of an extensive review of pollution and its possible effects on people. For the second year in a row, officials with the national Centers for Disease Control and Prevention traveled to Northern New Mexico with bad news. . . . Already, CDC officials say, evidence from soil-sampling seems to indicate that the amount of plutonium released into the environment might be "hundreds of times" higher than estimated. (Jeff Tollefson, "CDC Says Lab Withholding Documents," *Santa Fe New Mexican*, July 10, 2003)

The Centers for Disease Control eventually sifted through 40,000 boxes of documentation, managing to obtain enough insight to estimate radioactive and chemical releases for a significant number of lab experiments and activities. Reconstruction was based on experiment logs, research notes, reports, and eyewitness accounts, among other documents. The results were disturbing, and the potential impacts were greater than previously thought, as detailed in the following newspaper article:

> A recently filed lawsuit is alleging a man died of cancer as a result of years spent playing in contaminated canyons near Los Alamos National Laboratory as a child in the 1950s. The suit—which could be the first of its kind against Los Alamos—was filed Tuesday by the man's daughter. . . . Lowell Edward Ryman's exposure to radioactive wastes and plutonium as a young boy led him to develop multiple myeloma as an adult . . . . Ryman's mother also died of multiple myeloma . . . . Autopsies done on some residents who lived in Los Alamos and White Rock during the Cold War but who were not lab employees showed plutonium levels that exceeded what would be expected . . . (Raam Wong, "Lawsuit Blames LANL in Death," *Albuquerque Journal North*, April 11, 2008)

Employees who raised health and safety concerns were "non–team players" and were dealt with accordingly, as in the case of Eddie Lujan, who'd worked for Los Alamos for nearly twenty years. According to a 1993 article in the *Houston Chronicle*, high radiation readings outside Area G (LANL's radioactively contaminated waste disposal site)—in some cases four to five times the "background" levels typically found in the local Jemez Mountains—made Lujan uneasy:

> . . . [Per Eddie Lujan] "They said, 'We'll take care of it.' . . . Nothing ever happened." On Jan. 8 the lab finally acted. It fired Lujan after nearly 20 years of service. (Jim Morris, "Deck Stacked against DOE Whistleblowers," *Houston Chronicle*, September 26, 1993)

Nearly four years later, the Government Accountability Project released a press release announcing that a female LANL radiation technician, Frances McLeod, was wrongfully fired after raising safety and radiation concerns connected with her work at Los Alamos. The US Department of Labor (DOL) investigated, and then offered to prescribe her remedies. Typically this entailed job reinstatement and restitution for lost wages, but no payment for emotional pain or physical suffering, and no protection from the retaliation that would inevitably follow. And in the lab's case, there was always an appeal, and sustained resistance to complying with agency rulings of this type. LANL wasted lots of taxpayer money fighting labees, but nothing changed, and the list of victims just kept getting longer:

> Longtime House Speaker Ben Lujan announced to the opening session of the [New Mexico] Legislature today that he has Stage 4 lung cancer and will not seek re-election . . . Lujan said he believes the lung cancer was due to his previous work as an ironworker at Los Alamos National Laboratory. (Dan Boyd, "Speaker Lujan Reveals He Has Lung Cancer," *Albuquerque Journal*, January 17, 2012)

It was risky for a labee to express misgivings about a bad situation in Los Alamos, but every once in a while some still tried, including Joe Gutierrez, a quality assurance (QA) assessor for LANL's Assessment and Audits Division. Gutierrez was a professional associate of mine, and an expert on the Clean Air Act regulations. His refusal to cover up problems for the lab led to the following 1997 *Santa Fe Reporter* article, which Senator Pete Domenici then took Joe to task for:

> [Gutierrez] found that two technicians were compiling data on radionuclide air emissions at Tech Area 21 using different methodologies. . . . When he reviewed their calculations, Gutierrez said he discovered that the emission records for a complete year were missing. Among other instances, a report Gutierrez wrote on the tritium air monitoring system sat on the lab director's desk for a year while it was being revised to minimize the problems cited. . . . Another assessment, prepared by Gutierrez in 1995, of the plutonium processing facility warned that because of a defect in concrete walls, plutonium gases could escape . . . (Anne Constable, "The Truth about the Stacks," *Santa Fe Reporter*, January 15–21, 1997)

Workers, their families, and surrounding communities had all been exposed to far more than anyone could imagine, and nobody in authority ever got held accountable:

> Los Alamos National Laboratory released a critical self-evaluation Friday saying that the lab has been complacent, ignorant, and not accountable for protecting the

environment and workers. Those are among major "root causes" of lab environment, safety, and health problems, which range from lack of leadership to noncompliance. . . . Findings highlight noncompliance with state and federal water discharge rules, the lack of a worker occupational safety program, and inconsistent observance of radiation protection procedures. (Associated Press, "Los Alamos Admits Major Faults, Lists Causes," *Los Angeles Times*, August 31, 1991)

The lab was arrogant, but certainly not ignorant. Institutional leadership knew precisely what they were doing. It was the community that was being kept ignorant, not knowing to what extent they'd been exposed to plutonium (Pu) releases from the DP West site—the original Pu processing plant in Los Alamos. The amount and frequency of radioactive releases at that site, as reported by the Associated Press (AP), were among the worst in the DOE complex, something I wasn't told when I began working there in '78. According to the AP, plutonium releases at DP West between 1948 and 1955 could exceed airborne escape totals from the following Pu production facilities combined: the Hanford plant in Washington State, where nuclear reactors were used to convert uranium to plutonium; the Savannah River plant in South Carolina, where the material extracted from the Hanford reactors was processed to separate the Pu atoms from everything else; and in Colorado, at the Rocky Flats facility, where the plutonium concentrate from Savannah was then processed into the metal spheres used in nuclear warheads.

Documents discovered by the Los Alamos Historical Document Retrieval and Assessment (LAHDRA) Project and presented in 2010 say that airborne Pu releases from LANL before the 1970s were "significantly higher than had been officially reported." The documents also say that the releases from DP West "greatly exceed the independently established total releases from routine operations for all other DOE plutonium production facilities." And according to a November 1996 report in the *Albuquerque Journal North*, forty-two years after Los Alamos agreed to cede its position as the nation's nuclear weapons factory it had been targeted to become the next Rocky Flats. The Energy Department's justification was that LANL was the nation's only facility left for making plutonium "pits." But the lab had never manufactured Pu warheads on the scale anticipated, nor dealt with the quantities of waste stemming from that size of operation. According to the *Albuquerque Journal North*, discharges of liquid radioactive wastes into nearby Mortandad Canyon would increase by a fifth, or 45 million gallons, to 278 million gallons a year, with existing facilities being greatly expanded and waste hauling, within the lab, doubling to about 1,300 shipments annually. The *Journal* also reported an additional 10,600 cubic feet of plutonium-contaminated and mixed radioactive/hazardous wastes would be generated each year. Presumably, though not stated in the article, the risk to workers and communities would increase as well.

It's been said that those who forget the past are condemned to repeat it. At the Rocky Flats plant, established in 1952 thirty minutes outside Denver, Colorado, stacks of barrels containing radioactive waste had been left exposed to the elements for too long and began leaking out into the environment as early as 1959. It wasn't until 1970, when wind-borne particles of plutonium were detected in Denver, that public concern over Rocky Flats began to take root. But by then it was too late, and in the '80s whistleblowers began revealing more about what was occurring within the secretive facility, including on-site burning of contaminated waste, often done illegally and under the cover of darkness. As a result, the Federal Bureau of Investigation (FBI) and Environmental Protection Agency (EPA) conducted a joint raid of the plant in 1989. The abuses discovered were so widespread and serious that a special grand jury was impaneled. A related plea agreement, reached in 1992, had Rockwell International—the company contracted with the Department of Energy to manage Rocky Flats—admitting to ten federal environmental crimes. But the citizen-representing grand jury wasn't satisfied, accusing both the contractor and the DOE of "engaging in a continuing campaign of distraction, deception, and dishonesty." The grand jury followed suit by compiling indictments, charging three Energy Department officials and five Rockwell employees with crimes. The US Department of Justice, however, refused to sign off, and in so doing the legitimate outrage of the citizenry of Colorado was quashed. Once again the wealthy corporate interests represented by the DOE complex, and jealously protected by powerful allies within the DC beltway, had gotten a free pass to do as they pleased and get away with it.

With the city of Santa Fe located just twenty miles away as the wind blows, "Santa Fe style" would surely take on new meaning if a Rocky Flats–magnitude accident were to occur in Los Alamos. Million-dollar estates would become far more affordable overnight; city streets once lined with tourists would be far less congested.

Until the end of the Cold War, lab and university leaders pledged LANL would never become a plutonium warhead production site, but by the end of the '90s these same officials were having second thoughts. The search for sustainable funding had usurped common sense. The laboratory was now being touted as the logical replacement for Rocky Flats, and with this sudden change of heart the funding floodgates were reopened.

Following WWII we committed, as a nation, much of our collective wealth to the care and feeding of the military-industrial complex. We won the Cold War in the process, and in the aftermath were supposed to receive a peace dividend. But military-related expenditures went up instead; the LANL budget alone nearly doubled ten years following the collapse of the Soviet Union.

By 2014, even though the United States represented just 5 percent of the world's population, it was responsible for 65 percent of the planet's defense spending. It also possessed all ten of the world's functional aircraft carriers, and was still intent on acquiring one more. We the citizenry had been duped, like an abused spouse who wants to believe his or her partner has turned a new leaf but hasn't, and never will. War-making expenditures just kept climbing.

20

LEPERS AND LIES

WHISTLEBLOWERS ARE INDIVIDUALS WHO provide a service by informing elected officials, regulators, law enforcement, and the general public of suspected fraud, waste, and abuse of taxpayer resources, as well as practices that place workers, families, communities, or the environment at unreasonable or unnecessary risk.

Federal fraud is generally characterized as willfully misrepresenting a fact that results in the government making an undeserved payment or costly decision. With abuse, the person may be badly motivated, but not clearly in violation of laws regulating fraud. And with respect to waste, negligence or incompetence is implied, which in and of itself isn't a crime.

Institutional leadership is usually responsible for what's occurring under these circumstances, or unwilling, for whatever reason, to admit to the problem, much less resolve it. Because of this, and the associated risk to the individual, whistleblowing is protected under the law, or is at least supposed to be.

At Los Alamos, however, whistleblowers are often left to their own defenses—or worse. A 1998 *USA Today* article reported that former Department of Energy secretary Hazel O'Leary said, in a videotaped deposition, that workers who exposed flaws at nuclear weapons plants and labs were regularly harassed and undermined by their bosses.

According to the Government Accountability Project, which issued a press release on the matter, O'Leary went on to assert:

> [W]hat I then knew and know even more deeply after having spent four years in the Department of Energy . . . has been a practice of repeated and long-term reprisal that visits the employee in the place that he or she is most vulnerable and that is, first of all, in the questioning of the employee's competence to do his or her work . . . . [O]nce that happens to any employee, that individual is almost dead in terms of promotion. . . . I recall stories . . . of employees being stopped in the parking lot, threatened by some of their colleagues, and more often than not the theme of what they told me would be, "You are messing with our livelihood here. Don't you know that this is about our work?" . . . One employee believes that she or he was forced off the road, and others have told stories about driving home late at night from work and having people point shotguns at them and the like." (Bob Seldon, Press Release, "Liberty and the Workplace," Government Accountability Office, June 6, 1998)

In addition to being forthright in her revelations about whistleblower retribution, O'Leary, who was appointed by President Bill Clinton in 1993, would also receive praise for declassifying Cold War era records showing the US government used American citizens as guinea pigs in human radiation experiments. Thus the Department of Energy, in its own right, was notorious when it came to abuse.

In January 2003, according to the *Los Angeles Times*, Energy Department officials suspended Christopher Steele, a senior DOE safety manager stationed at LANL. He was let go without explanation after pushing for an investigation into the unsafe storage of plutonium-contaminated waste and other safety problems he discovered in Los Alamos.

Former DOE secretary O'Leary attested to what those employed at contractor facilities like Los Alamos Laboratory already knew—if they report mismanagement, they become targets for career-ending retaliation. And when that happens, there's no credible recourse for them except to endure, quit, or sue. Journeyman carpenter Rhonda McNeal learned this the hard way in 1997. After she warned of safety hazards and poor workmanship on a new experiment facility being built at LANL, her top supervisors "cursed" her, according to an article in *Albuquerque Journal North*:

> "Twenty years of my life, and I couldn't buy a job right now," a sobbing McNeal told Hecker [the outgoing laboratory director]. . . . McNeal and others pressed Hecker . . . for stronger protection for whistleblowers at the lab." (Ian Hoffman, "Whistleblowers Describe Harassment, Fear at LANL," *Albuquerque Journal North*, June 30, 1997)

In 1997, Hecker promised to "look at" McNeal's claims and "study" how to improve whistleblower protection at LANL. Apparently nothing came of it, for in truth nobody in charge was really all that concerned about those reporting fraud, waste, and abuse. This, despite what the law required, or public posturing to the contrary.

In biblical times, lepers were considered dead people. As they passed through the streets, they had to yell out, "Unclean!" so everyone knew their status. Thousands of years later, Glenn Walp, a Los Alamos National Laboratory employee who was fired for speaking up about corruption, understands what it's like to be a leper. "In parallel, when you become a whistleblower, you likewise become among the unclean and people avoid you," he told a gathering Tuesday . . . (Diana Heil, "Whistleblowers Share Hopes for Congressional Hearing," *Santa Fe New Mexican*, October 27, 2004)

Glenn Walp, a retired state police commissioner, had gained national notoriety following his termination from LANL. I was on hand the day he gave his whistleblower presentation in October 2004. Sitting next to me was Pete Stockton from the DC-based nonprofit Project on Government Oversight (POGO), an organization focused on helping whistleblowers. He was among those leading the fight inside the Washington Beltway to get meaningful protections in place for government whistleblowers. Decades earlier, as a staffer in the US House of Representatives, he'd investigated the puzzling death of renowned nuclear industry whistleblower Karen Silkwood. Silkwood was a chemical technician in a plutonium-processing plant managed by Kerr-McGee, an Oklahoma energy company that produced fuel rods for the nuclear power industry. She died in a 1974 car crash while on her way to meet a reporter. Twenty years later, an AP story made the shocking disclosure that Silkwood's bone fragments were in Los Alamos:

The disclosure that Los Alamos lab has had her bone fragments since 1974 outrages the family. . . [Silkwood] had promised to bring proof the [Crescent, Oklahoma] plant was unsafe; no documents were in the car. (Laura Trolley, Associated Press, "Karen Silkwood Case Returns to Haunt Parents," April 24, 1994)

In her work at Kerr-McGee, Silkwood had discovered rods with substandard welds were passing inspection after quality-control X-ray images were tampered with to hide defects. The rods were designed to hold cylindrical pellets of plutonium fuel, and were used in nuclear power plants. When grouped into assemblies, the rods were strategically positioned within the reactor core to generate intense radiation. The radiation created heat, and converted water to steam. The steam turned turbines, which, in turn, produced electricity. If a defective rod were to rupture during use, workers and equipment could be exposed to danger-ous levels of nuclear radiation, and in a worst-case scenario a meltdown of the fuel assembly might result, putting the entire plant and region at risk.

A 1980 study commissioned by the German government after the 1979 Three Mile Island reactor core meltdown in cen-tral Pennsylvania, concluded this type of accident was only likely to occur once every 30,000 years. But then it happened in 1986 at the Chernobyl nuclear power plant in Ukraine, and again in 2011 at the Fukushima nuclear power plant in Japan—three times in thirty-two years!

Silkwood's concern was justified, but nobody in charge wanted to hear about it. The additional cost associated with waste and redoing welds meant lower profits for the company, smaller bonuses for managers. She became a whistleblower, and soon there were death threats. Then one day Silkwood set off a monitoring station, which was designed to detect radiation on workers as they passed by. She was contaminated with Pu. A humiliating and physically painful high-pressure shower and full-body scrub ensued. But then it happened again—she was exposed to the lethal material once more. A few weeks later Silkwood was found dead alongside an isolated stretch of road. It appeared she'd lost control of her vehicle, but her rear bumper was damaged in a manner that suggested she'd been hit from behind. To a large extent the movie *Silkwood* was based on Pete Stockton's investigation:

> Peter Stockton and David Burnaham answer questions from the audience at the Whistleblower Film Festival last night. . . . Stockton was the senior investigator for the House of Representatives into the mysterious death of Karen Silkwood *and the mysterious termination of the government investigations into Kerr-McGee's falsification of safety X-rays* [my italics]. (Richard Renner, "Burnham and Stockton Answer Questions about the Silkwood Case," The National Whistleblowers Legal Defense & Education Fund, *National Whistleblower Center,* October 16, 2009)

For some, the axing of the investigation into Kerr-McGee's falsification of safety X-rays may have been a mystery, but for those who understand the relationship that the DOE has with its military-industrial stable of Fortune 100 contractors—the huge corporations that, in concert with high-level members of the military, ensure politicians in Washington are always at the ready to intervene on their behalf—it was no shock.

There is a high price associated with doing what's right: many whistleblowers end up unemployed and unable to pay their bills. All are marginalized. Some go bankrupt or get sick. A handful, given enough time and abuse, may even lose their will to live, as reported in a book that Glenn Walp later wrote about his lab experience. He gave an account of two LANL employees—Jaret McDonald and James Stewart—who brought to his attention the fact that a major theft was occurring within the institution. It was their duty to report this type of activity to Glenn, who at the time was in charge of a laboratory unit established to investigate such claims. Afterward, McDonald and Stewart became targets of death threats. McDonald endured; Stewart eventually committed suicide. And as for Glenn, the laboratory fired him for doing his job.

Joe Gutierrez and his wife lived less than ten miles downwind of the LANL plutonium plant. He was a labee, and reported problems he'd found at the facility, including an issue with tritium (a radioactive isotope of hydrogen) that was being released into the environment without proper monitoring. Like everyone else in the community they were part of, Joe and his wife drank from the same aquifer as Joe's coworkers at the lab. No one was immune to the looming threat, and though, in the minds of many, he'd done the right thing, among those in laboratory leadership he was a "leper":

> The Energy Department undermined its "zero tolerance" policy on retaliation against whistleblowers by helping its contractors fight nuclear site workers who raised legitimate safety concerns, whistleblowers and House lawmakers said Tuesday. . . . *Joe Gutierrez, a whistleblower at the Los Alamos National Laboratory, said he has spent about $50,000 of his own money to press his case. Gutierrez said he got an unfavorable job evaluation after he challenged lab officials' claim that the lab did not violate the federal Clean Air Act* [my italics]. (Matt Kelly, "Employees Challenge DOE," *Albuquerque Journal North*, May 24, 2000)

The US Department of Labor investigated Joe's situation and ruled in his favor, but the lab preferred digging in for litigation. Joe eventually prevailed, but before then had been called upon to address a congressional committee about his experience. His fifteen minutes of fame also earned him a guest appearance on the *O'Reilly Factor*. But his fate was already sealed, and no agency ruling, congressional hearing, news headline, or nationally syndicated TV show could change it. By 2010 Joe was ready to accept a severance package to leave the lab. The many years of unrelenting workplace marginalization and career-ending retribution he'd endured had finally achieved their aim.

Real improvement at LANL seemed impossible to accomplish. Even a former DOE secretary—Hazel O'Leary—openly admitting whistleblower persecution had no effect:

> The suit said a newly hired supervisor in the plutonium processing facility told [Marlayne] Mahar in 2009 that a boss could shoot a worker who says the wrong thing. Another female employee days later reported that the same supervisor got angry with her and told her he was going to "bring in a gun and take care of it himself." . . . The second employee called police, saying she felt threatened . . . (Associated Press, "Jury Awards $1M to Los Alamos National Lab Worker," *Contra Costa Times*, February 21, 2013)

The reports of lost computer drives containing secrets had no impact on politicians either. Nor did disclosures of one environmental contamination after another, the lab's refusal to release information to the Centers for Disease Control and Prevention, cost overruns, or embarrassing labor disputes. Indeed, not even workplace injuries or repeated exposures to hazardous materials could pressure politicians to demand legitimate change in Los Alamos. And as for the possibility of fines being imposed, it was an empty threat at best. Because the University of California, under its contract with the DOE, was protected from such penalties, the Department of Energy guaranteed taxpayers would pay the fine.

And as for local authority, the New Mexico state legislature lacked the stomach for holding LANL accountable, and by 2004 was resigned to accepting things as they were, not as they could be. Courage and conscience are qualities that keep public officials in league with concerned citizens; both are necessary for a functioning democracy. Some New Mexico legislators had one or the other, and a few possessed both. But the military-industrial complex was a formidable force in Northern New Mexico, and the laboratory's influence-peddling and propaganda machine was legendary in its own right. Small-town politicians were rightfully fearful of taking on either—LANL or the Department of Energy—even though failure to act might mean putting workers and communities in jeopardy:

> The US Department of Energy is thwarting a court-ordered independent review of Los Alamos National Laboratory's compliance with the federal Clean Air Act. . . . The DOE last year admitted 31 of 33 vents for radioactive contaminants at its weapons lab were not in compliance with the Clean Air Act . . . (Ian Hoffman, "Feds Hindering LANL Review," *Albuquerque Journal North*, July 25, 1997)

And despite official assurances always given to the contrary, the limited water supply of New Mexico—the driest state in the union—was in real jeopardy. The safety of the aquifer that, for centuries, the Pajarito Plateau watershed had always managed to replenish, could no longer be guaranteed:

> Los Alamos National Laboratory's first deep-testing well in almost 40 years confirms lab pollutants can travel fairly easily into ground waters as deep as 275 feet under Los Alamos Canyon. . . . Deeper still, a few LANL contaminants have penetrated hundreds more feet of rock and gravel to the regional aquifer, the drinking water source in Los Alamos. (Ian Hoffman, "LANL Pollutants in Water," *Albuquerque Journal North*, April 17, 1998)

> Los Alamos National Laboratory predicts the Rio Grande will be safe from contaminants on the lab property for a long time—anywhere from hundreds to thousands of years, depending on where the contaminants are located. But low concentrations of explosives and perchlorate have already reached the river, by way of springs . . . (Diana Heil, "Report: Lab Waste Reaches Rio Grande," *Santa Fe New Mexican*, August 22, 2004)

Without consequence there is no accountability—hence the old adage "Power corrupts; absolute power corrupts absolutely." But not everyone embraces responsible corporate behavior, least of all those who benefit from keeping things as they are:

> Thank you for your presentation before the [LANL] Oversight Committee at its October meeting in which you discussed your experiences with whistleblower retaliation and asked the committee to request a congressional

hearing on the issue. [T]he committee does not believe it has enough clear-cut evidence that LANL has broken the law or violated University of California procedures on whistleblowing and whistleblower retaliation to call for congressional hearings . . . (Letter to Charles M. Montaño from co-chairs Rep. Roberto Gonzales and Sen. Phil Griego, New Mexico State Legislature, November 18, 2004)

Alas, when it came to Los Alamos, too many elected officials were reluctant to engage, even in matters potentially impacting the health and well-being of their constituients. If the lab was involved, politicians tended to prefer diplomacy over enforcement, appeasement versus compliance, accommodation as opposed to accountability. And the last thing these officials needed was for whistleblowers to be pointing out this reality in public.

21

BROKEN PROMISES

Rules, regulations, and good business practices provide the foundation for policies and procedures in an organization, or at least that's the way it's supposed to be. Internal controls promote compliance with these rules, regulations, and good business practices, thus establishing that the legitimate goals and objectives of the institution are being pursued. The audit serves to independently evaluate the effectiveness and efficiency of the internal control environment, providing "reasonable assurance," which is what stakeholders require.

A missing control is analogous to a door without a locking mechanism, while an existing control not being utilized is like a door people can lock but choose not to. Both conditions were common in LANL, and the higher up in the lab's class structure, the more likely an individual could break rules and get away with it. This was why classified data could disappear and reappear without anyone being disciplined, costly trips to exotic destinations were taken without concern for need or cost, procurements got issued with little justification or oversight, and why taxpayers always paid no matter what. Plus if adherence was optional for

143

some, internal controls could be overridden for others. In the end, this was the root of the problem in Los Alamos.

Auditors gauge risk. They are relied upon to report truthfully so that stakeholders can make informed decisions about when and how much to invest, or where it's safe to work, live, and raise a family. To appreciate the need for good information, consider those who lost everything after relying on the false assertions of Wall Street Ponzi schemer Bernie Madoff, or the self-serving claims of those in charge at WorldCom and Enron. Consider the risks that banks and hedge fund managers took with the economy leading to the 2008 stock market crash, or the consequences to those living and working in or around the Rocky Flats nuclear facility, located on the outskirts of Denver, Colorado. Those living near Rocky Flats believed in false assurances that the risk associated with being downwind of a plutonium facility was negligible.

The common denominator in all these failures was a willingness of those in authority to misinform and, if necessary, hide reality, plus our own inclination to believe without challenging or questioning. Just as harmful as these lapses are the omissions of those we entrust to report truth, whose responsibility it is to validate what's accurate and relevant in order to expose the culprits who engage in these deceptions. Among the most culpable are officials we elect who fail to serve in the public trust . . . and their bureaucratic minions in government who also renege on their fiduciary duty to the taxpayer.

Arthur Anderson, the once-renowned international accounting firm, no longer exists because people relied on it to reveal the truth about Enron's business practices. Arthur Anderson's failure to do so resulted in retirement and investor portfolios collapsing, major spikes in energy prices, adverse impacts to the economy, and, in the end, Anderson's own demise. Consider as well the US Securities and Exchange Commission's unwillingness to respond to an insider's repeated attempts to expose Madoff, who ended up causing an estimated $18 billion in investor losses. Or the politicians so exclusively focused on appeasing their affluent donors who, because of this desire, can violate worker rights with impunity, sidestep health and safety laws, and ignore environmental protection requirements. These are the same campaign-contributing companies that repeatedly bilk taxpayers with contract extensions, change orders, inflated claims, and questionable and unallowable costs, and who retaliate against those blowing the whistle on such contemptuous behaviors.

On June 24, 2002, two labees—James Stewart and Jeret McDonald—reported a major theft occurring at LANL. They reported it to the FBI, because in 2001 they'd tried, three times, reporting it to authorities within the laboratory, and had gotten nowhere. Glenn Walp and Steve Doran were different, though. Their background was law enforcement. They'd been hired by the lab in early 2002, and were soon working closely with the FBI on what was to become a massive procurement fraud case. The fraud that was occurring involved a well-paid lab manager using his position of authority to orchestrate his illegal activities. But soon lab officials were interfering with their investigation, as though attempting to prevent Glenn and Steve from digging too deep, insinuating they would be exceeding their authority by revealing things that might bring into question the University of California's stewardship in Los Alamos.

Glenn and Steve had found a huge cache of stolen merchandise being secreted away in a vacant Cold War bunker situated on a remote stretch of lab property. It was crammed with camping, hunting, and ranching gear, including camouflaged clothes, boots, and gloves, as well as Coleman lanterns, portable heaters, sleeping bags, GPS units, topographic maps, compasses, polarized glasses, cold-weather socks, weather stations, walkie-talkies, Bushnell range finders, ATVs, remote-controlled survey drones with cameras—the list went on and on. It was a virtual sportsman's warehouse, with approximately $350,000 worth of inventory. And according to another labee and FBI informant—John Jennings, who worked for the suspect at the laboratory—on at least eight occasions he'd delivered truckloads of merchandise to the perpetrator's home. How many more deliveries had been made, and by whom, or where else? Were the items being sold for profit, or being utilized in some other way? Why would someone need dozens, even hundreds, of the same item . . . hunting knives, for example? How much had been taken over time, over how long of a period, and how many procurement contracts might be involved? Not only did LANL officials not want answers to such questions, they wanted the questioning stopped—halted dead in its tracks, which meant getting rid of those obligated to ask and get answers . . . Glenn Walp and Steve Doran.

On the eve of their firings, in November 2002, the two investigators received a tip that stolen merchandise was ending up at someone's ranch. They determined the primary suspect owned a cabin, which was situated on a small patch of forest on the outskirts of town. Had they not been forced out when they were, they might have discovered the alleged ranch existed, and that a high-ranking LANL executive was connected. By being fired in order to prematurely halt their investigation, Glenn and Steve were sacrificed. Stakeholders, including elected officials, were hoodwinked into believing the full extent of the scandal had been uncovered at that point, but it hadn't.

According to the Association of Certified Fraud Examiners (ACFE), by far the greatest damage from fraud is attributed to inappropriate behavior by those in charge—managers who have intimate knowledge of the control environment and its strengths and weaknesses, and who possess the authority to override internal controls. As noted in the following study by ACFE, these are typically high-ranking company officials, with the ability to initiate or oversee large-dollar transactions, such as multimillion-dollar contracts:

> Perpetrators with higher levels of authority tend to cause much larger losses. The median loss among frauds committed by owner/executives was $573,000; the median loss caused by managers was $180,000; and the medial loss caused by employees was $60,000. . . . Asset misappropriation schemes were by far the most common type of occupational fraud, comprising 87 percent of the cases reported. . . . Financial statement fraud schemes made up just 8 percent of the cases in our study, but caused the greatest medial loss at $1 million. (Global Fraud Study, "Report to the Nations on Occupational Fraud and Abuse," Association of Certified Fraud Examiners, 2012)

An unfortunate truth is that when it comes time to prosecute, the focus will almost always be on the ones least likely to have the political clout to rally support or the financial means to obtain legal representation. Those at the bottom of the organizational chart will receive a subpoena; those at the top may get a plea deal instead, or a payoff to keep them quiet and get them to leave.

The day Glenn and Steve were escorted off laboratory premises, the investigation they were pursuing came to an abrupt end. It was as though Sergeant Schultz, the "I see nothing" prison guard in the late-'60s WWII sitcom *Hogan's Heroes*, had taken over criminal activity review in Los Alamos. Nobody wanted to know anything anymore. Those responsible for Walp and Doran's firings received money to silently disappear. And the media frenzy that ensued in the aftermath was, for all practical purposes, a public announcement for those who may have been involved in the fraud. The cover for the investigation was blown.

Stolen merchandise could be hidden now, disposed of quickly; ongoing relationships could be severed; records could be altered or destroyed.

Whether intentional or not, the act of interfering with an ongoing criminal review is called obstruction of justice, which is what LANL officials carried out. But politicians, protective of their corporate benefactors, weren't about to jeopardize the status quo in Los Alamos, much less support the prosecution of someone at the highest levels of laboratory authority.

In the final analysis, an entity immune to accountability and rooted in privilege and arrogance will always tend to resist preventive, detective, and corrective controls that promote compliance with rules and regulations. This type of corporate culture will also resist generally accepted good business practices. Because of this, recurring violations will occur, including noncompliance with environmental and fair employment laws, health and safety rules, or, as is so vital to a weapons lab, security mandates.

Last, in order to protect auditors from reprisal, the audit function is normally placed under the auspices of the governing body for the institution or within the home office—never under those responsible for site management. To do so would be to put the fox in charge of the henhouse. Yet this was precisely what the university did in 1992, when it abandoned the internal audit function it had always overseen in Los Alamos, turning it over to LANL management. UC was the home office, and its board of regents was the governing body. The laboratory director and his leadership team together acted as the site manager. For three decades the University Office of the President had directed the audit effort in Los Alamos, but not anymore. UC's "eyes and ears" now belonged to the fox.

22

DECEIT

To ENSURE THE INDEPENDENCE and objectivity of the LANL internal audit team, lab auditors had always worked directly for the University of California Office of the President (UCOP). But this was no longer the case—they now, in 1992, worked for the lab. The activity still remained physically located in Los Alamos, as before, but was placed under laboratory management's control. By '96, all those who'd transitioned over with the audit function in '92 were gone, including the audit manager. LANL had applied the "best qualified" doctrine to execute his removal by 1994, the notion being that only the "best and brightest" were qualified to lead in Los Alamos. After his unceremonious dethroning, he left the laboratory to assume an audit leadership position at a Texas institution of higher learning. His downfall at LANL had been nothing less than an orchestrated coup, designed to ensure that someone with a more management-compliant mind-set took control of audit efforts in Los Alamos. Tommy Hook was the person chosen for the role.

In the early '90s Tommy was the institutionally designated whistleblower officer, and managed the lab's Internal Evaluation

Office—a group tasked to investigate reports of LANL fraud, waste, and abuse. Tommy also oversaw the effort to validate labor and material costs associated with lab procurement contracts, plus overhead rates. Placing the internal audit team under him made sense, but the overriding consideration was that institutional leadership felt comfortable with Tommy, meaning that the independence and objectivity of the audit effort might be in jeopardy. But he was an enigma—part of the director's inner circle, yet loyal to his underpinnings as a professional. His dual commitment would lead to his eventual removal from lab leadership, and his fall from grace would be far worse than I could have ever imagined.

In 2001, I'd just returned from lunch and was walking back to my office when a man called out my name. I didn't expect it to be Tommy, for I hadn't seen him since about '96, a time when my son was a member of the Los Alamos High School football team. I'd briefly worked for Tommy after the internal audit effort was placed under LANL in '92. Following that, Tommy and I would periodically cross paths at a home game, quickly exchange hellos, and that was about it. He was now standing at the LANL payroll service window, returning from extended sick leave after having suffered a stroke. It had cost him partial vision in one eye. Needless to say I was surprised to see him, and sorry to hear about his medical condition.

Tommy had been enduring relentless retribution in Los Alamos ever since he'd testified in connection with the 1995 layoff. One of the fired labees was an auditor who'd transferred with me from UCOP to LANL in '92. Both he and I were assigned to work for Tommy. Within months I was transferred to the Internal Evaluation Office, a unit also under Tommy's purview, and was tasked to investigate allegations of contracting irregularities. He now theorized, returning from medical leave, that his deterioration in health was a physical manifestation of what he'd been put through since he'd provided a deposition on the matter. Lab leaders had gotten upset with his testimony, and suddenly he was no longer in good standing among them, or "best qualified" to remain in management.

In quick order, Tommy had been maneuvered out of his leadership role. At 5'8" and 150 pounds, he was the picture of health. But being taken out of his position of authority so abruptly had served to marginalize him professionally, thus creating enormous stress in his work life. And this, in all likelihood, was what led to the stroke.

The deposition Tommy gave in '95 had sealed his fate. He'd done the unthinkable—told the truth, admitting that the internal audit function in Los Alamos was largely a farce. Lots of people would have lied to hold on to the responsibility and authority Tommy had at that point in his career, but lying under oath was something he apparently wasn't willing to do. His standing among his peers in institutional leadership collapsed because of his integrity, and so did his career . . . and then his health.

The "best qualified" doctrine was the cornerstone of laboratory hiring, promotion, and salary management practices, and was a way to ensure officials got what they wanted despite qualifications. Experience, achievements, credentials—all were incidental to personnel decisions being made. Job ads were placed by the hiring official, and he could target a specific individual by simply using the phrase "preference will be given to . . ." It was a way to game the system so that those in charge won every time. In its investigation of the '95 layoff, the US Department of Labor Office of Federal Contract Compliance determined the lab manipulated terminations in a similar way. This disregard for fairness—indifference with respect to accountability—was why labees could be targeted with impunity, why so few women and minorities were ever chosen for advancement, and why managers acted as though they were "bulletproof and invisible," meaning they could do as they pleased.

Once the internal audit effort was moved from UC to the laboratory, the mission was to "assist" management. Telling the truth under oath, as Tommy Hook had done, was obviously not an "assist," nor was accurate and factual reporting. Professional audit standards no longer seemed to apply, with auditors instead having to sign loyalty pledges guaranteeing not to report anything embarrassing about the university or the laboratory. This was the brave new world investigative professionals now faced in Los Alamos, a world that began taking root with UC's purposeful abandonment of the audit effort in 1992.

Audit independence, objectivity, and relevancy were what led to factual, useful, and meaningful reporting, but the new "investigative standard" for the institution enabled truth to become fiction, fable to become reality. Plus functional area managers now had the ability to stop an audit in its tracks, limit its scope, and prevent the validation of their self-serving assertions. What UCOP auditors feared in '92 would happen if the proverbial fox was put in charge had come to pass.

23

OUTRAGE

"The situation we begin to confront today is not your run-of-the-mill theft and misuse of taxpayer property, as much as that demands our urgent attention in its own right. We also must examine what our committee investigators have learned is a disturbing breakdown in management controls and oversight at, of all places, an institution that pursues research critical to the nation's security" (James C. Greenwood, chairman of the House of Representatives' Subcommittee on Oversight and Investigations. House Hearing, 108th Congress, "Investigation of Management Problems at Los Alamos National Laboratory")

The congressional hearings on LANL were held on February 26 and March 12, 2003, before the House of Representatives' Committee on Energy and Commerce. The purpose was to shine a light on the firings of Glenn Walp and Steve Doran, to determine why this had happened. Some committee members were furious that the two were ousted after discovering fraudulent activity at the lab—in other words, that they were let go for doing what they were hired to do.

Glenn grew up in northern Pennsylvania. He was a farm boy whose rural upbringing and family teachings led to his life-long interest in theology. But it was his great-uncle, a member of the first Pennsylvania State Police class, who inspired him to pursue a career in law enforcement. In time, Glenn would become police commissioner for Pennsylvania, the highest-ranking law enforcement official in the state.

Steve also had a law enforcement background. He was a former police chief, as well as a renowned firearms expert. At 6'5" and 250 pounds, he was an imposing presence, but had a reassuring demeanor that made him seem like just the person you'd want coming to your aid in an emergency. He was raised in a rural setting by a loving grandfather, who made it a point to spend countless hours hunting and fishing with his grandson. Steve grew up with an affinity for Mother Nature, and for guns.

While Glenn invited strangers close with an easy smile and a twinkle in his eye, Steve was more reserved, keeping people at arm's length until he got to know them better. Glenn and Steve were seasoned criminal investigators, the type both UC officials and Congress decided were needed to straighten things out in Los Alamos—particularly following the Wen Ho Lee affair, and the ensuing reported losses of storage devices carrying secret information. Years had passed since these headline-grabbing events, and so by 2003 the more pressing concern was whether the contract for running the Los Alamos National Laboratory would be put out for competitive bid. To prevent this from happening it was imperative that there be no further disclosures of mismanagement. Resolving deficiencies, therefore, wasn't the priority, and certainly not reporting problems. Making sure nobody heard about them, however, was.

The two investigators had survived less than a year at LANL before being fired for uncovering fraud. They became whistleblowers, and within days achieved national notoriety. Underlings were blamed for having done the "dirty deeds" that served to undermine them, and were then given lucrative separation packages to leave the lab quietly. UC officials claimed ignorance regarding the decision to terminate Glenn and Steve; preventing the university from being further tarnished by the scandal was all that mattered.

It was easy enough to blame the lowest person on the totem pole for wrongdoing. But on the day of the firings, high-ranking University of California officials were on the Hill meeting with the lab director and members of his inner circle to talk about the two former police officers and their investigations. The university's future in Northern New Mexico was at stake, and UC had sent a delegation to town to find out more. So it was hard to believe the university's claim that it had no advance knowledge of the planned terminations, especially given that Glenn and Steve were fired first thing that morning, with UC officials then claiming not being told about it until lunch. This version of events meant you'd also have to believe no one in the room that morning, including the LANL director or the head of laboratory legal, knew the firings were occurring as they spoke with these university officials.

I knew from my decades in Los Alamos that no disciplinary action was ever taken without layers of management and legal review, especially for a planned termination. Firings were rare. They never happened on the spot, and also never happened without lots of strategic planning and advance warning. The only exception was if someone was an immediate threat, which was not the case with respect to Glenn and Steve, unless the "threat" they posed was the potential for exposing things the powers that be preferred remain hidden. If the status quo was being jeopardized by Glenn and Steve's work, that would explain their prompt dismissal; otherwise it made no sense.

Personnel actions required guidance and involvement from the laboratory's human resources department, and all actions leading to termination required the blessing of laboratory legal. The lab's head attorney was at the same meeting that day, a clue the fate of the two investigators was decided at that point. Another indicator was the press-related item on the meeting's agenda—apparently media fallout was anticipated. Terminating two experienced criminologists in the midst of a major fraud investigation would be controversial. Establishing talking points, therefore, seemed prudent. Thus ordinary logic, common sense, and a smidgen of professional skepticism would suggest the determination to "get rid" of the two investigators was discussed that morning, on that November day, with the knowledge and full participation of the UC officials in attendance, and just as likely that the university had advance knowledge of the decision to terminate.

On the copy of the meeting agenda I managed to obtain, there were handwritten notes, including the name of the recently retired deputy director of LANL Operations. He wasn't in the room that day, so why had his name been jotted down? And then, adding to the mystery, two months later he was found dead—a gunshot wound to the back of the head.

As the congressional hearing convened, Glenn and Steve stood tall and straight to be sworn in. But politics was involved now—*Alice in Wonderland*-type politics—where up may be down, fantasy can be reality, and facts only matter when politically expedient.

Two former investigators at Los Alamos National Laboratory told Congress on Wednesday that several senior managers who blocked their efforts to uncover

theft and fraud at the nuclear weapons lab remain on
the payroll of the University of California. Glenn Walp
and Steven Doran, fired from the lab but since rehired
by UC, testified that despite the university's firing or
reassignment of more than a dozen lab officials, several
managers who stymied their probe are still working at
the lab and drawing hefty paychecks. (Zachary Coile,
"Lab Whistleblowers Testify in Congress," *San Francisco
Chronicle*, February 27, 2003)

Lab and UC officials attempted to rationalize the irratio-
nal, explain the unexplainable, and justify the unjustifiable.
But none of it made sense. Some committee members, for the
moment, were skeptical. Some even felt a need to express support for whistleblowers.

The accusations of fraud, mismanagement, and repri-
sals against whistleblowers at the labs managed by the
University of California, both Los Alamos and Lawrence
Livermore Labs, are extremely serious and sobering.
Clearly, *there have been errors* [my italics] that the Uni-
versity of California must take full responsibility for.
(Prepared statement of Hon. Anna G. Eshoo, congressio-
nal representative from the state of California)

The careers of whistleblowers were being destroyed due to
"errors"? Was this a joke? I'd been in career limbo at LANL for
years, so I sent Congresswoman Eshoo an e-mail to find out,
requesting help rectifying the "error" in my own situation. No
response. A follow-up e-mail with copies of relevant newspaper
clippings attached elicited an identical reaction—none.

Glenn Walp and Steve Doran, two seasoned criminal inves-tigators, were fired on November 25, 2002, while still investigat-ing the largest procurement fraud in Los Alamos history. A little more than two years later, in 2005, Harry Rodas—the LANL division leader overseeing all laboratory purchasing activities, expressed concerns regarding fraud and waste that might be occurring within the lab's procurement division, where over a billion dollars annually are expended in the acquisition of goods and services.

Glenn, Steve, and Harry Rodas were fired just prior to the completion of their probationary period as new hires, after all raised concerns about the same flawed procurement practices. With respect to all three, a laboratory spokesperson immedi-ately proclaimed that an employee could be let go for any reason whatsoever, so long as the individual was still on probation. It was a lame excuse, but the position the laboratory had staked out. Congress, however, wasn't buying it.

Since people rarely lost their jobs at LANL, what happened to all three men would be inconceivable were it not for the fact that they were trying to fix problems institutional leaders didn't even want to admit existed. What followed, with respect to all three, was the proverbial "shooting of the messenger." Whether believable or not, it was vital to shield the university from the decision to terminate.

Unfortunately, nothing has changed for the better. In early 2014, local news outlets reported allegations that the spouse of the lab's then–deputy director, the second-highest-ranking lab official, got a "sole source" (noncompetitive) contract, and that neither had disclosed the fact they were married, thus masking the potential conflict of interest rooted in their relationship. The deputy resigned as a result. The lab commanded negative media attention again when, in May 2014, a jury awarded $3.6 million in damages to Orion Technical Resources LLC, a company that sued the lab's overseer, Los Alamos National Security LLC, after a competitor won a contract to provide administrative services. According to an *Albuquerque Journal* report, Orion alleged that "secret policies and procedures" were used that were prejudicial to a fair and equitable selection process. The jury agreed.

Despite LANL, the university, and the Department of Energy spending millions on audits, legal fees, studies, congressional hearings, correction plans, and public relations spin-doctoring, procurement contracts were still being awarded unfairly in Los Alamos, vendors were still being paid inflated prices, and unallowable and questionable costs were still being incurred. In short, fraud, waste, and abuse, as alleged by Glenn Walp, Steve Doran, and Harry Rodas, were still significant problems in Los Alamos. And those expressing concerns about it were as likely as ever to find themselves unemployed, just for bringing it up.

The congressional hearings convened in 2003 provided officials the opportunity to feign outrage while the media paid attention and cameras were rolling. Promises were made to remedy weaknesses, assurances were given to protect whistleblowers, and all the right words were spewed—but it was all for naught. Expressing support for those whose careers were being ruined by doing the right thing was easy; coming to their aid afterward was something else. Politicians paid attention so long as journalists did; reporters reported if their management allowed them to; and editors, increasingly, worked for media outlets owned and operated by corporate interests. As for whistleblowers they, in reality, were typically abandoned and forgotten, relegated to an existence of perpetual career marginalization and ongoing retribution; essentially left to wither away and die on the vine, while those responsible remained largely unaffected, unrepentant, and forever unchanged.

The Pajarito Plateau was occupied before the arrival of the Manhattan Project. Photo courtesy of NM Historical Review/Dr. Carlos Vasquez.

Founding LANL director Robert Oppenheimer with General Leslie Groves, surveying the aftermath of the world's first nuclear detonation near Alamogordo, New Mexico. LANL photo.

Director Sig Hecker with US senator Pete Domenici. LANL photo.

Group photo for posterity: those targeted for termination in '95.
Photo by C. Montaño.

Labees confront their congressman, Bill Richardson, outside his Santa Fe office. Photo by C. Montaño.

CLER delegation heads to DC on the way to making history. Photo courtesy of NM Historical Review/Dr. Carlos Vasquez. Michael Mouchett photographer.

Testifying at the May '98 California/New Mexico joint legislative hearing. Director John Browne is at my side; the head of lab legal sits behind him. Photo by E. Montaño.

Wen Ho Lee, a free man, rejoices in the holiday season with his family. Photo courtesy of Lee family.

Glenn Walp and Steve Doran swear in for Congress.
Photo courtesy of Associated Press/Susan Walsh.

Senator Pete Domenici (center), unhappy with the decision
to open up the LANL contract to competition; Director
Pete Nanos stands to his left. Photo courtesy of
Los Alamos Monitor/Dissinger.

Director Michael Anastasio with Congresswoman Heather Wilson.
LANL archive photo.

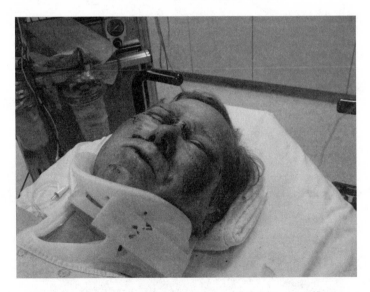

Tommy Hook, the lab's former whistleblower officer,
severely beaten the week before he was scheduled to
meet with congressional staffers. C. Montaño photo.

Deputy LANL director Richard Burick with his Flying Sigma brand. LANL News photo.

Glenn Walp and I, the day we met with Ken Gonzales, US attorney for the District of New Mexico. C. Montaño photo.

Our crusader for justice—Lynne Bernabei, framed by Glenn Walp, Steve Doran and me, wearing my UC Professional and Technical Employee organizing shirt. E. Montaño photo.

Topper Man mural and hand gesture in focus. C. Montaño photo.

24

FAILED TRUST

SEEING TOMMY HOOK IN 2001 made me wonder what it was about Los Alamos that kept people there. It was such a beautiful place on the surface, yet seemed so shortchanged in conscience. Perhaps that explained why there were so many churches in town. By the same token, there were many decent people who lived and worked at LANL—the vast majority of employees, in fact. Perhaps the excellent wages and benefits offered at the laboratory, coupled with the second-to-none retirement plan, made people fearful of offending those who were in charge, the ones responsible for much of the turmoil and abuse. It was as though it were less risky to live with the "disease" than to cure it, reminding me of my old college roommate's motivation for returning to Los Alamos. It *was* about economics, but that mentality had also cost Mike his life.

It was now 2002, and I was on the phone with Tommy. He'd just had a meeting with the laboratory's Associate Director for Administration (ADA) and the UC auditor. They'd made Tommy an offer he couldn't refuse. It was an opportunity that could help revive his standing at the lab, and his career. If it panned out as he'd been led to believe, perhaps I could join him at some point. My own career had been on life support since the mid-'90s.

The ADA, a former DOE official, later became "executive director," working directly for the lab's highest officer—the LANL director. This arguably made him the third-most-powerful person at the institution, after the director and deputy director. And as for the UC auditor, he was in Oakland, California, reporting directly to the UC Office of the President.

The congressional committee investigating Glenn's and Steve's firings was now interested in Tommy, who, as the lab's former whistleblower officer, once asserted under oath that LANL leaders sought to prevent auditors from reporting unallowable costs, related system weaknesses, and financial improprieties. It was testimony he'd given years before Glenn Walp and Steve Doran arrived in Los Alamos, corroborating some of what the two fired criminal investigators were now saying in the news about the lab.

"It may be an opportunity to get our careers back on track," Tommy said.

"Think so?" I asked.

"I think so," he responded.

"I'll head up a new function," Tommy said. "We'll perform assessments of all business activities, starting with procurements." During his meeting, he'd asked if he could hire his own staff, and was assured he could. The carrot had been dangled, and he'd taken it. And when the time came, I *did* join him.

Our assignment was to assess the internal controls of all LANL business operations, including accounting, budgeting, and property management. Our initial focus was the procurement arena, in direct response to Glenn's and Steve's terminations, as well as to related congressional demands that the lab's flawed material and service acquisition systems be fixed. Anyone could claim something was resolved, proving it required tangible verification, what auditors do for a living. There is no other way to provide reasonable assurance, in other words. But this wasn't what the laboratory's executive director wanted. He requested recommendations for improvement, but didn't want us documenting the existence of any problems, or reporting any shortcomings that could make the institution look bad.

"How can we recommend improvements," Tommy asked rhetorically of me, "if we don't know where the shortcomings are?"

Transaction testing—such as taking a sample of procurement orders and verifying that the supporting documentation demonstrates all policy requirements were met, including appropriate reviews and signature authorizations—establishes whether a process is working as intended and, if not, provides a sense of how to correct the weakness. Audit recommendations for improvement, therefore, serve to mitigate related exposures to risk. Accepting the assertions of managers at face value does not. To do so would be analogous to relying on those who have a vested interest in denying the existence of problems—essentially tasking the fox to inform you when hens are missing.

Lab legal was the perennial filterer of bad news, including internal control failures that auditors uncovered. The LANL executive director, who was also an attorney, had a similar mindset to that of the legal office. Unlike an auditor, who is required professionally to provide independent and objective assessments of reality, a lawyer's responsibility is to protect a client at all costs (i.e., to provide the best defense possible). For an auditor or investigator, having to appease the "client" is an untenable position to be in. Yet that's where Tommy and I were, in the same predicament that had gotten Glenn and Steve fired.

WHEREAS, The University of California (University), a
state university in California, as a non-profit organization; has managed the Los Alamos National Laboratory

(Laboratory) since its founding in 1943 as a public service to the nation, for no loss or gain, in recognition of which the federal government provides a general indemnification of the university against liability or losses associated with its role . . . ("Contract between The United States of America and the Regents of The University of California," Modification No. M359, Supplement Agreement to Contract W-7404-ENG-36, November 10, 1992)

The contract between the US Department of Energy and UC was changed in the '90s, under congressional pressure, to end the university's indemnification for mismanagement. The LANL executive director was a high-ranking DOE official within the Albuquerque Operations Office during that period.

[T]he DOE's Inspector General identified 21 standard DOE clauses that were omitted or modified in the University of California contracts, including the procurement and property management clauses. . . . [O]ther significant deviations omitted or narrowed the limited instances in which [the] DOE's policies would have required the university to incur a financial liability . . . . Liability is limited to six officers of the regents of the university . . . and the three laboratory directors. . . . DOE's contracting approach has fostered an environment that *provides opportunities for waste, fraud, abuse, and mismanagement* [my italics]. (GAO/RCED-94-202, "Report to the Chairman, Subcommittee on Oversight and Investigations, Committee on Energy and Commerce, House of Representatives—Modest Reforms Made in

UC Contracts but Fees Are Substantially Higher," US
General Accounting Office, August 1994)

The General Accounting Office (GAO), the investigative arm of
the US Congress, found that the Energy Department had made
numerous contracting concessions to the university over the
years. The University of California had agreed to accept more
risk in return for a larger management fee, but the department
had agreed, as well, to make it virtually impossible to hold UC
accountable by creating "opportunities for waste, fraud, abuse,
and mismanagement". . . and by limiting the university's exposure
to what the LANL director knew. In other words, unless it could
be demonstrated that the director had prior knowledge of a problem, whatever it may be, and did *not* take action, only then could
UC be liable. The bar to establish culpability had been raised so
high as to make it virtually impossible to impose any liability on
the university, and the lab's executive director had been among
the DOE officials who'd authorized the "concession."

Congressional demands that UC share in the risk of running the Los Alamos lab had been undercut by the department
as well, by it allowing the university to relinquish control over
the internal audit function in Los Alamos. A contractual bait
and switch is what occurred, with the US Congress being led
to believe the university had accepted greater responsibility for
running a nuclear facility in Northern New Mexico when, in
truth, it hadn't. By allowing UC to place the internal auditors
under laboratory management control, the independence and
objectivity of the function had been undermined. This, in turn,
meant auditors could no longer look into areas where problems
might exist, or report what they found if they did.

The Energy Department's willingness to concede was hardly
ever in the public interest, plus the DOE official largely responsible was the contract administrator. In a nutshell, while it

may have been to the university's advantage to give up its "eyes and ears" in Los Alamos and virtually eliminate its exposure to potential liability, the risk to taxpayers went up dramatically.

(Questioning of the LANL executive director by Lynne Bernabei, Esq.)

Q. And did you have any responsibility either for administering or awarding the contract to the University of California to run Los Alamos National Laboratories?

A. Would you repeat the questions?

Q. Yes. During the time you worked for the DOE in Albuquerque, did you have any responsibility for either awarding or administering the contract by which the University of California managed Los Alamos labs?

A. Administering? Yes.

(Deposition transcript, LANL executive director, September 15, 2010, starting on p. 14)

25

GAGGING

In 1997, TOMMY HOOK and I had given sworn testimony related to an auditor terminated in connection with the '95 lab-wide firings. In his testimony, Tommy, who was the audit manager at the time, described a disturbing interaction he had with his then-boss Katherine Brittin, who joined LANL in 1994. As the newly designated audit director, she mandated that laboratory auditors would no longer be allowed to share information with their counterparts at the US Department of Energy Office of Inspector General (OIG). Reining in the auditors was crucial, because the new contract between the University of California and the DOE made it possible for UC to incur liability for mismanagement and malfeasance—but only if it could be demonstrated that the lab director had prior knowledge and did nothing to address the underlying problem. It was about controlling information flow, preventing serious deficiencies from being reported, and keeping the director ignorant of things that might result in the university being held liable.

Prior to LANL taking over the internal audit effort, it was common practice for lab auditors to share concerns with their counterparts at the OIG. Thus, it didn't take long for an auditor under Tommy's supervision to violate Brittin's decree. His actions so enraged her that she wanted to "rip his fucking face off," as attested to by Tommy in his sworn statement. A few months later the auditor was terminated—a victim of the 1995 layoff that snared so many who'd lost favor with a lab manager.

Brittin, like the university auditor stationed in California, arrived on the scene after the proverbial fox was put in charge of all laboratory audits in '92. In the wake of their arrival came the unraveling of the internal audit program in Los Alamos. Brittin's directive—that contact with the OIG was prohibited—was followed by a "loyalty oath" for auditors, which was a written pledge that all of us were required to sign. The oath effectively destroyed the auditor's role as an independent and objective source of relevant information. Tommy, as audit manager, objected to what Brittin and the university auditor had done, and was quickly removed from his leadership role because of it.

The audit function in Los Alamos was no longer credible. Audit scopes, once used to plan audits by specifying objectives and related review steps, were now used to direct auditors away from potential problem areas. Audit reports could be manipulated as well by using the peer review process. This is where another auditor—one not involved in the audit being reviewed—goes through the audit report with a fine-tooth comb to ensure sufficient supporting documentation exists to prove what's being said. But now this process could be used to mandate the removal of findings, regardless of proof. And if all else failed, the release of a finished report could be held up by the audit manager, at the request of lab management.

Glenn Walp and Steve Doran were terminated for doing their jobs, but lab spokespersons claimed in related news stories they'd been fired for riding roughshod in Los Alamos. "Loose cannons" was the characterization that was used. Yet the two investigators were adamant in their denials. They insisted they'd been forced out, instead, for refusing to cover up theft, and claimed laboratory officials warned them not to report anything disparaging about LANL, or that might otherwise tarnish the university's image. The lab's Public Affairs Office was equally adamant in its denials of their claims. Someone was lying; I doubted it was the two who were terminated.

On December 2, 2002, I strolled into the Santa Fe office of the *Albuquerque Journal North,* carrying the depositions Tommy and I had given years earlier. I handed them over to Adam Rankin, the reporter who broke the story about Glenn and Steve. "Look at these," I said. "Those two guys you've been writing about . . . they're telling the truth." Important pages were paper-clipped, and sentences corroborating their version of events were highlighted. Rankin's article, which appeared the next day, was devastating to the lab's credibility:

> Allegations that Los Alamos National Laboratory man-
> agers covered up waste or mismanagement date back to
> the mid-1990s. Lab employees made such allegations in
> court depositions years before the current controversy
> over alleged purchasing and property-control problems
> at the lab. . . . Glenn Walp, head of the lab's Office of
> Security Inquiries, and Steve Doran, a security spe-
> cialist under Walp, have said the lab fired them in late
> November after less than a year on the job because they
> attempted to reveal wrongdoings that lab managers tried
> to cover up. . . . Tommy Hook, a former senior advisor for
> audits in the lab's Internal Evaluation Office, testified in
> 1997 that his boss [Katherine Brittin]—still head of the
> lab's Internal Audits and Assessments Division—"didn't

want to aggressively report findings" and "didn't want to see certain things put in reports," including "unallowable costs" and "embarrassments to the university." (Adam Rankin, "Charges Not New to LANL," *Albuquerque Journal North*, December 4, 2002)

In the days that followed, the university did a 180-degree turnaround, suddenly becoming allied with the two investigators. The tide for Glenn and Steve had shifted in their favor, as the University of California agreed to pay both a settlement. Glenn alone received a million dollars.

The offer to settle was an attempt to mitigate damage to UC's image. Tommy's old boss, Katherine Brittin, had to leave, as would others in time. All would be given generous incentive "parachutes" so that they could fall gently (and quietly), unlike the whistleblowers—Glenn and Steve—who, essentially, were tossed from a plane with lead weights attached to both feet.

Two security supervisors at Los Alamos National Laboratory demoted earlier this week as part of a lab shake-up over purchase and property control problems haven't had to take pay cuts. . . . Stanley Busboom and Gene Tucker, LANL's two top security managers, were demoted Tuesday. The two were responsible for the November firings of Glenn Walp and Steve Doran, two investigators who say they were dismissed for blowing the whistle on fraud and theft at the lab. Lab officials said Thursday that a search is under way to find new positions for Busboom and Tucker, whose demotions followed the resignation of former lab director John Browne last week. Busboom, who was director of LANL security, will get to keep his

> $180,000 annual salary and Tucker, the former deputy
> director, will retain his $165,000 salary. (Adam Rankin,
> "No Pay Cuts Came with Demotions," *Albuquerque Jour-
> nal North*, January 10, 2003)

Not a single sacrificial lamb was slaughtered. They were just moved to other green pastures. But the ploy didn't sit well in the press, or with some members of Congress:

> The former top two security officers at Los Alamos
> National Laboratory have agreed to leave the troubled
> facility amid continuing allegations that they were
> involved in fraud and retaliation against whistleblowers
> there, University of California officials said Tuesday. The
> announcement that Stanley Busboom, the lab's former
> security division director, and his one-time deputy, Gene
> Tucker, would leave Los Alamos in April came on the eve
> of a congressional subcommittee hearing in Washington,
> DC, at which the two men are scheduled to testify.
> (Rebecca Trounson, "Ex-top Security Officials to Leave
> Los Alamos Lab," *Los Angeles Times*, March 12, 2003)

Glenn and Steve, two seasoned criminal investigators, were fired for refusing to ignore problems in Los Alamos. The people responsible for their undermining received a full year's salary and benefits to leave the lab, under the condition they wouldn't say anything disparaging about the lab or the university. A few months later, as reported in *Wired* magazine, one of the culprits who accepted the arrangement resurfaced as a consultant, once again working at LANL:

In March, Los Alamos National Laboratory Security
Chief Stanley Busboom was forced to resign for his role
in ousting two whistleblowers from the world's best-
known nuclear weapons facility. Now, a little more than
six months later, Busboom is back—as a consultant to
the same Los Alamos division he was once compelled to
leave, lab officials confirm . . . Busboom was relieved of
his duties as head of the lab's security division in January, shortly after Walp and Doran were let go. A little
more than two months later, as Congress held hearings
into the lab's management, Busboom stepped down, in
exchange for $190,000 and health benefits for a year.
(Noah Schactman, "Ousted Official Back at Nuke Lab,"
Wired, October 1, 2003)

This was a classic "thumb your nose" moment—bringing Busboom back into the fold, even after being paid to leave. It spoke
to the arrogance of those involved, and the lack of commitment
on the part of those in charge to accept responsibility for much
of anything.

Rankin's news coverage in *Albuquerque Journal North* shed
light on what happened to Glenn and Steve, and in the process
Tommy Hook's deposition caught the attention of congressional
staffers. Everyone felt compelled, at that point, to express support
for whistleblowers . . . and auditors. One of those addressing the
congressional committee during the March 2003 Washington,
DC, hearing was UC's senior vice president of university affairs,
Bruce B. Darling. He emphasized that the university auditor
would be taking charge of the internal audit mess in Los Alamos
now and would clean it up, including getting rid of the "loyalty
pledge" auditors had been forced to sign. He talked as well about
making improvements that would enable employees to blow the

whistle without fear of retribution, and even came across as being bothered by the mistreatment Glenn Walp and Steve Doran received at the hands of lab leaders. But he failed to stress that he was in Los Alamos, meeting with the lab director and his inner circle, the very same day they were fired.

The undermining of audit objectivity and independence in Los Alamos was something UC had willingly done in 1992, when it gave up control of the internal audit function. The loyalty oath, which effectively muzzled auditors, was the university auditor's doing. And if Darling didn't know this, or didn't know about the undermining of the internal audit function in Los Alamos, then he presumably wasn't reading my e-mails to him, which were sent long before Glenn and Steve were in the news. Or perhaps he wasn't paying much attention to what was going on at LANL to begin with. To be telling a congressional committee, at this juncture, that the UC auditor was somehow akin to the army cavalry being sent to the rescue was disingenuous at best. A January 2003 article written by Adam Rankin, exposing the university's earlier decision to give up its "eyes and ears" in Los Alamos, suggested as much:

> Has the fox been guarding the hen house at Los Ala-
> mos National Laboratory? That's the question raised by
> several current and former LANL workers who say the
> seed for the lab's current problems in purchasing and
> property control was planted in 1992. That's when the
> University of California moved auditors keeping tabs
> on LANL operations from the university to the lab and
> made them answerable to the lab's top managers. (Adam
> Rankin, "Auditors Trace Plight to 1992," *Albuquerque
> Journal North*, January 12, 2003)

An earlier deposition from 1999, related to a DOE OIG ruling in my favor showing I'd been removed from the internal audit function in retaliation for my supporting the workers laid off in 1995, reveals the source of the loyalty pledge—the university auditor:

(Questioning of Ronald Rodriguez, LANL internal audit team leader, by Merit Bennett, Esq.)

Q: And the reason you decided to do this [have the auditors sign a loyalty oath] on August 23, 1996, was why?

A: Well . . . there was a standard Code of Ethical Conduct environment that was already prevalent in the Institute of Internal Auditors, things like that, so we felt we needed to make it evident to employees that they needed to abide by that same Code of Ethical Conduct.

Q: Why did this need to be made evident to employees and require their signature to come to fruition in August of 1996?

A: Well, the fruition part, I would say this matter was— been discussed over periods of time with UC, university auditor . . .

Q: Who was considering doing this?

A: Oh, the university auditor . . .

(Deposition transcript, Ronald Rodriguez, November 5, 1999, starting on p. 120)

The UC auditor, stationed in Oakland, California, had enabled the gag order to be placed on lab auditors 1,000 miles away in Los Alamos. And any notion that this might have been done in order to achieve adherence with a professional code of ethics is ludicrous. There is nothing ethical about gagging someone, much less a person required by his or her profession to report factually. Requiring the auditors to sign a loyalty pledge was as profane as having someone living and working in one state swear allegiance to another state as a condition of employment. But that, too, was the case in Los Alamos, as evidenced in my employment letter with the lab:

> We are pleased to offer you a position in Group NM as a
> Nuclear Materials Specialist. . . . Your employment will
> be effective upon completion of our hiring forms which
> include the Oath of Allegiance to the state of California.
> (Employment Offer Letter from Los Alamos Laboratory
> to Charles Montaño, May 14, 1979)

I'd been required to pledge allegiance to the State of California, and nearly twenty years later to proclaim my loyalty to LANL and the University of California exclusively. I had two competing oaths to abide by, with no idea as to which took precedence.

Because the UC auditor played an instrumental role in undermining my career, he was named a defendant in my whistleblower retaliation complaint. But a conservative federal judge in New Mexico prevented us from questioning him, and this went on for years. And so by 2010, when my attorney was finally able to dislodge the legal logjam, the university auditor, it seemed, had disappeared—he'd retired, moved, evaporated like a mirage. It was as though he'd gone into a UC-sponsored witness protection program; of course, nobody at the university seemed to know how to locate him.

Justice delayed, it's been said, is justice denied. But this was just part of the laboratory's accountability-avoidance game, one that LANL and its parent (the university), along with the DOE and its stable of military-industrial contractors, are experts at playing. The objective is simple . . . delay long enough for witnesses to disappear and for plaintiffs to become ill, go bankrupt, or die. Case in point—Rocky Flats whistleblower Jim Stone:

> Jim Stone, the troubleshooter-turned-whistleblower whose testimony helped shut down Rocky Flats, has waited a long time for his reward. . . . [H]e filed a whistleblower fraud case . . . [and] was awarded $4.2 million in damages. But he never saw a dime of it. After an eighteen-year fight, in 2007, the US Supreme Court denied Stone any damages. . . . By this time Stone is eighty-one years old and living in a nursing home. Two weeks after the decision, he dies from complications related to Alzheimer's. (Kristen Iversen, *Full Body Burden—Growing Up in the Nuclear Shadow of Rocky Flats*. Crown Publishers, 2012, 327)

In theory, while whistleblowers may be entitled to their day in court, in truth they're more likely to die or go bankrupt before that happens. This has nothing to do with justice being blind, but with a judicial system whose scales are balanced in favor of the powerful, and those beholden to them.

The University of California and Los Alamos National Laboratory were adept at playing with people's lives and twisting the judicial process into knots. The US Department of Energy's role was simple—to ensure the taxpayer paid for it.

26

BECOMING DILBERT

THERE WERE NUMEROUS PROCUREMENT activities in Los Alamos. One was as informal as having people walk into a local store, show their employee badge, and charge the purchase to the lab. These protocols were called "local vendor agreements" and were limited to buying specific items, though labees frequently purchased whatever they wanted with them, and the vendors got paid. At the other end of the spectrum were procurement orders requiring formal review and approval before being issued. Between the two extremes were procurement cards (P-cards) and "just in time" (JIT) acquisitions, the former enabling credit card holders to purchase essentially anything, the latter limiting people to specific items priced at preestablished rates. JIT acquisitions, however, were often billed at a higher level than allowed. For example, sometimes freight was charged when it wasn't supposed to be, or was charged at a premium, even though the contract stipulated a discounted shipping service. Whatever got billed typically got paid. As for P-cards, the organizations that received them were responsible for ensuring their proper use, but few were doing so.

LANL expended $1 billion in procurements every year, and with controls as lax as they were, it was inevitable fraud would occur—or, as the Association of Fraud Examiners might characterize the situation . . . weak control was an open invitation to cheat the taxpayer. Within the institution, therefore, it was known that questionable buying activity occurred in specific months: August was the school supply month, December marked the holiday gifting season, and June was the month for graduation presents. Tommy Hook and I found all these problems and then some, just as laboratory officials were openly and widely proclaiming they'd fixed related deficiencies in the lab's procurement processes.

Tommy's meeting with the LANL executive director and UC auditor just a few months earlier, and the "golden opportunity" he'd been offered then, was the seminal event that brought us to this point in 2004. One procurement order sampled in our testing revealed hundreds of thousands in taxpayer money being contributed to a university; perhaps it was an attempt to reward someone's alma mater, garner a scholarship or admission for a son or daughter, or maybe secure a faculty placement for the LANL manager who'd authorized it. Whatever the reason, and despite this being a clear-cut violation of the Federal Acquisition Regulations, we weren't allowed to investigate any further.

In total, millions of dollars of questionable and unallowable expenditures were identified through our assessments of the laboratory's procurement processes, something the lab executive director didn't want to hear. Our work established that internal controls were exceedingly weak. Yet instead of being concerned, the executive director became furious—not with the message, but with the messengers. Our assessments confirmed that the conditions contributing to the procurement frauds Glenn Walp and Steve Doran discovered in 2002 still existed. And yet by 2003, the powers that be were telling elected officials, the media, and whoever else would listen that these problems were fixed. Everyone was being misled. The question now was whether this reality, as reflected in our reports, should be shared with the Energy Department. The LANL executive director was adamant—he wouldn't allow it, meaning we were not authorized to provide the Department of Energy access to our assessment conclusions. And because of this, the laboratory would receive a higher performance score in the procurement arena than it otherwise deserved, and the University of California would get a larger annual performance award fee than was warranted. This was deception at its worst, and we were being mandated to go along with it.

Tommy and I immediately voiced objection to the suppression of information—a move that wasn't well received by the executive director. The first indication of this came with the removal of all our assignments. The next retaliatory act was to put an end to Tommy's supervisory authority. His entire staff was reassigned elsewhere in the lab without his knowledge, except for me. The two of us were left behind together, but a former colleague granted Tommy a reprieve—a temporary role, albeit at a dramatically reduced level of responsibility. It was better than having nothing to do, so Tommy packed up his office for the move. Before leaving he assured me he'd keep lobbying the LANL executive director, on my behalf, for an assignment. He felt bad leaving me behind without any role, responsibilities, or duty—not even a coworker to interact with. Neither of us, at that point, could anticipate the nine months of professional isolation that still lay ahead.

I was now living a *Dilbert*-like cartoon existence—cubicle detention, workplace segregation, punishment for doing my job in accordance with professional auditing standards. I spent my time surfing the Internet and sending e-mails to LANL and UC officials requesting an assignment. No response. Phone

messages were never returned either. Days were spent glued
to the computer—following the latest space mission, becoming
an expert on the most recent Wall Street scandal, glancing at
the clock every few minutes with hopes of speeding it up. Empty
days became weeks, then months, without purpose or meaning;
just sitting, reading newspapers, reviewing professional
journals, sipping more coffee than I should to stay awake . . .
flagging down old acquaintances in the cafeteria, taking long
walks, doing whatever was required to survive just one more
excruciating day of boredom. Each day was the same as the last,
as was each hour, almost like being buried alive—aware of my
situation but helpless to do anything about it, and at the mercy
of a merciless mind-set determined to achieve whatever its aims
might be. Outside of a comic strip this was something I'd never
imagined possible in a professional setting. My years of advocacy
on behalf of workers, coupled with my refusal to cover up serious
problems in the procurement arena, had turned me into a poster
child for whistleblower abuse.

One day I cornered the individual who'd been approving my
time sheet submittal every other week, a LANL procurement
leader. It was rumored that he'd recently impregnated one of
his employees. Both were married, but not to each other. Affairs
between managers and staff weren't that uncommon in Los Alamos, but pregnancies were. And so she'd been transferred to
another part of the laboratory, thus mitigating the risk of having
a scandal come to light, one that even the most hardcore contor-
tionist of truth—a lab public affairs spokesperson—would have
difficulty explaining. Ironically, the procurement leader in question was promoted soon afterward. It was a chance encounter that
day, bumping into him in a hallway. I'd been sending him e-mails
periodically for months, reminding him that I had no assignment,
so the only thing I had to say at that moment was, "I still have no
work to do." His response caught me off guard:

"I'm sorry, Chuck; I wish I could give you an assignment, but my hands are tied."

Before I could respond, he said he was running late for a meeting and walked past me, leaving me wondering . . . who was "tying" his hands? Was he being forced to keep me penned up, without anything to do or anyone to interact with? Was his promotion a reward for doing so? Unfortunately, I'd never get to find out, for two years later, just days before he was scheduled to be deposed in connection to the whistleblower retaliation complaint I'd eventually file due to my many months of cubicle isolation, he dropped dead from a massive heart attack. He would have been queried, under oath, about our hallway encounter, and about the affair with his employee, and about the promotion. He was only forty years old when he died, healthy by all measures—a dedicated runner, in fact. But stress is the disabler that spares no one. He left behind a grieving family, and the mystery of who was preventing him from assigning me work. His regret had been his burden; his misplaced sense of loyalty to those in charge, his undoing.

By now it was clear someone was trying to make an example of me, perhaps even hoping I'd quit the laboratory, or keel over from despair. In either case I'd be gone. A *Los Angeles Times* article titled "A Nuclear Lab's Cowboy Culture," dated July 25, 2004, referred to my plight. The story caught the attention of a lab scientist on assignment from another country, perhaps not yet in tune with the lab's leadership culture. Nonetheless, it didn't sit well with her that anyone would be kept idle without an assignment.

"I can use someone with your skill sets in my area," she said over the phone, putting herself at risk, unknowingly, by just offering to help. After a brief conversation we agreed that if she could convince the person who seemed to be most responsible for my situation—the lab's executive director—I'd be happy to join her effort. A few days later she called back. No luck.

I could deal with just about anything, but I couldn't accept being kept idle indefinitely. It was time to make a decision, the one I'd always advised others to avoid. A Washington, DC, law firm, Bernabei & Wachtel, was being mentioned in the news, as it was representing Glenn Walp and Steve Doran in their own struggle with Los Alamos. A principal from the firm was coming into town, and I'd managed to arrange a meeting.

"I can't spend the rest of my time here not doing anything," I said to Tommy Hook. "Maybe you need legal representation as well."

He remained silent for an uncomfortable amount of time. As former whistleblower officer for the institution, Tommy understood the lab's insatiable appetite for litigation. He recognized people could end up bankrupt, and their reputations and careers could be ruined as well. Knowing the nature of what we'd be up against, he had reason to pause.

I'd come to the conclusion that my laboratory career was over; the question was whether Tommy felt the same about his own. We both had a paycheck, but even that seemed tenuous. Plus Tommy had already suffered a stroke, and I doubted the people we were dealing with would care. I was relieved when he finally said, "I'll come."

27

PRINCIPLE

I'D BEEN SITTING EIGHT months in cubicle detention with no work assignment when I received the call. It was from a *Los Angeles Times* journalist who'd gotten my name from someone; I didn't ask from whom, I was just glad she had. The reporter wanted names of people to talk to, those willing to share personal experiences about the laboratory. I provided several leads, but one in particular stood out in my mind—Deesh Narang.

During the struggle stemming from the 1995 layoff, Deesh attended the Citizens for LANL Employee Rights (CLER) meetings regularly. He hadn't been targeted for termination, nor did he have a friend or family member who was, but he seemed interested in what CLER was doing. On occasion, at the end of a meeting, he'd pull me aside to talk privately. He probed for insight while revealing little about himself, as though working undercover for others.

Intelligence gathering was something LANL paid many people to do. That's what the Government and Community Relations Offices were about, and what Public Affairs did as well:

> Buffeted by accusations of leaking nuclear secrets, pub-
> lic-affairs staff at Los Alamos National Laboratory began
> sizing up influential government officials, media and
> academics as "pro," "con" or "neutral" to the laboratory.
> . . . In what might be called the strange bedfellows list,
> the lab rated environmentalists, reporters for the Wall
> Street Journal and the New York Times and most Senate
> Republicans as "cons": Their statements on China's sup-
> posed nuclear thefts were bad for LANL and its image.
> (Ian Hoffman, "Lab Lists Its Foes, Friends," *Albuquerque
> Journal North*, August 17, 1999)

There were also freelancers—those who vied for the approval
of the powers that be while undermining their own community's interests in the process. But the laid-off workers still
had friends, colleagues, and family members at the laboratory
as well, and on occasion a LANL memorandum or e-mail surfaced at a CLER meeting, providing insight and perspective
on what upper management might be thinking. Rumors, also,
were brought to the group to analyze. But for every one of our
sleuths, the lab had multiple, so to think we weren't being
scouted as well was naive.

In time it became apparent Deesh wasn't spying, but was
having difficulty at work. The laboratory had brought him on
board years earlier for his expertise with nuclear regulations.
Ever since, he'd been repeatedly passed over for advancement,
and recently decided to file a complaint. The retribution began
immediately. Though he hadn't been targeted for termination
this time, there were still two more rounds of firings to go. My
notoriety, stemming from the layoff dispute, made him think I
perhaps had some wisdom to share regarding his predicament.
Other labees regularly came to me in a similar fashion, and my

advice was always the same: "Move somewhere else within the lab, stay away from lawyers, and get on with your life."

Like so many things at LANL, the internal complaint resolution process was an illusion—not objective, not independent, and certainly not intended to promote responsible behavior. The goal was simple—discovery—to make it possible for attorneys to locate evidentiary material and identify potential witnesses. For LANL it was about building a defense, targeting those who complained in the process. For the employee it was a minefield that needed to be navigated, and failing to try could cause more difficulties down the road.

Judges looked unfavorably on workers who didn't exhaust existing administrative remedies before seeking judicial relief. So after using the lab's internal grievance process and failing to achieve resolution, the next step was filing a formal complaint with the appropriate state or federal authority. For labees, the state route was a waste of time since neither California nor New Mexico labor laws seemed to apply. Filing federally was the alternative. The first step in the process was to submit a detailed complaint for the laboratory to respond to, and that normally entailed a formal denial of all allegations. Months of agency inaction typically followed, sometimes years, until one of two things happened—the employee requested a "right to sue" or the agency, on its own, issued a notice of dismissal for lack of proof. The latter didn't mean an investigation was done, just that there was no evidence in the agency's case folder to support a determination.

The good news was the individual was entitled to file a complaint; the bad news was the agency didn't necessarily do anything with it. In the process, the employer had months, even years, to retaliate, which sometimes included finding a way to engineer a dismissal or force the employee to quit. In either case the complaint was, at that point, moot.

The practical value in filing a formal complaint, besides satisfying a judicial expectation, was to prevent the statute of limitations—the time allowed to take legal action—from running out. Even then there was no guarantee, because there would still be many court filings to come—motions for dismissal, counterclaims, appeals, and other maneuvers designed to harass, confuse, delay, and exhaust the claimant financially, physically, and emotionally.

The system was designed this way by lobbyists and attorneys who constantly tug on political levers to ensure the interests of their well-to-do clients are protected, and by those we elect, who seem perennially focused on just carrying out the biddings of their wealthy donors. And since the financial burden for litigation, regardless of merit, always fell on the taxpayer, the military-industrial Goliath on the hill had no incentive to resolve disputes outside the judicial process. And yet, for all practical purposes, it was the only complaint resolution process even remotely capable of holding LANL responsible—somewhat akin to the gladiator needing to defeat the tiger with a dagger in order to win freedom; assuredly high risk, but unavoidable given the objective.

Without a practical means of enforcement, including ways to prevent continuing delays that keep people's lives in limbo for years on in, laws on the books were, at best, illusions of rights—a cyberspace-like matrix of make-believe and self-delusion. And so litigation was a last resort, and even then I didn't recommend it. But Deesh was already feeling cornered, like an animal surrounded by predators closing in for the kill. In his mind, he'd run out of options.

Finding a good lawyer is challenging, especially one willing to take a case on a contingency basis, meaning he or she only gets paid by winning or settling. It's a risky venture that few legal counsels are willing to invest in, particularly if the adversary is as protected and well financed as LANL, the University of California, and the US Department of Energy combined. These entities are like the feudal systems of old—inextricably allied through common interests and the interrelationships that stem from the "revolving door" between corporations, and the agencies that are supposed to be overseeing them.

Los Alamos Laboratory and its parent, the university, preferred litigation to resolution because it could. Win, lose, or draw, the Energy Department always had taxpayers foot the bill. Plus the lack of risk to institutional leaders meant there was zero incentive for them to consider alternatives, much less be concerned about expense. One day, after a Saturday morning CLER meeting, Deesh pulled me aside to inform me that he'd hired an attorney. But his lawyer's practice was on the Hill. And to make matters worse, it was not a contingency arrangement.

Los Alamos is a closed community and company town, with everyone seemingly connected in one way or another to the laboratory, or each other. It was hard to fathom why anyone taking on LANL would choose a lawyer from the lab's home turf, except for the fact that the laboratory had every major law firm in the state on retainer. Perhaps settling for an attorney based in Los Alamos had been Deesh's only option. Regardless, it wasn't the ideal choice.

Months went by, thousands of dollars were spent, and Deesh's attorney suddenly stopped working on his case. Finding a replacement lawyer for a lawsuit already on track for trial would be difficult. But in his dogged determination, Deesh did find someone—a young, energetic individual from a midsized Albuquerque law firm. He was the glimmer of hope that Deesh was in dire need of. But the matter was still slated to be litigated in Los Alamos, and LANL, for all practical purposes, *was* the community. Finding an objective jury on the Hill for a case like this would be virtually impossible.

Like most folks ensnared by litigation, Deesh was lost in an unfamiliar maze of confusion, frustration, and misunderstanding, and didn't know whether his previous counsel had even bothered requesting a change in venue. Hopefully his new attorney would, but the trial was just days away. The imperative, now, was to get the unfairness of his predicament out into the open. Local newspapers were a godsend, as they reported the impending slaughter within hours, and a few days later the venue for the case was moved to Santa Fe. In protest LANL immediately filed a motion for reconsideration by the court, opposing the change, asserting it wouldn't get a fair hearing in Santa Fe. The appeal was denied, but it said volumes about the laboratory and its relationship with neighboring communities.

The Narang trial lasted a week, and on the last day a member of the lab's in-house legal staff sat at the entrance to the courtroom. She was thick-lipped, small-framed, thin, and wrinkled, wearing a "little Dutch boy" hairstyle—straight blond hair, cropped slightly below the earlobe, with bangs. As I walked in I noticed her feverishly scribbling notes on a pad. She looked up at me, her face turning beet red in anger. The contempt was obvious, but irrelevant. I was there for Deesh, not her.

The wait for the decision wasn't long. Somehow jury members had managed to navigate through the fog of courtroom proceedings to come out on the side of justice:

> Deesh Narang, a specialist in nuclear regulatory compliance, said he had been "unassigned" for seven years since suing the lab for passing him over for a promotion. Awarded more than $500,000 in that case, he later won an internal retaliation grievance that accused the lab of wasting taxpayer money for paying his $100,000 annual salary but giving him nothing to do. Narang, who applied for 50

positions, remains nothing more than a "demoralized" file clerk. He has filed another grievance against the lab, which he says has already spent more than $1.5 million fighting him. (Ralph Vartabedian and Christine Hanley, "A Nuclear Lab's 'Cowboy Culture,'" *Los Angeles Times*, July 25, 2004)

Deesh had overcome insurmountable odds. In the same *Los Angeles Times* article, Senator Pete Domenici expressed regret for enabling LANL to become what it was, referring directly to the lab's defiance of accountability:

Los Alamos has acquired "a reputation as being both dysfunctional and politically untouchable," according to its chief benefactor, New Mexico Republican Sen. Pete V. Domenici. . . . On Friday, Domenici issued an open letter that acknowledged he wrongly had protected the lab for years. "I have found myself increasingly defending the laboratory for failures of basic management . . . and security. While critics have carped, I have worked to ensure that none of the attacks harmed the laboratory, but that effort has come at great cost. Today, in Washington, Los Alamos' reputation as a crown jewel of science is being eclipsed by a reputation as being both dysfunctional and untouchable." (Ralph Vartabedian and Christine Hanley, "A Nuclear Lab's 'Cowboy Culture,'" *Los Angeles Times*, July 25, 2004)

For those who had lost their health, their careers, and their professional standing because of the lab's machinations, Domenici's belated acknowledgement rang hollow—or, as the famous maxim goes, "A day late and a dollar short." His words, at this point, were of no value to anyone but himself.

28

INFLUENCE

BEFORE THE US DEPARTMENT of Energy existed, there was the US Atomic Energy Commission (AEC). And at the end of WWII, before the University of California became committed to the nation's nuclear weapons program, the university actually didn't want anything more to do with Los Alamos. But renowned UC physicist and Nobel laureate Ernest O. Lawrence needed a sustainable funding source to support his research, and his close association with a powerful university regent provided the lever to nudge UC in the "right" direction. Lawrence got his funding and the AEC, in turn, got the university's mantle of academia to use, as cover, in bolstering recruitment efforts. In his book *The National Labs: Science in an American System, 1947–1974*,[1] Peter Westwick states:

> The inexperience of the federal government in the administration of basic research programs, the desired

---

1. Peter Westwick, *The National Labs: Science in an American System, 1947–1974*. Cambridge, MA: Harvard University Press, 2003.

> participation of academic students and faculty, and pri-
> vate industry in atomic research, and the difficulty of
> separating some labs, such as Berkeley, from their con-
> tractors argued against direct operation [by the federal
> government]. The main drawback, however, would be the
> difficulty of recruiting staff . . . [given that] scientific per-
> sonnel consider direct employment by the government
> highly undesirable.

From the onset, the concern among those put in charge of developing the world's first atomic bomb was that the best and brightest in academia would not want to work directly for the military. A way to convince them, though, would be to place the weapons research component under the University of California. In return, UC would enjoy a federal funding stream that would never go dry. Thus government money, earmarked for the State of California and for UC-specific research, was the bonding agent for the university's involvement from the onset. Yet the debate would continue for decades afterward, as to whether the relationship was appropriate:

> It is recommended that the university inform the Atomic
> Energy Commission that it does not plan to continue the
> operation of these laboratories beyond the expiration of
> the present contracts on September 30, 1972. (Paul E.
> Zinner, Chairman, "Report of the Special Committee on
> University Research at Livermore and Los Alamos," Uni-
> versity of California Academic Senate, 1970)

Over the years there have been many assessments by University of California stakeholders—students and faculty alike—reaching a similar conclusion: there is no valid or compelling reason for an institution of higher learning to be managing facilities whose primary mission is the development and maintenance of weapons of mass destruction (i.e., nuclear bombs). For example, a 1989 study commissioned by the UC Academic Senate recommended that the university "should, in a timely and orderly manner, phase out its responsibility for operating the laboratories." A 1996 Academic Senate study reached a similar conclusion.

Student concerns about the university's relationship with the military-industrial complex didn't fare any better. But the attitude of those in charge, with respect to UC and the facilities it managed for the US government, was, perhaps, symptomatic of much deeper problems within the university, as the following series of *San Francisco Chronicle* excerpts suggests:

The University of California's second in command, who resigned three weeks ago under the cloud of a conflict-of-interest investigation, has taken a sabbatical but remains on the university payroll—at more than $25,000 a month . . . (Tanya Schevitz and Todd Wallack, "UC Still Paying Ex-no. 2 Official $25,000 a Month," *San Francisco Chronicle*, November 26, 2005)

The University of California gave most of its top executives bonuses, housing allowances or other perks that weren't publically reported or approved by the governing Board of Regents . . . (Tanya Schevitz and Todd Wallack, "Most UC Execs Got Sweet Deals," *San Francisco Chronicle*, April 25, 2006)

Lawmakers harshly criticized the University of California's pay practices. . . . [A]n audit revealed scores of violations of university policy and UC President Robert Dynes admitted to a culture in his office of "trying to get away with as much as possible and disclose as little as possible." (Tanya Schevitz and Todd Wallack, "UC Chief Raked As New Pay Deals Are Revealed: Latest Audit Shows Scores Were Made in Secret," *San Francisco Chronicle*, May 18, 2006)

"Get away with as much as possible and disclose as little as possible." That was how UC president Bob Dynes—whom I'd met in Sacramento, the day before lab director Pete Nanos said he planned to "drain the swamp" on the hill—described the leadership culture of the university. It was the same attitude I'd perceived among those in charge at LANL, perhaps explaining why UC seemed so willing to accept conditions in Los Alamos without much question, or legitimate audit scrutiny.

Twenty-six individuals, known collectively as the Regents, run the University of California. Eighteen are appointed by the governor. Like the directors of corporate boards, most serve because their interests, typically allied with business, stand to benefit through their service. There may be a smattering of community-oriented appointments in the mix, but too few to alter the primary role of appointees, which is to carry out the wishes of those who appoint them, in this case the governor of the State of California. University presidents are politically astute as well, which is why faculty and student outcries are readily drowned out by the whispers of backroom wheeling and dealing—politics— where the 1 percent wins 99 percent of the time.

United States military expenditures in 2012, according to the Stockholm International Peace Research Institute, were

$682 billion, more than the next dozen countries with the largest national defense budgets on the planet, combined. And the lion's share of the economic benefit associated with US defense spending goes to California.

As documented by GovernmentContractsWon.com, there are more than 25,000 employers in the State of California receiving defense contracts. Between 2001 and 2011 the contracts totaled $415 billion, with nearly $44 billion being awarded in 2011 alone, plus the billions associated with the three UC-managed federal labs. In the final analysis, regardless of what the University of California stakeholder community may prefer, or what the legitimate needs of society are, it's unlikely the university will ever voluntarily sever its ties to the military-industrial complex and nuclear weapons establishment; certainly not so long at those in control continue to benefit so lavishly at the expense of everything else, including the planet, i.e. climate change.

29

COLLAPSE

I‌T WAS THE FALL of 2004, ten years since the lab-wide lay-off. So much had transpired since then, and the glow of hope I once had working for Tommy was now a cold ember. The former deputy director who once predicted I'd never be given the opportunity to have a satisfying career in Los Alamos was right. I was now commuting ninety miles daily, round trip, from a recently acquired Santa Fe residence to my basement cubicle on the Hill.

In August, after nearly nine months of sitting idle with nothing to do, I received notice that I'd been given an assignment. This was thanks to my attorney, Lynne Bernabei, who essentially forced the issue with the lab and the university. But my new job, effective the start of September 2004, placed me back in the lion's den, this time working in the director's office, under the watchful eye of my nemesis—the laboratory's executive director. My assignment was to recruit unsuspecting young college accounting and business school graduates to work at LANL—a cruel joke, given my own sad state of affairs. I had a graduate degree, four professional certifications, thirty years of professional experience, and a laboratory career that was anything *but* rewarding. Besides that, the human resources (HR) division did the laboratory's recruiting, and was staffed specifically for this purpose. But after nine months with no duties, anything was better than just sitting around twiddling my thumbs.

"In addition to the recruiting, we also need an MBA program in Los Alamos," said lab controller Jay Johnston. This was to enable others to advance professionally (another dig perhaps). But getting out of Los Alamos to recruit and lobby for an MBA program did have some appeal. I began by scheduling meetings with the accounting, economics, and business school department heads of various state universities, and representing LANL at recruitment fairs. I was determined to put a good face on a bad situation; plus I enjoyed working with bright young people. But after a couple of months I was done, as there were only so many recruiting events to attend, only so many university department heads to visit with, and only so many student résumés to review. It was time to focus on bringing an advanced degree program to Los Alamos.

The University of New Mexico already had a satellite campus on the Hill. The campus director was enthusiastic about the prospect of establishing an MBA program at his facility, but doubted his superiors in Albuquerque would support it. After a few days we found out their decision; as anticipated, the answer was no. Such programs were expensive to establish and run; plus the main campus in Albuquerque, ninety miles removed, already had one in place. The commute was difficult but doable— I'd earned my graduate degree from UNM in 1989 doing so.

Since New Mexico's largest university, UNM, had rejected outright the notion of expanding its MBA program into Los Alamos, it was now time to approach the state's second-largest—New Mexico State University (NMSU). In 2003, at a state-sponsored dinner held at the New Mexico governor's mansion, I met Bob Gallagher, president of the New Mexico Oil and Gas Association, and also chairman of the NMSU board of regents. It was a chance encounter that now came in handy. Garrey Carruthers, former New Mexico Republican governor, was the dean of the NMSU School of Economics and Business. I decided to approach Gallagher for a leg-up assist in setting up a meeting with him, and within days was with Carruthers in his Las Cruces, New Mexico, office. By December 2004, a contingent of NMSU department heads was at LANL, dialoguing with lab accounting and budget leads. And by the start of the following academic year, NMSU had a master's in business administration program in Los Alamos.

I'd done the recruiting and established the MBA program. Now what? This was the question I posed to my immediate supervisor, who reported directly to the LANL executive director, which meant she'd have to find out from him. The response threw me for a loop. I was to become a trainer—another HR function. The objective was to establish learning programs for accounting and budgeting professionals—basically teach others how to navigate the lab's maze of business systems and processes so they, in turn, were prepared for job advancement in Los Alamos. My own career was as stale as a decomposing corpse, yet I was supposed to be helping others with theirs . . . in essence pouring salt on my own open wound. A few days later, while driving to Los Alamos and contemplating how dysfunctional things had become for me at work, I suddenly felt an invisible weight bearing down. My breathing became labored; my vision clouded as I came up alongside the community airport. I pulled off the road and laid my forehead on the steering wheel to compose myself. Hundreds of commuters passed by in the morning rush. A few weeks later my primary care provider surmised I'd had an anxiety attack, and was perhaps now suffering from depression. I was nearing the end of my rope.

"We have no choice," Mike, my old college roommate, once said. "We have to endure." He was talking about Los Alamos, and the unfairness that permeated the community and lab. He was gone, silenced forever by hidden truths he'd never come to terms with. Tommy tried to endure as well, and had suffered a stroke. I didn't want to follow in either's footsteps, but I wasn't about to start popping pills for anxiety if there were other options. A few weeks of Family Medical Leave (FML) might do the trick. I now had three months to inch back from the edge.

30

SIMILARITIES

My time away from the lab helped me regain footing, which was fortunate, because word was out regarding the LANL procurement process assessments Tommy and I had done in 2003, and related lab efforts to cover up the problems we'd found. The Washington, DC–based Project on Government Oversight (POGO), a whistleblower protection advocacy group, had taken note, and I was now slated to appear on national TV.

Like the energy company Enron, Los Alamos had become a gross distortion of reality. Enron had lied to its investors and lenders about its financial condition. Arthur Anderson, the world-renowned certified public accounting firm, had blindly accepted Enron's self-serving assertions. Federal regulators were equally negligent, and in the end both the company and its accounting firm ceased to exist. Shareholders, including thousands of Enron employees who lost their jobs in the aftermath of the scandal and whose pensions were heavily vested in their employer's stock, lost nearly $11 billion dollars in company stock value. Energy markets across the nation were destabilized as well, with consumers being forced to pay hundreds of millions of dollars more for electricity than would have otherwise been the case.

The Los Alamos National Laboratory, like Enron, had mastered the art of giving the impression things were far better than they were, and that was precisely the point I wanted to make on the *CBS Evening News* in 2005. The interview had been arranged by POGO.

The CBS studio was unassuming, marked by a single-door entrance and a small sign above it with the news organization's logo. A security guard stationed immediately to the left of the doorway took down our names and reason for being there. Perhaps ten feet away, directly across the small foyer, was the entrance to the inner sanctum. The woman standing there was an assistant correspondent, and she promptly led me, and the POGO representative accompanying me, down a narrow corridor. In the distance an array of monitors flashed images of TV personalities I recognized, including the legendary news anchor Dan Rather. We were ushered into a small furnished room that had set pieces for a couple of talking-head programs. Switching out furnishings and changing camera angle magically produced backgrounds for different shows. A technician wired me up with a microphone for the interview, testing the sound reception with someone in an unseen control room, while another worked at positioning the background and lighting. In the midst of this flurry of activity, the cameraman readied himself, a makeup person popped in to powder me up for my *CBS Evening News* debut, and then investigative journalist Sharyl Attkisson walked in the room. We spent a few moments in casual conversation as she sought to settle my nerves. Then, in preparation for going on the air, she asked, "So what is it that you want to say?"

I held in my hand copies of the assessments Tommy Hook and I had done of the LANL procurement processes. "These reports were covered up by lab management," I said. "Congress is being misled," I continued, "like Enron did with its investors."

"Enron," she said thoughtfully. "You think what the laboratory's doing is similar?"

"Absolutely," I responded. After a couple of more brief exchanges, the interview began:

> On Friday, CBS News' Sharyl Attkisson had another remarkable story about the almost laughably corrupt business practices at the world's most important nuclear center . . . [Montaño] found: "Vendors could charge whatever they wanted." 10,000 purchases out of 56,000 shouldn't have been allowed. Another 38,000 were questionable. [According to Montaño:] "Vendors routinely overbilled and double-billed . . ." (Noah Max, "More Los Alamos Shenanigans," *Defense Tech*, March 20, 2005)

The CBS exposé was a last-ditch effort to get someone in authority to pay attention. A few weeks later, Tommy Hook followed suit with his own public appeal. Going into these interviews, both of us were already in institutional leaders' crosshairs for refusing to lie about systemic deficiencies we'd found in the laboratory's procurement processes. Taxpayers were paying a heavy price as well.

Tommy had been asked to testify in the February/March 2003 congressional hearings related to Glenn Walp and Steve Doran, but that testimony never happened. The university, instead, quickly settled with Glenn and Steve after Tommy's deposition made headlines—the one given years earlier serving to corroborate claims Glenn and Steve were making at that point. The quick resolution served to bring an immediate end to the lawmakers' inquiry, enabling UC and the lab to avoid further embarrassment, simultaneously derailing the plan to have

Tommy testify. But in 2005, once Sharyl Attkisson shined the proverbial camera lights back on us, congressional interest was revived. All of a sudden there was a renewed commitment on the part of congressional staffers to talk to the lab's former whistleblower officer—Tommy Hook.

The call came about 4:00 in the morning.

"It's Susie," my wife said as she handed the phone over to me. "Tommy's in the emergency room."

"What?" I asked.

"Tommy's in the hospital," she repeated. "It's his wife on the phone, Susie."

I took the phone.

"Come to the hospital," said the voice quivering on the other end. "Tommy needs to talk to you. He's badly beaten. Oh Chuck, please."

I had received an e-mail from Tommy just a few hours earlier, electronically time-stamped around 9:30 p.m. This meant that six hours earlier he'd been in his White Rock home; now he was in a Santa Fe hospital.

Susie's words cycled in my head as we drove; my mind churned, trying to figure out what was going on. Tommy had informed me a couple of weeks earlier that someone declaring himself to be a laboratory auditor had called him, sounding scared over the phone and claiming to have information to provide for Tommy's upcoming meeting with congressional staffers. But he was only willing to disclose what he had in person, so the conversation ended with the caller promising to get back with a time and place to meet. I hadn't heard from Tommy since then.

My wife and I were allowed into the hospital treatment area only after Susie came to escort us in. She was in a controlled panic. "Tommy . . ." she said. "You won't recognize him." Tears clouded her vision. "They left shoe prints on his face," she continued. "Why . . . why did they do this?"

It was a rhetorical question. How does one rationalize the merciless beating of another person? The numbness of the moment turned to disbelief when we saw him. Tommy *was*, as Susie had pointed out, unrecognizable. His face was swollen, bruised, and stained with blood, his eyes barely visible through ballooning eyelids and a broken jaw. On his cheek was a ghostly imprint—the tread mark of someone's shoe. Suddenly, with a slight movement of his hand, Tommy waved me in closer to hear him. Speaking softly through lips that barely moved, he said, "Be careful . . . They kept telling me to keep my fucking mouth shut; they kept telling me to keep my fucking mouth shut," he repeated.

"Who did this to you?" I asked.

"Don't know," he said. "Be careful."

"How many were there?"

"Two," he said. "Maybe more . . . I don't know."

"Do you think this had anything to do with the congressional thing?" I asked.

Unable to shrug his shoulders, Tommy shook his head weakly. "Don't know," he whispered. "Just be careful."

Tommy began to sob quietly. I had no idea what to say. The thugs who did this had done their job only too well. Decency no longer seemed possible; the world, all of sudden, felt less safe. I stared at my wife in disbelief, unable to express in words what I felt. Tommy had asked Susie to call me, to warn me about something neither of us could have ever expected. She was in Albuquerque that evening and had been called to the hospital after the beating, where she then called me. According to her, Tommy had gotten a telephone call at home as he was preparing for bed. The person on the other end requested they meet immediately, claiming he had information for Tommy to pass on to the congressional staffers he was slated to meet the following week. It sounded familiar.

"I should probably call Bob and Lynne," I said, talking to nobody in particular. Robert "Bob" Rothstein was a Santa Fe lawyer working with my attorney, Lynne Bernabei, who was located in Washington, DC.

"Should I take pictures?" I asked Susie and Tommy.

"Yes," Tommy whispered. "People need to know."

It was clear he'd been attacked by someone who wanted to shut him up, but why? Maybe it was people who were scared for their jobs, or perhaps fearful of being exposed for something? As Los Alamos's former whistleblower officer, Tommy probably had more than a few enemies, and even more so now as an actual whistleblower.

Later that morning my wife returned with a digital camera. Once word of the beating got out, there'd be questions . . . Tommy gets beaten up one week before meeting with congressional committee staffers, and all the while his attackers are telling him to keep his mouth shut? Words alone would never come close to describing his condition; pictures would help. But upon seeing them, I was having second thoughts. "Are you sure, Tommy—do you want these made public?" The photos were gruesome.

"Yes," he responded.

I still wasn't convinced. "Why should we let whoever did this see how they left you; why give them the satisfaction? Are you certain of this?" I asked again.

"Yes," Tommy reiterated. "People should know."

The attack occurred at a strip club about 2:00 a.m. on a Sunday morning. Tommy was carted away in an ambulance, and his car was left in the parking lot. Later that morning I drove by to check on it. The inside was exceptionally clean, and the outside appeared to be recently washed and showed no signs of damage. The establishment was closed, but a notice posted at the entrance indicated it would open that afternoon. I took a moment to check the parking lot for clues. Tommy's assailants had managed to escape before police arrived; perhaps they'd left something behind that could identify them. I noticed security cameras strategically positioned on the roofline, pointing at the parking lot and building entrance. Unfortunately, as determined later on, they weren't functioning. Recording patrons being beaten up so attorneys could later analyze the video perhaps wasn't smart, but maybe displaying a few dead cameras to deter break-ins was.

That afternoon I returned to the club with my daughter and son-in-law in tow, and as we drove into the parking area, a small pickup truck pulled in as well. A ponytailed male stepped out, keys in hand, along with a female. Both headed toward the front door.

"May I ask you a few questions about what happened this morning?" I asked. "I'm a friend of the guy that was attacked."

"The beating," the man began, "was like nothing I've ever seen before." He explained that he'd witnessed many bar fights in the past, but this one was different. "They wanted to kill him."

The woman chimed in, stating that Tommy had arrived the evening before, sat at the end of the bar alone, and looked toward the door as though waiting for somebody.

"Did he interact with anyone?" I asked.

She shook her head no.

"Did anyone get a license plate number?"

The man indicated that there were two cars filled with men. "We got some numbers off the plates . . . One of the cars was a Chrysler 300," he said.

"What were the numbers?" I asked.

"Don't recall," he responded. "We gave that information to the police." He continued, "Our bouncer saved the guy's life . . . If he hadn't come out when he did, they would've killed him."

Tommy's photos went viral over the Internet the next day; the press conference, twenty-four hours afterward, was well attended. Keith Olbermann, host of the TV news magazine *Countdown*, was among those taking an interest. This was the televised interview:

> OLBERMANN: Even in these days of superheated politics and business, we still think of the risks of whistleblowers as being confined to those of finance and career, those who have told on big tobacco, those who have claimed they were telling on presidential administrations.
>
> But in our fourth story on the COUNTDOWN tonight, every once in a while, there is a Karen Silkwood, a worker at an Oklahoma plutonium plant, herself contaminated, gathering evidence of safety violations for her union, and then suddenly dead in an inexplicable one-car accident. That was in 1974.
>
> Today, the name of the whistleblower, for whom the risk may have been far more tangible than just money, is Tommy Hook, an auditor at the Los Alamos National Laboratory. He was scheduled to testify later this month before Congress about possible financial waste and fraud at the lab.
>
> Mr. Hook and his wife say on Saturday, he was lured to a nightclub in the town of Santa Fe, New Mexico, with the promise of being given further evidence confirming his claims. When no one turned up, Hook went back to his car. There, he and his wife say, he was pulled out of the driver's seat by several assailants, kicked, punched, and told to keep his mouth shut.

SUSAN HOOK, WHISTLEBLOWER'S WIFE: He has a fracture down on his jaw down here, and under his eye. He was swollen really, really bad. His teeth are pushed back. He has a therapist coming in to help him talk. And he has a loss of memory right now. But, you know, it's starting to come back, because he's had a terrible concussion.

OLBERMANN: Law enforcement sources are telling *NBC News*, though, that the FBI says it's already investigated, [and] found an alleged perpetrator, who claims that he says it was just a bar fight. Mrs. Hook says the assailants did not take her husband's wallet. They did fracture his jaw. The Los Alamos lab, which conducts classified work on nuclear weapons, released a statement saying it's outraged by the attack and is cooperating fully with the police.

Mr. Hook had also filed a lawsuit against Los Alamos, claiming that since he started voicing complaints in 1997, managers had created work conditions designed to make him and another auditor quit.

That other auditor, who joined Mr. Hook in that suit, is Chuck Montaño, who joins us now.

And thank you for your time tonight, sir.

CHUCK MONTAÑO, LOS ALAMOS EMPLOYEE: Thank you for having me.

OLBERMANN: The report here says that the FBI says this was just a bar fight, unconnected to Los Alamos—your thoughts on that statement?

MONTAÑO: Well, we haven't seen the report. I don't believe it. I believe what Tommy Hook said initially. We were with him at 5:00 a.m. in the hospital. There was no—he did not look like he was intoxicated. That's not in his nature. Anybody that knows Tommy Hook knows he's very credible. And what he was telling me at the time was that, to be careful, because these people were telling him to shut up and to stay quiet if he knew what was good for him.

OLBERMANN: Yes, Mr. Montaño, it would be an extraordinary coincidence if, on the eve of his testimony, virtually, he had been beaten up in a totally unconnected bar fight, obviously. But do you have any other evidence besides that logic that would suggest that these events were indeed connected, besides the logic of the thing and what he told you?

MONTAÑO: Well, I think the logic is the big thing, because he had told me about a week ago that he had received a call indicating that there was an auditor that had some information, he was—that he had uncovered some fraud at the lab, but he was being pressured by his—by the lab management that he was under, to not report what he had uncovered.

But he was scared for his job. And he wanted to meet with Tommy in private so that he could provide him with the information. Tommy is the kind of person that likes to help people if they—if he feels he can help them. I've had several calls as well, because I have been somewhat visible at the lab. And I've had calls from employees that have been concerned. And I've met with them.

And so to me, that's not unusual that he would get a call like that.

OLBERMANN: Are you still going to testify, and is Mr. Hook going to testify?

MONTAÑO: Well, I do hope that he testifies, because he wasn't just a mere auditor—he was the lab's whistleblower officer. And he had daily interactions with the director's office, with lab legal. He was the point of contact. He was the person that basically had the staff that did the investigations related to fraud, waste, and abuse.

Those responsibilities were removed from him several years ago after he testified in another case and told the truth. And basically, the truth that he told was what [Glenn] Walp and [Steve] Doran were saying. These were the two investigators that revealed the procurement fraud. Walp and Doran were saying that they were being told not to reveal what they had found, because they didn't want to embarrass the university and put the contract in jeopardy.

Well, Tommy had testified in a related—in an unrelated case years earlier that he was being instructed to cover up problems for the same reason.

So Tommy has paid a very high price professionally, because he told the truth. And so this doesn't surprise me, being that he is—he was at such a high level within the lab, that he would be targeted, that there would be people very nervous about his testimony.

OLBERMANN: Chuck Montaño, Los Alamos lab whistleblower, we thank you for your time, and good luck with this.

MONTAÑO: Thank you very much.

(*Countdown* with Keith Olbermann, June 7, 2005) http:// www.msnbc.msn.com/id/8144282/ns/msnbc_tv-count-down_with_keith_olbermann/t/countdown-keith-olber-mann-june

Susie was phenomenally composed at the press conference, answering the media's questions truthfully and without hesitation. Then a reporter suddenly queried me with, "Do you think the laboratory was responsible?"

"Do I think the laboratory issued a procurement order to have Tommy beaten up?" I responded glibly. "No."

A couple of reporters chuckled.

"But if you're asking whether I think it shoulders responsibility for putting people like Tommy at risk, my answer is yes, because we become targets when the laboratory refuses to fix problems and instead forces us to become whistleblowers . . . So yes, the lab is responsible in that respect."

Institutional spokespersons immediately denied LANL or UC had any involvement in the beating. Local law enforcement—the Santa Fe Police Department—concluded as much within hours, their determination apparently based on interviews with club patrons. But the parties responsible for the attack were still on the run; thus it seemed presumptuous to be concluding much of anything at that point. Nonetheless, the picture painted by the two nightclub workers a couple of days earlier was starting to change. Others who claimed to be in attendance described Tommy as consuming alcohol and enjoying the entertainment along with other patrons, as opposed to sitting quietly at the end of the bar, waiting, as initially described. His time of arrival changed as well. Some claimed he'd come in around 7:00 that evening, versus three hours later, as would be expected based on the e-mail I'd gotten from him. Within days I no longer knew what to believe, except for the fact that Tommy had been viciously assaulted.

Tommy Hook was soft-spoken, wore glasses . . . the stereotypical accountant, both in appearance and demeanor. We'd never socialized much during working hours at LANL, or even after 5:00 p.m. But from what I could tell he was a dedicated professional, conservative in appearance and outlook, well liked among his peers—which is why it surprised me, later, to learn during his deposition that on the night in question he'd had several beers. I was even more taken aback when he admitted to patronizing strip clubs in the past with other LANL officials, while on business trips.

Suddenly the university tossed a bone into the fray, deciding to admit that the lab had in fact retaliated against Tommy on the job. But it was a qualified admission, because according to the official statement the retribution had been "unintentional":

University of California officials say an independent investigator found a single instance of retaliation against federal whistleblower Tommy Hook, the Los Alamos National Laboratory auditor who was severely beaten at a Santa Fe strip club last weekend. But UC officials say the retaliation was unintentional. (Adam Rankin, "Retaliation Was 'Not Intentional,'" *Albuquerque Journal North*, June 11, 2005)

For Tommy, it was little consolation that UC and the lab were willing to concede his career was derailed by LANL officials, albeit unintentionally. It was the epitome of the "day late, dollar short" apology. Plus the notion that someone retaliates "unintentionally" was absurd. None of it mattered anymore, though, for the cumulative effect of the stroke and beating, coupled with the emotional scars from years of unrelenting workplace marginalization and abuse, left Tommy disabled and suffering from post-traumatic stress disorder (PTSD), a clinical term that applies to shattered lives.

The scheduled meeting with congressional staffers became a pipe dream after the assault. Tommy's testimony was no longer needed or wanted. Beltway allies of Los Alamos and the university would have turned his appearance into a circus. Following the beating, my contact with Tommy gradually diminished, both of us, perhaps, wanting to put the memory of this horrific event behind us. I've not seen or heard from him in several years, and can only hope that he's doing better now.

The individuals who did the attacking were finally arrested, prosecuted, and found guilty, but denied any connection with LANL or the University of California. Out of several suspects, only two were charged. Both of them were known local troublemakers. According to them, Tommy had been brutalized for hitting someone with his vehicle while backing up that morning. But I'd inspected the car the day of the attack and had found no dents, scratches, smudges, or bloodstains to support the claim. It was the victim's word against the several who'd victimized him, and against powerful interests anxious to put the matter to rest. Case closed.

31

WHISTLING

THE PROCUREMENT ASSESSMENTS TOMMY Hook and I prepared at the end of 2003 were never handed over to the US Department of Energy. Nor was the cumulative report, which was what DOE field personnel needed in order to know whether LANL procurement processes were fixed. Instead of receiving our report, the department was given a dramatically watered-down version. This, we learned, was done at the instruction of the lab's executive director. Tommy and I found out about the deception after the fact, but we could still be implicated for knowing about it and not reporting it.

The executive director, a former DOE official placed in the Albuquerque Operations Office, assumed a leadership position at LANL after retiring from government service. During my first meeting with him, he made it clear that while with the Energy Department, it was his responsibility, as contract administrator, to determine whether to keep UC at the helm in Los Alamos. He made a similar claim later, while addressing a roomful of laboratory team leads, so apparently he *had* been a good friend of the university. UC, it appeared, had returned the favor by providing him a lucrative postretirement career at LANL. It was the quintessential revolving-door transaction.

Compliance enforcement was the responsibility of Energy Department personnel working in the trenches and at ground level. Above them, in the DOE executive wing, political influence ruled. John Gustafson, deputy for laboratory public affairs and a lab spokesperson, provided a sense of how this worked in a 1996 letter to the editor of the *Santa Fe New Mexican*:

> The *New Mexican's* editorial "LANL Need Not Go to Mat on Layoff Ruling" demonstrates flawed, shallow thinking on a topic that requires more careful consideration of all the facts. . . . News media also have neglected to consider the preliminary nature of the report by the Office of Federal Contract Compliance Programs, mistakenly viewing the report as conclusive. In fact, this report is the product of staff at a field office and does not bear the authority of the entire agency. (John Gustafson, LANL Public Affairs, "Letter to the Editor," *Santa Fe New Mexican*, October 26, 1996)

The further up the political food chain an investigative report went within an agency, the less likely it was issued with the views of field personnel intact, which is what laboratory officials banked on. Gustafson was my neighbor, the one who brought a pie to my doorstep years earlier as events were unfolding related to the '95 layoff. Apparently things hadn't turned out the way he'd anticipated. As suggested by his letter, the proverbial tortoise had won the race.

The university maintained a satellite office within the Washington Beltway to ensure constant contact with elected and government officials, including political operatives within the Department of Energy complex adept at intercepting field reports before they got finalized and issued. It was in this realm that UC and LANL were at their best, in an environment where field reports got wordsmithed to mush, unallowable or questionable costs got negotiated out of existence with the DOE contract administrator—the LANL executive director's old job.

The procurement assessments Tommy and I did exposed widespread internal control weaknesses within the lab's procurement arena, meaning the associated risk for fraud, waste, and abuse was high. Plus the assessments demonstrated that there'd been virtually no improvement since Glenn Walp and Steve Doran were fired for uncovering the consequence—theft. The lab's executive director was preventing our reports from being released; our cumulative report had been redone to blur reality. In accordance with official DOE orders, which are the regulatory mandates that contractors and their employees are required to follow, I was now obligated to blow the whistle:

DOE Order 221.1A, "Reporting Fraud, Waste, and Abuse to the Office of Inspector General":

Regardless of the performer of the work, the contractor is responsible for complying with the requirements of this contractor requirements document . . . [and to] notify employees annually of their duty to report allegations of fraud, waste, abuse, misuse, corruption, criminal acts, or mismanagement relating to DOE programs, operations, facilities, contracts, or information technology systems to an appropriate authority (e.g. OIG, other law enforcement, supervisor, employee concerns office, security officials.

DOE Order 221.2A, "Cooperation with the Office of Inspector General":

The Administrator of the NNSA [National Nuclear Security Administration, DOE] will assure that NNSA employees and contractors comply with their respective responsibilities under this Order. . . . [E]mployees must cooperate fully and promptly with requests from the OIG [Office of Inspector General] for information and data. . . . [They] must also comply with requests for interviews and briefings and must provide affidavits or sworn statements. . . . [They] must not impede or hinder other employees' cooperation with the OIG . . .

I was required by these official orders to report fraud, waste, and abuse to the Energy Department. Failure to do so also meant I'd be putting my career certifications in jeopardy, because related codes of conduct were strict when it came to matters of fraud. Loyalty oath or not, going to jail just to protect the university's image wasn't part of my job description, nor was ruining my professional standing just to keep UC in Los Alamos.

In late 2003, the DOE field representative tasked to assess the lab's procurement processes had been requesting copies of our reports for weeks. Tommy was instructed not to release them or he'd be fired, the dire warning coming directly from the executive director. It was one thing not to release a report; watering down a report for release was another thing entirely, which was what the lab did. The latter was misleading. And by not providing the level of insight needed for department personnel to reach an informed conclusion regarding LANL's performance in the procurement arena, the laboratory was able to garner a larger award fee for the University of California.

The award fee, of course, was paid for with taxpayer dollars. It was the incentive carrot that the US Department of Energy used to motivate contractors to achieve specific outcomes (performance goals and milestones). But if the achievement bar was set low to begin with, or if the contractor could be misleading about what was being accomplished and nothing was being done by the department to validate the contractor's claims, then the entire exercise was pretty much meaningless. And even more so if the DOE was also inclined to deny the public (the media) access to any of the supporting documentation related to its award fee determination.

In mid-2004, after being in cubicle isolation for months, I assembled an information package, including copies of our assessments, and shoved everything into a large manila envelope, which I then hand-carried to the local DOE Office of Inspector General (OIG)—the semiautonomous investigative arm of the Department of Energy. I left the material with the OIG receptionist and within days received a call from the office leader requesting a meeting. A few days later I signed a statement affirming the truthfulness of my disclosures. At that point, I was an official Energy Department whistleblower. After many months, the OIG initiated an investigation to determine whether the assessments Tommy and I had done were sufficient, and whether related conclusions were valid. They were. As reported in a July 12, 2006, *Los Alamos Monitor* article by Roger Snodgrass, the OIG not only agreed we'd complied with professional standards when it came to documenting our claims, but based on our work, the University of California needed to reimburse taxpayers $8 million.

Workpapers are what auditors assemble during an audit, and are used to support their conclusions. In late 2003 Tommy and I were directed to relinquish control of our procurement assessment workpapers. We turned them over to a lab manager and never saw them again. They were properly organized and cross-referenced at the time, in accordance with professional audit standards. But later, when lab officials were required to provide them to the OIG for its review, they were a jumbled mess—loose piles of papers tossed into boxes, and in no particular order.

Experienced evaluators recognize that being swamped with piles of paper, lacking in order or organization, is an attempt to frustrate them and obscure reality. It takes more time and effort to uncover the truth in "swamped" scenarios, but the inspector general managed to do so. And to make matters worse for the lab, the OIG's field report validating our results was issued before LANL operatives inside the DC Beltway could intervene. It didn't matter, though, for in the aftermath there were no consequences for the university or the laboratory. The management award fee to UC, as authorized by the Energy Department's upper echelon, remained the same. Nor was the university required to reimburse taxpayers for the $8 million in unallowable and questionable costs that the OIG believed should be paid back. This was proof that even the DOE's own investigative arm had little influence with the agency's contact administrator, or with the department's cadre of politically connected executives.

By keeping the military-industrial complex happy, politicians got contributions for their reelection bids, Department of Energy executives kept the revolving door well lubricated for themselves, and lower-level bureaucrats ensured their own longevity in government service. Society suffered the effects, taxpayers paid the tab, and, when all was said and done, nothing changed.

32

"MOURNING" AFTER

FOR NEW MEXICO'S REPUBLICAN US senator, Pete
Domenici, Los Alamos was a symbol of triumph in a largely poor
and heavily Democratic Northern New Mexico. So when any
outside force challenged the lab and its practices, he naturally
felt threatened.

In 1997, CLER board member Joe Gutierrez and I had
scheduled a meeting with Domenici in his Santa Fe office to talk
about a layoff-related matter. When Domenici walked into the
conference room, it was apparent he was upset. He took the most
current issue of the *Santa Fe Reporter*, which he'd been carrying,
and tossed it on the table from a standing position. He leaned
over to tap the cover with his forefinger and in a slightly elevated voice said, "This is the kind of stuff I don't like." No formal
introductions were required; the senator knew us and we knew
him. Though we were there to talk about other things, Domenici
needed to make his point first.

The focus of the senator's concern was an article about
a federal judge's ruling against LANL in a Clean Air Act case.
A local watchdog group, Concerned Citizens for Nuclear Safety

(CCNS), had initiated a legal action to force the lab to comply with the act. According to CCNS, the laboratory had failed to identify all sources of its radionuclide released emissions, or install monitoring equipment on vapor-release stacks (chimneys) already known to emit radioactive gases. In some cases, the equipment didn't even meet regulatory standards; plus the lab's quality assurance program was simply inadequate.

LANL spokespersons adamantly denied the institution was in violation but Joe, who was a quality assurance (QA) assessor for LANL's Assessment and Audit Division, had provided incriminating evidence proving otherwise. Lab officials were caught in a lie, and the judge was angry about it. Now the senator was furious as well, but not about the lying. He was upset at Joe for exposing the truth.

"No matter what," Domenici said, "I'll do whatever it takes to protect the lab." It was an astonishing Richard Nixon–esque "It's not breaking the law if the president does it" moment.

Joe had done the right thing, as his family, home, and neighbors were only a few miles downwind from LANL facilities working with dangerous materials. His sin was providing evidence his employer was venting canisters of tritium into open air without monitoring, meaning there was no measuring of the amounts being spewed into the environment. Tritium is a carcinogen, a radioactive isotope of hydrogen, having chemical properties that enable it to readily combine with other atoms to form molecules we ingest in air, food, and water. Tritium release monitoring was needed in order to ensure regulatory compliance with respect to health and safety standards. But to properly dispose of radioactive waste was costly to a program, so the incentive for some was to cheat—to sidestep compliance in order to save money.

Too many decisions were based on the notion that it was too inconvenient to follow the rules. The true cost of noncompliance, however, was far greater for those made sick because of it. Joe's concern for the health and well-being of his family and others was valid except, apparently, in the eyes of the lab's patron saint.

Senator Domenici fought hard to protect the status quo in Los Alamos but by April 2003 was resigned to the fact that things might not stay the same. When the decision finally came, he and laboratory director Pete Nanos were holed up in a lab office preparing for an announcement neither wanted to make:

> In the wake of several years of controversy about the national weapons labs, DOE has said that for the first time, competitive bidding will be used when the contract with the University of California (UC) to manage and operate Los Alamos National Laboratory expires in 2005. In addition, the House has added a rider to an appropriations bill that requires competition. . . . A host of problems has resulted in intense scrutiny. . . . Allegations of espionage; lost hard drives containing classified information; and, most recently, accusations of financial mismanagement. (Staff writers, "Issues in Science and Technology," *National Academy of Sciences* 20, no. 1, September 22, 2003)

Since 1943 the University of California had been given the contract to run LANL. The Energy Department always resisted the notion that UC should compete for the contract, but there'd been too many scandals. Congress was now more insistent than ever about putting the contract out to bid, thus forcing DOE secretary Spencer Abraham to capitulate, albeit reluctantly. UC insisted it would never compete, claiming it oversaw the three federal facilities under its umbrella as a "service to the nation":

> After weeks of harsh criticism of the University of California for financial mismanagement at the Los Alamos National Laboratory, a senior UC official said Tuesday that if the federal government were to seek new bidders on the contract to manage the nuclear weapons lab, UC would simply end the role. "We do this because the federal government asked us to do this," said Bruce Darling, a senior UC vice president who was recently given responsibility for clearing up the management problems at Los Alamos. "We will not compete for the contract because it is a public service; it is something we do for the nation." (James Sterngoal, "UC Won't Compete to Keep Los Alamos Contract," *San Francisco Chronicle*, January 15, 2003)

Suddenly the university was having second thoughts. National security, perhaps even the future of the free world, demanded it—or so UC officials would have us believe:

> "My instinct continues to be to compete—and to compete hard—in order to continue the university's stewardship of excellence in science and innovation. We believe, with every fiber of our institutional being, that continued UC management is in the absolute best interests of the nation's security." (Richard Atkinson, Press Release, University Office of the President, April 30, 2003)

"Service to the nation," coupled with the "best interests of the nation's security," plus millions of dollars in annual royalties from laboratory patents and licenses, and the hefty multimillion-dollar annual management fee UC received, might be worth fighting for after all. But not everyone was so enthralled with the university's change of heart:

> "Every year we are told that the problems are going to get better, and every year they seem to get worse," said Ken Johnson, spokesman for the House Energy and Commerce Committee. . . . "From our perspective UC's management of the labs has been woefully inadequate." (James Stern-goal, "UC Won't Compete to Keep Los Alamos Contract," *San Francisco Chronicle*, January 15, 2003)

The decision to bid the contract was based on the university's failed stewardship, yet UC was still going to submit an offer to continue running things in Los Alamos. This was done in deference to Senator Domenici, who demanded the related request for proposal (RFP) be written accordingly. To accommodate his request, the Department of Energy solicited input from UC to construct the RFP. It was akin to an employee fired for poor performance being permitted to rewrite the job description and reapply.

In a July 25, 2004, *Los Angeles Times* article, the senator had reflected on his role in relation to the lab, lamenting in an open letter that he'd wrongly protected the laboratory for years. His regret likely stemmed from the realization that he'd lost credibility among his Capitol Hill colleagues for steadfastly defending Los Alamos despite decades of scandal, and for his dogged insistence that UC remain in the picture. But Domenici's mea culpa proclamation didn't alter anyone's behavior, and the only change came in the form of personnel movements. Former laboratory director Sig Hecker jokingly referred to the practice as "same monkeys, different trees."

It was time for admiral-director Pete Nanos to step down. His mission had been to turn LANL around and avoid the contract being put out for competitive bid. But the command he'd been given was too deeply mired in the "swamp" he'd once promised to drain. The outgoing director now had to sign a "transition agreement"—a gag order by any other name:

> When the director of the Los Alamos National Laboratory resigned last year, the University of California, which runs the lab, agreed to keep him on the payroll in a new job for up to 28 months so he would qualify for the university's retirement plan. . . . The terms of Nanos' departure were negotiated last spring, while UC was preparing to bid for a new contract. . . . As part of the agreement Nanos, an outspoken former Navy admiral who was appointed director in January 2003 and promptly vowed to "drain the swamp" at the lab—agreed not to say anything disparaging about the university or the lab. Indeed, the agreement calls Nanos' silence "a fundamental and substantial part of this agreement." (Tanya Schevitz and Todd Wallack, "UC Pays Salary of Ex-lab Chief in Virginia Job," *San Francisco Chronicle*, April 23, 2005)

The Energy Department's 2003 decision to compete the LANL management contract put the university's sixty-plus-year occupation of Northern New Mexico in jeopardy. But by 2005, it was clear the only thing likely to come out of the decision was another round of musical chairs.

33

MUSICAL CHAIRS

On Jan. 17, 1961, President Dwight Eisenhower gave the nation a dire warning about what he described as a threat to democratic government. He called it the military-industrial complex, a formidable union of defense contractors and the armed forces. (Staff writers, "Ike's Warning of Military Expansion, 50 Years Later," National Public Radio, January 17, 2012)

AFTER WORLD WAR II the corporate war machine came into its own, due in no small measure to the wartime effort called the Manhattan Project—a military, scientific, and industrial collaborative to develop the world's first atomic bomb. A new cash cow was born—big science. These interests together comprised a potent lobbying force, and the cloak of national security was used to sidestep any related accountability. Ensuring a steady flow of funding was the ultimate goal, and with minimal oversight relationships between these interests and elected officials multiplied and grew. In time, this segment of the economy was no longer subject to normal market swings. Nor did it make any difference which political party was in power. The end result was always the same—more funding. Under these conditions, it was inevitable the military-industrial complex would grow exponentially in terms of wealth, power, and influence . . . and arrogance:

> For the second time in as many months, a blue-ribbon report on espionage and lax security at America's weapons labs failed to find a likely culprit: the University of California. "The DOE's performance throughout its history should have been regarded as intolerable," [Senator Warren] Rudman wrote. "The panel found a department saturated with cynicism, an arrogant disregard for authority and . . . denial." (Jack Anderson, "LANL Manager Escapes Spy Blame," *Albuquerque Journal*, June 28, 1999)

The University of California was the essence of big science run amok, providing the cover of academic legitimacy to justify wasteful spending that kept the coffers of corporations full. And the US Department of Energy never wavered in assisting:

> [The] estimated cost of a new radioactive waste treatment plant at Los Alamos National Laboratory has ballooned, from $100 million to $350 million. . . . What did the NNSA [DOE] know about the risk that the project would run over its budget, and when did it know? How and why did the agency repeatedly provide Congress with cost estimates so out of touch with reality? With the arrogance of a federal agency that has become accustomed

to a lack of accountability for its breathtaking history of delays and cost overruns on big nuclear projects, the National Nuclear Security Administration [DOE] refuses to release key documents that might answer these questions . . . (John Fleck, "Agency Keeps Public in the Dark," *Albuquerque Journal North*, September 15, 2010)

As for the politicians, who were perpetually indebted to the weapons establishment, they too never waffled in their support:

The University of California is tired of the bad press it gets as the manager of three national laboratories. . . . When [New Mexico] Governor Bill Richardson visited Los Angeles on Wednesday, the UC Regents raised many of these points. They have a chance to bow out. . . . Richardson came to dissuade them . . . (Diana Heil, "Governor Pushes UC to Bid for Lab Contract," *Santa Fe New Mexican*, November 18, 2004)

The LANL Employee Advisory Council (EAC) was composed of labees handpicked by management to serve as worker representatives on what was basically a powerless association of lab employees. The EAC met periodically to mull over whatever the worry of the moment was, and on September 29, 2005, the meeting's concern was whether UC was going to vie for the right to stay in Los Alamos. The university's contract transition officer, Bob Kuckuck, was at the meeting that day to allay fears, announcing UC's intention to compete as part of an industrial consortium, but only if the arrangement enabled it to maintain a "controlling interest."

The University of California had just finished a sixty-year flirtatious affair with the military-industrial complex, and from the start received enormous benefits from the relationship. But now it was time to commit, a figurative "tying of the knot," and if a "prenuptial" agreement in the form of a limited liability partnership was needed, then so be it.

The newly minted limited liability corporation (LLC) formed by UC was called Los Alamos National Security LLC, or LANS. It included industrial partners, but the university, as planned, was the dominant interest. In adherence with Energy Department requirements, a new benefits program would have to be established under LANS; this program would end up replacing the more generous (for labees) retirement plan already in effect. This was to bring Los Alamos in line with what other DOE contractors managing other sites offered. What occurred, in effect, was a redirection of wealth, with the DOE reducing worker benefits to offset the dramatic increase in management salaries, and to finance a doubling of the multimillion dollar annual performance award fee that UC and its industrial partners would soon be getting.

Under the partnership agreement, UC got to choose the LANL director, the president of the LLC, and the chair of the LANS board of directors. The university also got to influence the board of directors' composition for LANS; plus it remained the sole overseer of all laboratory research and development. Most important, the university would still be the beneficiary of royalties from patents, fees, and licenses.

LANS was the illusion of change the Department of Energy needed in order to justify keeping the University of California in Northern New Mexico, and at the same time significantly reduce the DOE's retirement benefit commitment to Los Alamos workers. Bechtel, the huge California-based engineering firm, was the lead business interest. Two other industrial partners, Babcock & Wilcox Technology (BWXT) and the Washington Group, were also brought into the mix. The Washington Group, an engineering and construction firm with 25,000 employees worldwide, was based in Idaho and named after its founder, Dennis Washington. BWXT, headquartered in Lynchburg, Virginia, was already managing other department facilities. The political prowess of these three industrial giants, combined with that of UC, would come in handy in the competition for the prime contract to manage the Los Alamos National Laboratory.

The Department of Energy's Albuquerque Operations Office, where the LANL executive director once worked, was the administrator of the bid process and would decide who'd be awarded the lab contract. On the day of the September 2005 meeting, labees were crammed into the laboratory's largest auditorium, anxiously awaiting the arrival of the Energy Department official overseeing the competition. I'd met him ten years earlier, when he testified on the lab's behalf in connection with the '95 layoff. At the time, he represented the DOE's position in that dispute. The judge issued an injunction, ordering a halt to the firings, but within days the New Mexico Supreme Court reversed the injunction.

At the front of the auditorium the LANL executive director waited for his former DOE colleague, Tyler Przybylek. As they approached each other their smiles broadened, and then came the endearing bear hug between friends—the revolving door on full display. The purpose of the visit that day was to provide labees a status report on the contract competition. The visiting official stressed that the process was still under way and that a related announcement would be forthcoming in the near future. The objective, it appeared, was to allay fears among those having a vested interest in keeping UC in the picture. But his visit, at that late stage in the process, also hinted of a decision perhaps already made but just not yet announced. Needless to say labees were disappointed that the uncertainty regarding their futures would have to continue.

Besides the UC-established LLC, two competing consortiums had been formed: one led by Northrop Grumman Corporation, the other by Lockheed Martin Corporation. On December 21, 2005, the Department of Energy announced its choice: the UC-led consortium—LANS. But not everyone was pleased:

> The questions began almost as soon as Energy Secretary Samuel Bodman announced the University of California would continue to lead the New Mexico nuclear laboratory that built the atomic bomb. After a run of embarrassing financial and security lapses, how could the US Department of Energy return Los Alamos National Laboratory to the university? (Jennifer Talhelm, Associated Press, "Critics Question LANL Contract Award," *Albuquerque Journal North*, December 25, 2005)

The university would remain in Northern New Mexico despite its decades of failed stewardship. Numerous US General Accounting Office and DOE Office of Inspector General reports documenting those failures were ignored. Congressional hearings and related calls for the university's ouster from Los Alamos had fallen on deaf ears. The practice of absorbing former Department of Energy executives into the UC fold had, it seemed, paid off for those determined to keep the status quo intact.

Los Alamos National Security LLC took control of the laboratory on June 1, 2006, and within a year another layer of management was added to represent Bechtel and the two other industrial partners now wedded, as well, to the university. The management fee for running the lab quickly doubled to $80 million. Executive salaries shot up as well, with the director's alone going from $450,000 a year in 2005 to over $1 million in 2013.

The UC consortium's LLC status could also be used as a shield against the public's right to know. Access to previously available records, such as salary information related to LANL activities, could now be kept hidden. Hard-won advances made in 2000, such as granting work protections under California law to UC employees stationed in Los Alamos were, too, null and void. The DOE could have, in its contractual agreement with LANS, preserved these gains and insisted on transparency. The New Mexico congressional delegation could have also intervened in this respect, but didn't. And to add further insult, the Energy Department was now refusing to reveal its rationale for awarding $80 million per year in taxpayer dollars to the new military-industrial alliance on the hill:

> Federal officials this week awarded a Bechtel-University of California team $83.7 million for its management of Los Alamos National Laboratory in 2011, plus a one-year extension of its lab management contract as a bonus, but refused to release the performance evaluation report on which the decisions were based. (John Fleck, "LANL Managers Rewarded," *Albuquerque Journal North*, January 12, 2012)

Under the new arrangement, the LANL director was an employee of the LLC, meaning that in addition to managing a plutonium-laden nuclear weapons facility for the US government, he was beholden to the for-profit interests of the university's corporate partners. This was a gross conflict of interest that put workers, communities, taxpayers, and the environment at greater risk, and that under any other circumstance would have been deemed unacceptable. But with respect to the secretive military-industrial complex rooted on the hill, where the priority had always been to ensure nothing ever changed, not so.

Michael Anastasio, who came from Lawrence Livermore

National Laboratory, became the first LANL director under the UC-led LANS collaborative. He'd arrived in Los Alamos on the heels of the admiral-director's departure, and had quickly embraced the LANL executive director as his "personal attorney."

Anastasio's "personal attorney" joined the laboratory in 2001, via the lab's legal office, and served as "special advisor" to Frank Dickson—head of that office. But the person rumored to have actually brought him in was another retired DOE executive—Joseph Salgado—who at that point was the laboratory's second-in-command. Two years later Salgado was summarily dismissed, after admitting he'd authorized the firings of Glenn Walp and Steve Doran. Salgado, according to the LANL executive director's deposition, was his supervisor during that time.

The executive director escaped being tarnished by what happened to Glenn and Steve, and then went on to help spearhead the university's successful bid to regain its foothold in Los Alamos. Institutional leaders took note of his survival skills, and in his success at keeping UC in place. It was Anastasio who elevated him to the position of executive director, aka his "personal attorney."

During Anastasio's tenure at the Livermore laboratory, a number of controversies came to light, including a class-action discrimination lawsuit brought—and won—by a group of female employees. The lawsuit cost taxpayers tens of millions of dollars. In another instance, an LLNL employee was fired after testifying truthfully in a coworker's sexual harassment case. Livermore officials didn't appreciate that she testified in support of her tormented colleague. Retribution, in the form of a "witch hunt" investigation, ensued, and in the process it was determined that she'd incurred, using lab equipment, under $10 in personal phone charges. She was terminated, nonetheless, because of it. A lengthy court battle ensued. A jury, appalled by what had happened to the woman, awarded $1 million in damages, plus her job back. True to form, institutional leaders appealed, and, for whatever reason, the appellate court ordered a retrial. The second jury concluded the same, except this time doubling the award to $2 million.

Anastasio's past was also linked to the national stockpile stewardship program—a pot of money established to develop state-of-the-art nuclear weapons diagnostic techniques and facilities, in response to international treaties banning nuclear weapons tests. The objective was to assure the reliability and safety of the nuclear arms stockpile, without having to explode a nuclear bomb every so often to make certain the weapons still worked. The incoming LANL director, under LANS, had also played an instrumental role in selling the stockpile stewardship program to policymakers, and getting hundreds of millions in funding for the National Ignition Facility (NIF)—a mammoth laser system intended to provide diagnostic capabilities in connection with stockpile assessment.

In 1992 the NIF project was projected to cost $400 million, but by 2012 taxpayers were out of pocket $7 billion without "breakeven"—the point where the amount of energy extracted from a laser-induced fusion reaction would match the energy invested to initiate it. Fusion is the power of the stars, and if the NIF project had worked as intended, it could have reduced our dependency on coal and oil. But, like so many big-ticket projects funded by the Department of Energy, the National Ignition Facility failed to live up to the promises made.

Behaviors adopted by those at the bottom of an organization reflect the attitudes of those at the top, and the common denominator for both nuclear weapons facilities was the University of California. The admiral-director once characterized LANL as a swamp, but its sister laboratory in Livermore didn't seem to be in any better shape. Leadership sharing between labs didn't help, nor did the revolving-door relationship between the university and the US Department of Energy.

34

SHELL GAMES

ALTHOUGH FRANK DICKSON WAS the lab's chief lawyer, his immediate supervisor—his boss—was located at the university's headquarters in Oakland. Dickson was involved in every serious legal matter related to LANL, and it was his responsibility to keep his overseers in Oakland informed on these issues. Thus the head of lab legal was present in the November 25, 2002, meeting where Glenn Walp and Steve Doran were discussed—the very day they were fired for doing their jobs. Bruce Darling, the highest-ranking UC official for laboratory oversight, was in the same meeting as well. It was hard to believe there'd been no prior mention of the plan to terminate the two, or the effect it would have on the investigations they were still doing in conjunction with the FBI. Adding to the intrigue was that Darling, during his June 15, 2010, legal deposition, couldn't recall who'd been at the November gathering except for himself, the lab director, the other university colleagues who'd traveled to Los Alamos with him, and the individual who ultimately took the blame for Glenn's and Steve's firings—Joseph "Joe" Salgado.

According to Darling's sworn testimony, he and his UC colleagues first learned of the terminations from Salgado, but only
after the fact. To make matters worse, after learning about the
firings, no attempt was made, by Darling or anyone else in the
room, to reverse course. It was an astonishing admission—that
Glenn and Steve were discharged while still investigating the
largest procurement fraud ever known to occur at LANL, and
the highest-ranking UC official for laboratory oversight hadn't
attempted to intervene. But there was an even greater con-
tradiction. According to Glenn Walp, in his book titled *Implosion at Los Alamos*, it was at about 8:00 a.m. on the morning
of November 25, 2002, when he and his investigative partner,
Steve Doran, were terminated. They were fired without warning
or right to appeal, on that bitterly cold New Mexico high-desert
fall morning, but Darling claimed he didn't learn about it until
lunch—hours later—on that same day. Here he'd been meeting
with laboratory officials all morning, and no one in the room,
presumably, knew that Glenn and Steve were being escorted off
lab premises as they spoke? Not even the director, or the head
of lab legal? What about Joe Salgado, the other person Darling
seemed to recall being at the gathering that day? He must have
known something, given that he later accepted responsibility
for authorizing the firings. But yet, for whatever the reason, he
didn't see any need to bring up the matter until lunch?

Salgado was, at one point, the deputy secretary of the
US Department of Energy, meaning he was the second-
highest-ranking official in the department. How does an
experienced executive like him, so skilled and proven when
it comes to briefing generals, admirals, corporate executives,
US presidents, and members of congress, not consult with his
colleagues in advance when deciding to terminate two former
law enforcement officials in the midst of a high-profile fraud
they're still investigating? Indeed, given that Glenn and Steve

were fired at about 8:00 a.m. the same morning UC officials were meeting with lab executives, how could no one in the room have known, well before lunch, that they'd been fired? The purpose of that day's gathering had been to discuss Glenn and Steve, and the fraudulent activity they'd discovered. Thus it made no sense that Salgado would have acted entirely on his own, or that nobody in the room would have known, first thing that morning, that the firings had occurred.

> As federal agents were looking into reported fraud and theft at Los Alamos National Laboratory last summer, the facility's chief lawyer warned in-house investigators [Walp and Doran] to "look out for the lab and its image first, not the FBI investigation." . . . [L]ab counsel Frank Dickson immersed himself in the details of the investigation. . . . He reports directly to the Oakland headquarters of the university. . . . "The general counsel is not really a lab employee," [LANL Director] Nanos told the Mercury News. "He works for the university. I think he was being inappropriately used . . ." (Dan Stober, "UC Lab Lawyer's Alleged Role in Probe Criticized," *San Jose Mercury News*, February 7, 2003)

Salgado was a politically astute Washington insider, a former law enforcement officer himself, who'd managed to work his way to the very top of the DC bureaucratic hierarchy. It's inconceivable, therefore, that he would have fired Glenn and Steve without first notifying the LANL director, or consulting with the lab's lead attorney. Yet that's precisely what officials of the University of California seemed to be saying.

Lynne Bernabei was a principal in the Washington, DC, firm representing Glenn and Steve—Bernabei & Wachtel, PLLC.

The law was her passion, which in and of itself doesn't equate to justice, but for much of her waking hours her singular focus was trying to achieve it. She was an idealist, yet the equal of a half dozen LANL attorneys combined. That's because outside law firms were paid exceedingly well to do the actual legal work, while lab attorneys employed as labees essentially tagged along and approved their monthly billings for payment. Because outside counsel made lots of money through protracted litigation, lawsuits inevitably dragged on for as long as possible.

I was fortunate to have Lynne's dedication and talent in my corner, but not so lucky with respect to the federal judge we were dealing with in regard to my 2005 whistleblower complaint. Justice Judith Herrera had been handpicked for the New Mexico federal judiciary by the lab's "personal" US senator—Pete Domenici. A judge with the senator's seal of approval meant LANL had an ally on the bench. This meant justice was going to be harder to achieve. Plus, according to the following OIG audit report (DOE/IG-0825), regardless of merit the DOE reimbursed contractors for virtually all litigation-related expenditures:

> According to Department of Energy Acquisition Regulation (DEAR) 970.5228-1(h), contractors shall not be reimbursed [for litigation expenses] if the cause of action was due to contactor managerial willful misconduct, lack of good faith, or failure to exercise prudent business judgment. . . . the Department did not fully implement processes for managing the cost of legal services . . . (DOE/IG-0825, "The Department of Energy's Management of Contractor Fines, Penalties, and Legal Costs," US Department of Energy Office of Inspector General, September 2006)

And contrary to what regulatory mandates stated, the DOE complied only if it wanted to:

> The Energy Department spent $330 million in taxpayer money to reimburse its private contractors for legal bills over a 5½ year span, including for lawsuits they lost. . . . "When a contractor for the DOE gets sued, 95 percent of the time its legal fees and settlement costs get reimbursed by the federal government," said Rep. Edward Markey, D-Mass . . . (Associated Press, "Sued for Wrongs, Contractors Give Bills to DOE," *Salt Lake Tribune,* December 30, 2003)

In his book, *Implosion at Los Alamos: How Crime, Corruption, and Cover-Ups Jeopardize America's Nuclear Weapons Secrets,*[1] Glenn Walp describes his own experience dealing with lab attorneys. He uses the alias Gayle Rollins for a staff lawyer. He writes:

> Gayle Rollins walked into my office unannounced and asked for copies of the FBI's NIS [LANL Nonproliferation and International Security Division] report so that she could take them back to her office and review them. . . . I [Glenn Walp] respectfully refused. . . . "If [the head of lab legal] contacts the FBI, and the FBI agrees to allow me to give you the reports, you can have them," [said Glenn] . . . Rollins continued to argue with me. She was adamant about getting the reports even though I kept insisting that her request could potentially interfere with a suc-

---

1.   Glenn Walp, *Implosion at Los Alamos: How Crime, Corruption, and Cover-Ups Jeopardize America's Nuclear Weapons Secrets.* Justice Publishing, LLC, 2010.

cessful FBI investigation. At that point, she snapped. "Our job is to determine if there is enough evidence to fire or suspend an employee, not whether we have the evidence to arrest and prosecute. *I'm not concerned whether we violate anyone's constitutional rights or interfere with an FBI investigation; our job is to protect our employer,*" she said. (Pgs. 85–86; italics added)

In his book, Glenn Walp describes a concerted effort by institutional leaders to prevent him and Steve Doran, his investigative associate, from engaging the FBI in their criminal reviews, even though he and Doran were mandated by law to do so. When that failed, the lab then attempted to derail their work by requiring them to divulge all they'd discovered thus far, even though the Federal Bureau of Investigation by that point was advising them not to. Too many people knowing too much about an ongoing investigation could undermine the effort, which was the FBI's concern. A tense confrontation then occurred with the head of laboratory legal, during which Glenn and Steve were directed to turn over all evidence they'd assembled to an outside firm, hired by LANL to take over the investigation. This would include the release of interview notes, witness lists, and related files and documents. At that point Glenn reminded the lab's lead attorney that obstruction of justice is a crime. The chief attorney turned pink with rage, and as he did bellowed, "Remember who you work for—your boss is the lab, not the FBI, and you will tell everyone in this room everything you know about these cases, because that's the way it is."

He continued, "We look out for the lab first, not FBI investigations."

Glenn's discomfort was justified, because paying outside "experts" exorbitant sums to endorse LANL's official position was a common practice in Los Alamos. It was a tactic right out of the Enron playbook, where Arthur Anderson, a world-renowned public accounting firm, was paid handsomely to legitimize the company's financial schemes.

By the start of 2003, the media was paying attention to what had happened to Glenn and Steve. Because of it, the Energy Department's quasi-independent Office of Inspector General was able to do its job. The two fired investigators, according to the OIG's findings, had been undermined:

> On November 18, 2002, the Office of Inspector General began a fact-finding inquiry into allegations that senior management of the Los Alamos National Laboratory engaged in a deliberate cover-up of security breaches and illegal activities, in particular, with respect to reported instances of property loss and theft. . . . Our inquiry disclosed a series of *actions by laboratory officials that had the effect of obscuring serious property and procurement management problems and weakened or overrode relevant internal controls* [my italics]. (DOE/IG-0584, "Special Inquiry: Operations at Los Alamos National Laboratory," US Department of Energy Office of Inspector General, January 2003)

Lab officials had interfered with Steve and Glenn's efforts to root out criminal activity at LANL. And as for those who assisted them, they became targets for retribution:

> For months, John Jennings led two lives. On the surface, the longtime Los Alamos National Laboratory employee continued his relationship with his boss, Peter Bussolini.

... But at the same time, Jennings was tormented by the work he secretly performed for the FBI, which was investigating suspected fraud and theft of laboratory property. ... Now he blames the laboratory for turning on him ..." (Adam Rankin, "Lab Worker Aided FBI in Theft Case," *Albuquerque Journal North*, May 30, 2004)

Jennings, for all practical purposes, was a whistleblower—someone whose conscience had gotten the better of him. He was courageous for doing what was right, but would suffer career-debilitating retaliation because of his actions. He retired from the lab because of the retribution, sooner than he might have otherwise. Others who assisted Glenn and Steve in their efforts suffered as well:

As part of an overhaul of Los Alamos National Laboratory's business operations, two employees instrumental in calling attention to weaknesses in the lab's credit card system were told earlier this week they were going to be reassigned. Arleen Roybal, administrator of LANL's purchase card program, and Eric Martinez, a contract employee assigned to analyze the program's weaknesses, were told by their supervisor Tuesday they were being reassigned as part of a "cosmetic" change. (Adam Rankin, "Two LANL Workers to Stay in Jobs," *Albuquerque Journal North*, June 25, 2003)

Fortunately, the "cosmetic" change planned for Roybal and Martinez was rescinded after the media got wind of it. Years later I asked them how things turned out. One was still suffering repercussions; the other just didn't want to talk about it anymore. Both were frustrated.

Roybal, Martinez, and Jennings paid a steep price for believing they were required, by DOE order, to report fraud, waste, and abuse, and that protecting taxpayers from such behavior was their professional and fiduciary duty. Glenn and Steve had been hired to respond—to take action against those misusing public resources—and were fired for trying.

35

STACKING THE DECK

JIM HIRAHARA WAS THE University of California's whistleblower officer, and was situated in Oakland, California, within
the Office of the President. Because of his role, he was the primary recipient of the many e-mail messages Tommy Hook and I
began sending the university in 2004. At issue was the cover-up
and retribution following the procurement assessments we'd
done. As whistleblower officer for the university, and in accordance with related policy, he was obligated to investigate. He
ignored us, however, until my attorney, Lynne Bernabei, arrived
on the scene. And once that happened, the "glacier" that is institutional resistance began moving.

Policy is like any mandate, regulatory or otherwise—it only
matters if enforced. Just because something is required doesn't
mean it has to be done legitimately. Case in point—the state
and federal agencies that are supposed to investigate employee
complaints but rarely do. UC did the same with whistleblowers.
The university had violated its own rules from the outset, failing
to initiate the investigation within the prescribed time frame.
An employee's failure to adhere to established policy could result

in his or her claims being dismissed, but since it was UC's own misstep, it was a simple matter of the university granting itself an exception.

As 2004 came to a close, Jim Hirahara announced that a California law firm would be doing the investigation of the whistleblower complaints Tommy Hook and I had filed. This meant UC was turning an administrative review into a legal matter— another violation of the institution's whistleblower protection policy, which mandated informal review of the complaints. It was a signal that the university was digging in for battle.

The outside investigator, an attorney from the contracted law firm, made several trips to Los Alamos, first to get his marching orders from the laboratory, then to interview dozens of potential witnesses—fellow auditors, DOE personnel, members of management, and others I'd come in contact with over the years. The legal dragnet was intense, requiring so much extra effort that the university needed to grant itself yet another extension, this one in 2005, thus giving its outside counsel more time to finish.

The final report was released, ironically, on April Fools' Day 2005. It cost taxpayers nearly $500,000. But for the price, the university and the lab got the conclusion they wanted. According to the report, my nine months in cubicle isolation was incidental, a mere oversight by an institutional leadership too distracted to notice I had nothing to do. This, despite all my e-mails proving otherwise, and the fact that time sheets I submitted on a biweekly basis during the entire period were reviewed and approved by a line manager who, in doing so, was improperly authorizing my salary, with nothing to show in return. Gifts and donations, in accordance with the Federal Acquisition Regulations, were unallowable costs. So what else was new?

UC's outside counsel concluded that since no laboratory official would admit to any wrongdoing, there was no basis for claiming whistleblower retaliation had occurred. It was *Alice in Wonderland* logic, but it served its purpose—providing institutional leaders a way to weasel out of responsibility. It was akin to being in a room when a decision is made to fire someone, then later claiming not to have known the termination would occur. Or as was done with the salary disparity analysis, aka the Welch Study, where an outside expert was paid lots of money to include variables he couldn't justify . . . except for the fact that those paying him had an interest in doing so in order to achieve a desired outcome. It was a waste of taxpayer money to be doing any of this, or to be paying people to sit idle for months on end. And to do so with the intent of misleading others is fraud, but the Energy Department—the taxpayer's blind and toothless watchdog—never failed to authorize payment, regardless.

In 2010, after years of legal wrangling, my attorney and I were finally sitting in a conference room in downtown Oakland, waiting to depose the well-paid "outside" evaluator of my whistleblower complaint. He'd started the effort in 2004, released his report in 2005, and it was now five years later. My attorney made the moment possible, but it hadn't come easy. Institutional lawyers had fought hard to stop this from happening, and a hostile federal judge assisted them by blocking us from obtaining documents or conducting depositions all these past years. This is the underbelly of the legal system—providing advantage to the affluent and powerful at the expense of the public and the few who dare to challenge "city hall."

Over the course of my attorney's questioning, it was apparent that the evaluator's task had been carried out in a manner that served to intimidate people. LANL attorneys had sat in on witness interviews, and were allowed to coach them as need be. The investigator himself injected bias by telling individuals at the start of their testimony nothing they said was under oath, thus implying they could testify falsely or revise their recollections later, if they wanted. Transcripts appeared tampered with as well, with print fonts changing abruptly in the middle of sentences and paragraphs, suggesting editing had taken place long after the interviews were done.

When my attorney, Lynne, asked the outside counsel if LANL provided him direction in any way regarding the final wording of his conclusions, his answer was unequivocal: "No."

"Are you sure?" Lynne asked.

"Yes," the response came back, "I'm sure." The trap was set:

(Questioning of the outside investigator by Lynne Bernabei, Esq.)

Q: Now, you said that in your—you never received any information from Ms. Chris Chandler [LANL legal office attorney] about what you should put in your report, right?

A: That's correct.

Q: And you're certain about that?

A: Absolutely certain.

Q: Take a moment to look at what's marked as . . . Exhibit 26. This is a letter from Chris Chandler to you dated March 9, 2005; is that correct?

A: That's what it says, yes.

Q: And that's a date before you finished your fact-finding report dated March 31, 2005?

A: Correct.

. . .

Q: So it does appear that—contrary to your earlier testimony, it does appear Ms. Chandler provided you with the substantive position of the lab prior to the time you finished your report, right?

A: Well, I see on page 2, Ms. Chandler is making an argument based on the document referenced above.

Q: Can you answer my question?

A: I am, ma'am.

Q: Is the answer yes, it appears that contrary to your earlier testimony, Ms. Chandler is providing you with the lab's position on certain disputed issues of fact?

A: This appears to contain argument with respect to the lab's position, yes.

Q: So you were incorrect when you said Ms. Chandler never gave you—never provided you with a letter or documentation setting forth the lab's position on certain issues, right?

A: Well, I would amend my response to saying this letter contains argument with respect to the lab's position.

. . .

Q: Now, if you take a look, she said, "Upon the reassignment of Hook in May 2004, there was a miscommunication between [LANL procurement official] Vern Brown and senior management regarding Montaño's assignment," right?

A: Correct.

Q: "In Brown's witness interview, he stated that he under-stood that [the LANL executive director] had committed to reassigning both Hook and Montaño and he believed those reassignments occurred at the same time." Do you see that?

A: I do.

Q: Thus, when he heard Hook had been reassigned, he assumed Montaño had been as well, right?

A: Correct.

Q: "Brown did not realize this was not the case until early July when Montaño e-mailed Brown a request to attend professional development training which Brown approved." Do you see that?

A: Yes.

Q: That's precisely the argument that you make or the facts, as you call them, the findings of fact that you make in your report in the paragraph we've just discussed. That's on page 84, paragraph 12. Exactly what Ms. Chandler gives to you on March 9, 2005.

(Deposition transcript, External UC Investigator, June 16, 2010, starting on p. 165)

Despite the investigator's initial claim that he was "absolutely certain" no lab attorney had dictated his final report, Chandler, a laboratory lawyer, had done that very thing—literally provid-ing verbiage the investigator ultimately used in his conclusion.

When all was said and done, potential witnesses had been intimidated, coached, and assured subconsciously it was safe to lie. The so-called investigation was a sham, and a total waste of taxpayer money. But there was still one more policy violation to contend with. Under California law, the university could decide the complaint had no merit, and use its decision in this regard to petition the court for a dismissal of related legal claims. UC, in effect, was judge, jury, and executioner.

The university's motion for dismissal fell flat due to another turn in the maze—a twist that UC itself had apparently forgotten. Its hired gun missed the reporting deadline by a day, which meant the report's distortions of truth could no longer be used as a basis for requesting dismissal of my legal claims in a court of law. The University of California had violated its own rules not once, but four times, and my attorney skillfully used the slipups to our advantage. After five wasted years of judicially imposed delay, my state legal claims could now, finally, proceed to trial, meaning the federal judge who'd imposed the blockade could no longer prevent us from questioning laboratory and UC executives under oath. It was time to track down those officials.

36

CAT AND MOUSE

BRUCE DARLING, THE HIGHEST-RANKING university official responsible for laboratory oversight, was the first UC executive my attorney managed to schedule for a deposition (i.e., an interview under oath). Darling was the individual who'd once told me, during a Los Alamos Foundation banquet held in downtown Santa Fe, that he was impressed that Hispanics in New Mexico spoke English so well. He was also one of the UC officials I tried reaching about not having any work to do for nine months, and he was no help in that regard. Darling also happened to be in Los Alamos on November 25, 2002, attending a meeting with lab officials regarding procurement fraud activity occurring at LANL—the same day Glenn Walp and Steve Doran, the two individuals who were investigating the fraud, were terminated for doing their jobs..

Darling was effective in his deposition, which occurred June 15, 2010, in a downtown Oakland high-rise. He denied saying that he thought Hispanics in New Mexico spoke English well. He seemed unable to remember anything when it came to me. All in all, we didn't end up getting much out of it, except one thing— Darling admitted to being in Los Alamos the same day Glenn

Walp and Steve Doran were fired. We had a copy of the agenda for the meeting he'd attended that day, and he was among those listed as being there. Given this, it would have been foolish for him not to recall that.

Forgetfulness can be useful in sidestepping accountability. Keeping responses open-ended and indefinite is a tactic as well; it's a way to ensure an escape route is available in the event you're inclined to be deceptive, or worse. Providing an unequivocal yes or no response to a question is, also, something to avoid. Typically, those occupying the highest echelons of large entities are adept at tap-dancing around questions they'd prefer not answering. UC, LANL, and the DOE were no different.

Frank Dickson, head of lab legal, was in the same meeting as Darling the day Glenn and Steve were fired, along with the lab's executive director and his supervisor, Joe Salgado—the laboratory official who took the fall for approving Glenn's and Steve's terminations. Dickson and the executive director were noted on the agenda as "presenters." And near the end, time was reserved for "Communication Strategy." Why were talking points necessary, unless something controversial was being decided at the meeting that would attract media attention?

The last scheduled topic of discussion was: "Close-out with John C. Browne . . . By Invitation Only," a private session with the LANL director to discuss something in confidence. Equally intriguing were notations on the copy of the agenda that we had, which my attorney had obtained when she was representing Glenn Walp and Steve Doran in their own case against the lab. Among the cryptic handwritten notes was the name of someone not in the room. Had his name come up during the meeting? If not, why, then, had it been written down?

"Whose handwriting is this?" Lynne asked Darling during his deposition. At that point she wasn't referring to any particular notation.

"Bob Van Ness," responded Darling. His answer was immediate and unequivocal, which surprised me. Perhaps he'd been caught off guard, or hadn't seen any significance in the question at that juncture. Van Ness was another high-ranking official within the University Office of the President, responsible for overseeing all business and administrative activities at the three federal labs run by the university, including procurement activity. He reported directly to Darling.

On the agenda the name "Brittin" was written several times, and the names "Busboom" and "Wallace" each appeared once. Katherine Brittin, director of the Audits and Assessments Division, and Stanley Busboom, the lab's security chief, later received payments to leave LANL quietly after being implicated in the scandal surrounding Glenn's and Steve's firings.

Wallace was a procurement group leader, so it made sense that his name would show up. But there was one other handwritten name, someone never mentioned before in connection with the work the two seasoned criminal investigators were doing at the time of their terminations. The curious reference was *Burick*, and alongside the name was a number—C412, perhaps a location or room.

As the deputy director for laboratory operations, Richard "Dick" Burick had been LANL's second-in-command. He'd retired in January 2002, the same month Glenn arrived in Los Alamos. The meeting that determined Glenn and Steve's fate was held eleven months later, in late November. The media latched on to their story following their discharge, igniting public outrage. By January 2003, a congressional inquiry was under way. That same month Burick was found dead, faceup on a snow-covered ski lift parking lot about five miles outside Los Alamos. This is why seeing his name appearing on an agenda for a meeting that occurred eleven months after he retired—and two months before his demise—seemed unusual.

Lynne, my attorney, had done a masterful job of setting the snare, getting Darling to confirm the notations were in Van Ness's handwriting. Now it was a matter of determining the reason for the Burick reference. Van Ness's deposition followed two days later, but in his case there was no surprise. Apparently he'd been prepped for the question about Burick, and because of it was ready to admit the notes were his. Except for one:

(Questioning of Robert Van Ness by Lynne Bernabei, Esq.)

Q: Take a moment to look at Van Ness Exhibit 13. Have you seen this document prior to today?

MR. BOHNHOFF [Outside Legal Counsel for UC and LANL]: It says Darling Exhibit 11 at the bottom. Is that your handwriting from two days ago?

Q: You can answer the question, Mr. Van Ness.

THE WITNESS: Would you ask that again?

Q: Have you seen this document prior to today?

A: Well, this is my handwriting on here. So on that basis, I must have seen it. But I wouldn't be able to tell you from memory that I saw it.

Q: Now, if you take a look at the left-hand corner is the word "agenda"; is that correct?

A: Yes.

Q: And then it says "procurement and investigation overview"; is that correct?

A: That's what it says, yes.

Q: And then it lists a number of people, yourself included, right?

A: Yes, that's right.

Q: And those were the people on the team that went down from the University of California to look at these issues?

A: Yes, that's correct.

Q: And that was pursuant to President Atkinson's charge to you that's reflected in Exhibit 12?

A: Yes.

Q. Now, are those, in fact, the four people including your-self that came down?

A: Best of my recollection, yes.

Q: And there is certain handwriting, and leave the exhibit numbers for the moment or the handwriting in the lower right-hand corner. Would it be correct to say that the other handwriting appears to be your handwriting?

A: That's what it looks like.

Q: If you take a look, the date on this is Monday, November 25th, 2002; is that right?

A: Right.

Q: Now, do you recall that it was a Monday shortly before Thanksgiving that you went down?

A: No.

Q: Now, if you take a look, up in the right-hand corner, it says "Burick," and then it says "ID office."

. . .

A: I see that, yeah.

Q: It says Burick.

A: That's what it appears to say, yes.

Q: And then it says and something "ID office." Do you see that?

A: Yes.

Q: Do you know what that says?

A: Do I know what it says?

Q: Do you know what's written? There's some letter that isn't—is that "old office" or something?

A: I don't know. That would be one way to guess it.

Q: And then there's an initial C and 413; is that correct?

A: That looks like a room number to me.

Q: Do you recall why you wrote "Burick old office C413"?

A: I didn't write that.

. . .

Q: Do you know whether or not you met Mr. Burick at this time period?

A: I can't, no.

Q: You don't recall?

A: No.

Q: Do you recall if you met Mr. Burick at any time after this meeting?

A: No.

Q: Take a look at what was—what follows below. You would agree that all the handwriting other than what appears on the bottom is Darling Exhibit 11, other than that, all the handwriting on this is yours?

MR. BOHNHOFF: Object to the form.

THE WITNESS: No, not the top part. I didn't write that up on the top.

BY MS. BERNABEI:

Q: Oh, you didn't?

A: No.

Q: Did you know whether, when the document was given to you, that was written?

A: I don't know. I don't know. That doesn't look like my handwriting. The other ones are mine.

Q: Well, to my eye it looks exactly like the others. It looks like the same form.

A: Not to me. But I'm just me.

Q: But you can't remember at this point—you can't remember whether you may have written that, right?

MR. BOHNHOFF: Object to the form.

MS. BERNABEI: Mr. Darling identified that as your handwriting as well, all the handwriting on the page?

MR. BOHNHOFF: Object to the form.

THE WITNESS: Well, I don't believe that's my handwriting.

(Deposition transcript, Robert Van Ness, June 17, 2010, starting on p. 120)

The university's lawyer (Bohnhoff) objected repeatedly to the line of questioning Lynne was pursuing. It was as though the wagons were beginning to circle Burick. During a deposition, such objections serve to warn the person being questioned to be careful. It's a way to slow down the process, a time-out if you will . . . a signal for the individual to stop, reflect, and think carefully before answering. All notes on the agenda seemed to be in the same handwriting, but Van Ness was adamant—they were all his, except for the Burick notation.

In 2003, university officials claimed in congressional testimony, and in statements to the press afterward, that UC played no role in determining the fate of Glenn and Steve on the day they were escorted off lab premises. But yet the LANL officials responsible for firing the two men were in the same room on the same day, meeting with the same previously mentioned UC officials and discussing Glenn and Steve. To accept the notion that UC hadn't played a role would be akin to believing Japan's Emperor Hirohito had nothing to do with the bombing of Pearl Harbor, and that the signature authorizing the attack wasn't his. Yet this, in effect, was the position university officials staked out with respect to Glenn and Steve . . . and now Burick, who had apparently been mentioned during the same meeting that November day. But why would he have been brought up?

The remainder of the Van Ness deposition proceeded along the lines of not recalling, not knowing, not remembering, not being sure. Van Ness, like Darling, was unfazed with the rigors of the process. Both of their careers were seemingly secure no matter what the outcome. With the full backing of the US Treasury in their corner, there was, in reality, little risk to them. This is why during their questioning I saw in my mind's eye the unflappable Alfred E. Neuman of *Mad* magazine fame—the kid with the toothy grin and front tooth missing, all the while proclaiming, "What, me worry?"

Indeed, whistleblowers walk the minefield. And as for those doing the mining? They just look on, and smile:

(Continued questioning of Van Ness by Lynne Bernabei, Esq.)

Q: I guess my question is, you said you recommended getting the director of Los Alamos out because you didn't think he was capable of leading the lab out of this situation?

A: Yes.

Q: What was the situation you saw the lab in?

A: A variety of management and leadership failures.

Q: And what did you understand were the management and leadership failures at that point in time?

A: I can't recall.

Q: Do you recall any of them?

A: I can't recall.

Q: You can't recall one management or one leadership failure of the lab at this point in time?

A: Well, Mr. Browne or Dr. Browne had turned over the management largely to Mr. Salgado at that point. Mr. Salgado did not have the support of the laboratory employees.

Q: What do you mean?

A: Well, he wasn't regarded with credibility.

Q: Okay. So why did you remove him, Browne?

A: Dr. Browne had delegated significant responsibilities to Salgado. Salgado was, in my opinion, not capable of discharging those responsibilities effectively.

Q: And what were the responsibilities that you thought Salgado was not capable of carrying out?

A: Providing leadership and being a credible leader at the laboratory.

Q: And what incidents had shown that?

A: I can't recall.

Q: Well, what had he done that led you to that opinion?

A: I can't recall.

Q: You say that you were probably the person at University of California that had the most knowledge of what was going on in the laboratories?

A: Yes.

Q: And it would be fair to say that you were the most familiar with all the different reviews going on?

A: At least one or two.

Q: And you can't recall what it was that led you to believe that Salgado was not a credible leader?

A: That's right.

Q: Is there any reason that your memory isn't so good today?

A: Yes, I'm 69 years old and I'm experiencing aging.

(Deposition transcript, Robert Van Ness, June 17, 2010, starting on p. 197)

Within hours following Van Ness's deposition my attorney retained the services of a private investigator to find out more about LANL's former deputy director, and why university officials now seemed to be distancing themselves from him. The PI that was hired? Steve Doran.

37

SMOKE AND MIRRORS

IN 1999 I SETTLED a ruling by the Office of Inspector General, confirming my charge that LANL managers were retaliating for my workers' rights advocacy. After meeting with then–lab deputy director Joseph Salgado, I received assurance that the retribution would stop, and was given a new role as project leader for accounting internal controls. So I signed off on the resolution agreement. Five years later, using federal judge Judith Herrera to their advantage, university and lab attorneys filed a motion in her court asserting the '99 agreement prohibited me from claiming LANL later violated the commitment it made, in conjunction with the settlement, to end its retaliation campaign against me. It was a ridiculous notion, but the judge concurred, ruling in a manner that lacked foundation in legal precedence or common sense, effectively rendering out-of-court resolution meaningless. This meant a labee could be conned into resolving a complaint, and then the lab could retaliate with impunity the very next day. To add insult, institutional lawyers doubled down by asserting employees should be liable for challenging the employer's violations. Once more the judge agreed, placing my case on a legal trajectory that could end up shattering what little whistleblower protection still existed within the Department of Energy complex.

What it boiled down to was this: auditors identified millions of dollars in unallowable and questionable costs that were incurred at LANL. The Department of Energy never made UC reimburse the taxpayer, but was willing to bankroll a concerted effort by the university to establish a legal precedence imposing financial penalties on those who reported fraud, waste, and abuse in Los Alamos. It was as though I'd fallen through the *Alice in Wonderland* rabbit hole, landing in judgment before her Highness the Queen of Hearts, who at every turn decreed "Off with his head!" as the solution to everything.

My attorney immediately appealed the court's bizarre rulings, but it was going to take years, perhaps decades, of litigation to deal with the latest judiciary-imposed distraction. Money and attorneys were what the Energy Department furnished the military-industrial complex with in abundance, essentially providing contractors resources to engage in delay tactics and judicial sleight of hand for as long as necessary.

When the day of Jim Hirahara's deposition arrived on June 16, 2010—he seemed nervous. The UC whistleblower officer had previously worked with the Los Alamos executive director, who was at the center of my complaint. Both had retired from the Department of Energy. After retirement, Hirahara landed in the University Office of the President, while his colleague ended up on the Hill. The two former DOE officials had been instrumental in awarding contracts to UC, Hirahara with respect to the Lawrence Livermore National Laboratory, and his former colleague with regards to LANL. Now they both had lucrative second careers, thanks to the university.

As the university's whistleblower officer, Hirahara was responsible for investigating my whistleblower retaliation claims.

Since the executive director was at the epicenter of everything going wrong in my laboratory career, it was difficult to believe Hirahara hadn't been in contact with him. At first Hirahara sought to portray his relationship with the lab's executive director as distant, suggesting his trips to Los Alamos were infrequent and communications with him rare. But as the deposition proceeded it became increasingly apparent that neither was the case.

The LANL executive director's reputation at the US Department of Energy had followed him to Los Alamos (i.e., rumors of alleged indiscretions with female employees). That would, perhaps, explain Hirahara's reluctance to answer questions about him. But Lynne was insistent:

(Questioning of Jim Hirahara by Lynne Bernabei, Esq.)

Q: Did you become aware during the time that he [the LANL executive director] was at DOE that [he] had a number of sexual harassment complaints against him?

ATTORNEY: Object to the form.

Q: Did you become aware of that?

A: I wasn't privy to those kinds of problems that he had. He was in a different office than I was.

Q: Did you hear, though, that he had a number of sexual harassment complaints?

A: I heard a lot of things.

Q: Did you hear that, whether they're justified or not? People file complaints for all kinds of reasons. Did you hear he had a number of sexual harassment complaints?

ATTORNEY: Object to the form.

Q: You can answer.

A: I'd rather not answer that question.

Q: I'm sorry. You have to answer. Did you hear that [the LANL executive director] had a number of sexual harassment complaints against him while he was at DOE?

A: A number, no.

Q: Did you hear he had one?

A: I heard about alleged sexual harassment claims against him.

(Deposition transcript, Jim Hirahara, June 16, 2010, starting on p. 30)

Under oath, Hirahara admitted to knowing about the employee abuse allegations linked to his former DOE associate. He tried sidestepping Lynne's questions by pausing for long moments between responses, as though contemplating the consequence of stumbling in his answers, and perhaps pondering if we had copies of records, transcripts, statements, maybe even one he'd given at some point before. For whatever reason, instead of sticking to his initial claim of not being "privy to those kinds of problems," he decided to recall.

Hirahara, it turns out, knew about the sexual harassment allegations involving his former Energy Department colleague, but did he ever tell his UC bosses about it? Hirahara reported directly to Bob Van Ness, who was tasked with monitoring all administrative affairs in Los Alamos. Hirahara's duty was to keep him informed, but apparently he'd failed to do so with respect to the lab's executive director's past, or the fact that he'd been put in charge of all LANL investigation and complaint resolution activities, including those dealing with sexual harassment complaints and other worker abuse. And if Hirahara did by chance say something, it apparently had made no difference.

In public, LANL director Michael Anastasio fondly referred to the executive director as his "personal attorney." His predecessor, Pete Nanos, the admiral-director, didn't have much to say about him, while the previous lab director, John Browne, allegedly claimed not to have had anything to do with his hiring. If so, then the decision to bring him into the fold was made by someone else. According to Van Ness's remarks during his deposition, Browne "turned over the management [of LANL] largely to Mr. Salgado." Then perhaps it was Joe Salgado—a retired DOE executive as well—who'd orchestrated the lab executive director's arrival in Los Alamos, essentially swinging the "revolving door" from one Department of Energy official to another.

Salgado, along with Glenn Walp and Steve Doran, came to Los Alamos in the wake of the Wen Ho Lee debacle. It was rumored that Salgado had been brought into the lab at the urging of LANL's foremost defender—Senator Pete Domenici. But after three years on the job he was gone, fired for authorizing Glenn's and Steve's terminations. Others escaped unscathed, most prominent among them the executive director, and now Anastasio's "personal attorney." Indeed, the executive director was a lawyer, but perhaps more important, a "favorite son" among those in charge, both at the university and within LANL, maybe even with respect to the senator.

In graduate school I learned there were expressed values of an organization, and then there were the real values of the institution. The former was reflected in employee handbooks, mission statements, and recruiting brochures, and the latter in everyday behavior and decisions. At LANL, employee surveys helped distinguish between the two:

2004 LANL Checkpoint Survey Result Highlights:

Group morale continued to draw low marks: 40 percent of employee respondents said morale in their group is high, a drop of 2 percent from 2003 and 10 percent from two years ago. In the area of communication, 64 percent of employee respondents said the lab keeps them informed about matters affecting them. This was a drop from 72 percent on the same question in 2003. . . . [O]nly 30 percent of respondents said they believe division management seeks their opinion on important issues impacting their jobs. . . . And 59 percent of employee respondents said they were satisfied with their involvement in decisions that affect their work, down from 65 percent in 2002.

Checkpoint Surveys had been conducted every year—the one in 2004 was the third in a series. Questions were reworded each time, and attempts were made to highlight even the slightest improvement. But distrust in the workplace was still very evident in the results. It was one thing to proclaim zero tolerance for employee abuse, another thing to keep those responsible in charge. Indeed, the difference between "walking the talk" and "talking the talk" is as stark as good and evil, as obvious as day and night.

38

COVER-UP

GLENN WALP, WHO WAS recruited to establish an investigative unit for rooting out criminal activity at the lab, started his lab employment in January 2002. Like most new labees, he was enthralled with the idea of working for the storied nuclear weapons laboratory on the hill. His partner, Steve Doran, joined him soon after. Both were seasoned law enforcement professionals.

LANL had made an institutional commitment to hire them after a series of high-profile incidences attracted national attention. The last straw was the Wen Ho Lee scandal, which led to congressional calls for UC to clean up its act in Los Alamos or get out.

Peter Bussolini, one of the LANL employees Glenn and Steve were investigating, was a laboratory manager earning $150,000 a year. He and an employee, Scott Alexander, were suspects in a major procurement fraud. Alexander was a procurement specialist whose father—since retired—was rumored to have been in charge of the laboratory's engineering organization. And it was rumored, as well, Alexander's father had hired Bussolini, who was also an engineer by trade. If so, then the son now worked for his father's former employee. But this wasn't unusual for Los Alamos, where extending favored treatment to friends, relatives, and old school chums was a long-standing tradition.

Glenn and Steve located a huge cache of merchandise Bussolini and Alexander had apparently acquired for themselves using the lab's procurement process. It was hidden on lab property, in an out-of-use Cold War bunker. The two suspects would eventually plead guilty:

> Two men implicated in a Los Alamos National Laboratory purchasing scandal in 2002 pleaded guilty Monday to charges stemming from improper buys of items ranging from television sets to power tools to bathroom fixtures. Peter Bussolini, 66, and Scott Alexander, 42, formerly highly paid LANL employees, each pleaded guilty in federal court to mail fraud and to conspiracy to commit a felony . . ." (Martin Salazar, "Men Admit to LANL Purchasing Scam," *Albuquerque Journal North*, October 19, 2004)

Bussolini and his coconspirator worked in the Nonproliferation and International Security (NIS) Division, a sensitive area of the lab dealing with national security issues. Glenn and Steve were fired while in the midst of determining if anyone else might be involved. They still needed to find out, as well, where the stolen merchandise was going. As required by regulation, the two seasoned criminal investigators were cooperating with the Federal Bureau of Investigation (FBI) in the matter, and got into trouble with LANL officials because of it. Soon they were being pressured by institutional leaders, including the head of laboratory legal, to reveal their findings to others, even if in doing so their investigation could be jeopardized. It felt like obstruction of justice, but officials were adamant, the concern being that the university could lose the prime contract to run Los Alamos if another headline-grabbing scandal were to come to light.

A related issue Glenn and Steve discovered was the significant quantities of "missing" equipment written off annually as misplaced, rather than lost or stolen. This meant the lab manager assumed the item was missing, perhaps sent to salvage for disposal, and the accounting record simply hadn't been updated. The corresponding conclusion, conveniently enough, would be that nothing was stolen, hence no further effort would be required. Plus items costing less than $5,000 weren't subject to tracking, much less investigation. Two articles from 2002 and 2003 sum up the situation, as well as the security threat that missing equipment could pose:

An internal lab document obtained Wednesday by the *Journal* indicates that in addition to items considered "lost or stolen"—which totaled nearly $3 million in value over the past three years, according to LANL documents—the lab has records of still more goods that are not accounted for. Equipment in this loss category—for items considered "missing" from inventory rather than lost or stolen—was worth an additional $723,000 in the 2001 fiscal year, the document states. (Mark Oswald, "Another $723,000 in Items Missing," *Albuquerque Journal North*, November 21, 2002)

Department of Energy Inspector General Gregory Friedman couldn't assure Congress on Wednesday that no classified or sensitive information from Los Alamos National Laboratory was contained in more than 236 lost or stolen computers still unaccounted for by the weapons

lab. . . . Friedman also told members of the House Energy
and Commerce Committee that he didn't have enough
confidence to say exactly how many computers were
missing or lost, or how LANL would ever know because
some may have never been entered into inventory . . .
(Adam Rankin, "Testimony on LANL Called Outrageous,"
Albuquerque Journal North, February 27, 2003)

Lots of equipment, including computers, was lost and replaced
each year at LANL. Glenn and Steve needed to determine why.
And so they pulled the "string" to see where it led, and discovered
nobody was "minding the store." Internal controls were too
weak to be useful, weren't being followed, or were nonexistent.
As professionals, they needed to determine if patterns of
behavior suggested illegal activity (i.e., if certain organizations
and individuals were more prone than others to "misplacing"
equipment). Lists were compiled to investigate—many pages
with line after line of missing items, plus questionable and
unallowable acquisitions. The missing items needed to be found,
people needed to be questioned, and documents needed to be
reviewed, but the executive director had other plans:

A top Los Alamos National Laboratory official has
instructed employees to provide the lab with copies of
any documents they give to federal investigators. . . .
[The LANL executive director] said in the e-mail that
employees providing any documents to the inspector
general's investigators should "provide copies of a
set of those documents to the [LANL] Audits and
Assessments Office" to the attention of two officials,
including Katherine Brittin. . . . [T]he Department of

Energy's Office of Inspector General began looking into allegations about LANL's purchase and property control systems. . . . [C]ongressional investigators have started mobilizing in Washington, DC to look into accusations of fraud, lax security and cover up. (Adam Rankin, "Lab Wants Copies of Documents," *Albuquerque Journal North*, December 10, 2002)

The lab's executive director once more was in the middle of things. Worse yet, he wanted evidence sent to someone with a questionable past, and who answered directly to him:

[Katherine] Brittin and her office have been accused of trying to cover up information that would embarrass the lab. Allegations against Audits and Assessments date to the mid-1990s when Tommy Hook, a former senior auditor, testified that Brittin tried to kill reports that would embarrass the University of California or cost the lab money. . . . Pete Stockton, a consultant for the Washington-based government watchdog group Project on Government Oversight, said having employees send Brittin copies of documents provided to investigators didn't make sense. (Adam Rankin, "Lab Wants Copies of Documents," *Albuquerque Journal North*, December 10, 2002)

Brittin was the individual Tommy Hook had indicated, under oath, directed him to hide problems. She was now monitoring the two sleuths and the frauds they were investigating, while someone else was assigned to keep tabs on their probe into lost and stolen merchandise. Both were keeping the executive director informed about Glenn's and Steve's comings and goings. The lab's executive director was masterful at remaining engaged, while ensuring someone always buffered him from potential controversy. It was a strategy that allowed the person at the top to feign ignorance, while the person in the middle took the blame. In Brittin's case, her punishment was a lateral transfer within the laboratory—a move that enabled her to continue drawing her six-figure salary:

> Katherine Brittin will step down as chief of Audits and Assessments effective Monday, the lab announced . . . although at least for now, she'll keep her $168,000 annual salary. (Adam Rankin, "LANL's Head of Audits Reassigned," *Albuquerque Journal North*, January 11, 2003)

Some members of Congress weren't pleased. Brittin would have to go—she'd have to take the fall. But unlike the two former law enforcement officials, who were fired outright, she received a separation package and was gently prodded out the door. Others were extended similar treatment:

> . . . Several [congressional committee] members questioned the large settlement packages given to departing implicated [LANL] managers. For example, the security director and deputy director were retiring with settlement packages upward of $190,000 and $140,000, respectively. . . . Others questioned why the Energy Department hadn't caught problems when it had given Los Alamos business practices an "excellent" ranking a few months before the scandal broke. Ralph Erickson, the Los Alamos site manager for the department's National Nuclear Security Administration [DOE], said his reviewers knew

about "very few" of the problems and he was "astounded, amazed, disappointed" when he learned about them. (Andrea Widener and Jessica Guynn, "Ex-Los Alamos Officials Defend Conduct During House Hearing," *Contra Costa Times*, March 13, 2003)

If those higher up the chain of command within the DOE didn't know about problems at LANL, it wasn't because department personnel out in the field weren't telling them; that's what their audit reports did. And it certainly wasn't because employees weren't submitting concerns to the Energy Department hotline, or whistleblowers weren't blowing the whistle. Those in charge simply preferred not to know and were better off, politically, pretending they didn't.

Faced by irate congressmen, the Bush administration's chief nuclear-weapons executive condemned recent losses of two drives of nuclear secrets at Los Alamos National Laboratory, saying "there is something about the Los Alamos culture that we have not yet beaten into submission." But on paper, where contract fees for Los Alamos manager University of California are most at stake, his agency—the National Nuclear Security Administration [DOE]—has awarded top marks to Los Alamos for its handling of classified data for the last four years. (Ian Hoffman, "Los Alamos Lab's Security Appears Great on Paper," *Oakland Tribune*, July 31, 2004)

Glenn and Steve were terminated to stop their investigation into the Bussolini/Alexander procurement fraud. That much was clear. Less apparent was why institutional leadership chose not to complete their investigation. In June 2010 Lynne Bernabei, my attorney, and I spent several days in California deposing some amazingly forgetful UC officials. Three months later, in New Mexico, we had the laboratory's executive director in the hot seat. It had taken years of legal wrangling to get him there, and like his colleagues in California, he was astute at tap-dancing around questions. But now Lynne had him cornered regarding the work Glenn and Steve left unfinished the day they were fired. At issue was whether lab executives ever assigned someone to finish their review. The answer to this question would establish to what extent taxpayers were defrauded.

(Questioning of the LANL Executive Director by Lynne Bernabei, Esq.)

Q: Okay. So as you sit here, you don't know if anybody at the lab ever looked at all the purchases Bussolini and Alexander made over their time at the lab?

A: I don't know that.

Q: Okay. And it's fair to say that you don't know a figure of what those—what those purchases would be as you sit here?

A: Again, I would ask you for clarification. On the Mesa contract?

Q: No, on all of the contracts, all of the purchases they made on whatever contract.

A: No, I don't know.

Q: Okay. And as you sit here, you can't tell me how much of what they purchased was used to [taken elsewhere] on other than lab property, right?

A: No.

Q: Okay. And you can't tell whether it's in the hundreds of thousands or millions of dollars, right?

A: I can only tell you what the FBI publicly released.

Q: Right.

A: When they were indicted.

Q: But I'm talking about your—

A. No.

Q. So as we sit here today, nobody knows at the lab how much these two individuals purchased over their tenure at the lab that was not authorized?

A: I don't know that.

Q: Well, does anybody at Los Alamos know that?

A: I don't know that either.

Q: Okay. So as far as you know, nobody at Los Alamos knows how much improper purchases these two men made?

Q: Over your entire tenure at the lab?

A: Yes.

Q: And we don't even know the range, whether it's millions or less than that, right?

A: That's right.

(Deposition transcript, LANL executive director, September 15, 2010, starting on p. 130)

Extracting the truth from laboratory and UC executives was like pulling teeth from a non-sedated lion—difficult at best. Taxpayers had been ripped off in a huge way, but nobody in charge seemed to know by how much, or cared to know. Was it in the thousands of dollars, or millions? For how long had the fraud been going on? Were others involved? No one in charge seemed to have answers to these types of questions. And if they did, they weren't talking, which only made sense if the objective was to prevent something else from being discovered.

Before his retirement in 2002, Richard "Dick" Burick was the laboratory's deputy director for LANL Operations. In January 2003, he was found dead on the outskirts of town with the back of his head blown off. According to two engineers I knew, their onetime boss had allegedly attended a meeting at the lab that morning, and had left it visibly upset. While having coffee with them I learned of Burick's apparent association with Peter Bussolini, one of the LANL employees implicated in Glenn and Steve's procurement fraud investigation. Joe Gutierrez—the labee who years earlier provided lab-incriminating evidence in a Clean Air Act dispute, made the show-stopper revelation:

"I bumped into Bussolini one day," Joe said. "I asked him what he was going to be doing when he retired, and he said Burick owned a ranch in southern New Mexico, and that he [Bussolini] was planning to run a hunting operation for him [Burick], on that ranch. He said something about using remote-controlled planes to locate game."

Suddenly, the hidden stash of stolen merchandise being attributed to Bussolini in the media—mostly hunting and camping equipment, including remote-controlled planes—now seemed to make more sense.

At one time, Burick was the Engineering Science Applications (ESA) Division leader, and in this regard had followed in Scott Alexander's father's footsteps. But labees, in general, knew of Burick because prior to his retirement in 2002 he was the lab's deputy director—the institution's second-highest-ranking executive. Plus he was the official who'd reportedly terminated Wen Ho Lee, albeit at the behest of then–DOE secretary Bill Richardson. Burick was also the command and control officer during the devastating May 2000 Cerro Grande fire, which destroyed most of the forest surrounding Los Alamos and 235 homes. It was during that disaster that two highly classified computer drives were determined to be missing. (The drives were later found behind a copier, in a room that had been searched twice in the previous forty-eight hours.) These headline-grabbing events made Burick a household name around town and perhaps, as well, within the entire DOE complex. It also suggested he had insider information on any number of national security matters, which meant he was probably widely known within the Washington, DC, Beltway as well, and among those at the upper echelon of UC leadership.

Laboratory and university officials questioned under oath by my attorney in 2010 no longer seemed able to remember much about Burick. It was as though a new form of amnesia had spread among institutional leadership. Their recollections about much of anything during depositions were vague at best. But there were others at LANL who still seemed to remember, and Joe Gutierrez was one:

In the early 1990s I worked in an organization in which Peter Bussolini was the Group Leader. In that capacity we occasionally met to discuss work-related issues. In the early 2000s I encountered Mr. Bussolini and an informal discussion ensued regarding our respective retirement plans. During that encounter Mr. Bussolini revealed his intent to participate in the management of a ranch and hunting operation with Deputy Director Richard Burick. I knew Richard Burick from past assessments I performed in areas falling within his purview. In 1998 Burick was appointed Deputy Director of LANL operations. Mr. Burick remained in that capacity until his retirement in 2002. (Joe Gutierrez, Affidavit, New Mexico District Court No. D0101-CV-2005-00489, September 1, 2010)

Another person who remembered was Robert "Bob" Ortiz. He was the top business and administration official in the ESA Division, where all the individuals now being discussed seemed to have crossed paths at some point. Bob corroborated Joe's claim regarding Bussolini and Burick:

(Questioning of Robert "Bob" Ortiz by Lynne Bernabei, Esq.)

Q: Okay. So at some point, you learn that there are—Bussolini and Alexander are making—are stealing property from—or allegedly stealing property from the lab?

A: No, they were convicted, so they were—

Q: But they were allegedly at this point in time. In 2002, they were allegedly—we can say now they were—

A: Right.

Q: But at that point in time, they were alleged to have been stealing property through this Mesa contract, right?

A: Yes.

Q: And Walp and Doran investigated that, right?

A: Walp and Doran investigated.

Q: Now, at that time—and at that time, you knew it was Bussolini and Alexander that were involved in that?

A: Uh-huh.

Q: Or alleged to have been involved?

A: Yes.

Q: And they were convicted in 2004 or thereabouts, right?

A. Yes.

Q. Now, did you have any conversations with Mr. Burick before he left the lab in 2002?

A: Yes.

Q: And if you can just tell us approximately when did you have any conversations with Mr. Burick?

A: I had gone to the Ad Building for a meeting that John Ruminer and I were attending for ESA [Engineering Sciences and Applications Division] on some financial matter.

Q: And who was this John Ruminer?

A: John Ruminer is the deputy director of ESA Division.

Q: Were you a friend of his?

A: I went there as the lead financial person for ESA Division. It was a budget meeting.

Q: And he went there as deputy director of the—

A: Correct.

Q: —ESA Division? Okay. And—

A: After the meeting broke up, we decided to go get lunch in the cafeteria at the Otowi Building. When we were in the cafeteria, we ran into Dick Burick. Dick Burick and John Ruminer were very, very close friends. They hunted together, although John did not hunt. He went and kept the camp and stuff, but they were very close. When Dick Burick was the ESA Division leader, John was his deputy, so they were very close. They invited me to have lunch with them, and we sat down. And Burick was talking about retiring, and I asked him what he was going to do. And he said that he had a camp that he was going to turn into a hunting lodge, and that he was going to spend some money to fix it up, and him and Peter were going to run it. And I asked him Peter who, and he said Peter Bussolini.

Q: Okay. And did he explain exactly what role Mr. Bussolini would have in this project?

A: He was going to run the place for him.

Q: So he was going to run this camp?

A: Yes.

Q: And if you recall, prior to that meeting, had you known that Mr. Bussolini and Mr. Burick were involved in this business venture together?

A: No. That was the first time I had ever heard Peter Bussolini's name at all.

(Deposition transcript, Robert Ortiz, June 29, 2010, starting on p. 68)

The large cache of ranching-related merchandise, as well as camping and hunting equipment, discovered in a decommissioned laboratory bunker a few months earlier was a red flag. If Glenn and Steve had known Bussolini's plan to manage a hunting venture on Burick's ranch, alarm bells would have been ringing loudly in their ears. But they'd been terminated before they could know.

Within hours after Burick's body was found the Los Alamos Police Department ruled the cause of death a suicide, a determination made days *before* the completion of the autopsy. The rush to judgment was neither necessary nor appropriate, especially given conditions at the scene:

[Los Alamos] PD Det. Dewayne Williams, who investigated the case, says it is possible that Burick's hand released the cylinder latch after he fired the shot. Williams tells SFR [*Santa Fe Reporter*] that he has investigated "a couple" of homicides in his career. He says he's

never seen a revolver in that condition at a suicide scene,
nor read about such a thing happening in any other case.
"But I can certainly imagine that is a possibility." (Wren
Abbott, "Who Killed Richard Burick?" *Santa Fe Reporter*,
February 15–21, 2012)

Local police could "imagine" something like this happening?
Why assume, if it can be determined for certain by having the
crime lab run tests? If the condition and location of the gun can
be recreated in a laboratory setting, then indeed it could be suicide. If not, other possibilities needed to be considered.

It would have made sense to engage the FBI in this matter,
as the deceased was a high-ranking official at a facility engaged
in national security matters. Plus it wasn't as though the bureau
hadn't assigned resources to look into what was going on in Los
Alamos before. In 2000, the FBI dedicated nearly sixty agents
to determine why classified data had been lost at the lab, then
found behind a copier. In 2006, local police solicited the FBI's aid
after responding to a domestic disturbance and finding classified
documents in a Los Alamos residence.

As deputy director for LANL, Burick had been privy to classified documents and national security discussions. His demise
occurred in the midst of a major procurement fraud examination
gone awry, and on the eve of related congressional hearings. But
then, it wasn't the first time a UC-run federal installation had
escaped scrutiny for a suspicious death:

Frustrated Livermore police detectives are accusing
Lawrence Livermore Laboratory of stonewalling an
investigation into the slaying of a reclusive designer
who uncovered a serious flaw in the lab's troubled $1
billion weapons testing program. Lee Scott Hall, 54, was

discovered beaten and repeatedly stabbed in the bedroom of his Livermore home October 20 by two co-workers. Hall was a lead designer on the $1.2 billion National Ignition Facility. . . . Hall had been trying to bring attention to a miscalculation in a multimillion-dollar installation of super laser beams that is part of the ignition facility. (Mike Weiss, "Livermore Engineer's Mysterious Death/ Investigators in the Brutal Slaying of Lee Scott Hall— Who Found a Flaw in a Billion-Dollar Project—Are Exasperated by the Lab's Lack of Cooperation," *San Francisco Chronicle*, February 15, 2000)

Something didn't smell right in Los Alamos. A high-ranking nuclear weapons facility official dies suddenly and mysteriously, but his demise is labeled a suicide hours after the body is found and days before the New Mexico Office of the Medical Investigator has completed the autopsy. In short, there was no investigation. It was like having security cameras on display that don't work, or a vault that's accessible by everyone. Why was any of this done unless there was a hidden rationale . . . perhaps something not intended to be apparent . . . a cover-up?

39

BURIED SECRETS

I obtained an official copy of the police report and photos of the crime scene where Mr. Burick allegedly committed suicide. After reading the police report I was surprised the investigation was discontinued and the incident was ruled a suicide. (Steve Doran, "Confidential Investigative Report," August 16, 2010)

STEVE DORAN WAS AN expert marksman and a survival specialist. After his premature departure from the lab, he took on the role of hosting a popular Internet survival series called *Trail Boss*. He was also tapped by the History Channel as an expert marksman for the hit cable show *Top Shot*. In addition to his educational and entertainment endeavors, Steve was a licensed private investigator.

Over the course of Steve's law enforcement career, he'd investigated hundreds of crimes. He was now working for my attorney. Lynne hired him to see if there was a hidden rationale for why institutional leaders, when being deposed, had sought to distance themselves from Burick.

The first step in Steve's investigation was to obtain a copy of the police report associated with Burick's mysterious demise. Photos taken at the death scene provided the initial clue that something might be wrong:

> [T]he revolver was at the feet of Mr. Burick . . . with the cylinder open. All but one of the unfired cartridges was firmly seated in the cylinder. The spent cartridge was sticking out of the cylinder. There was no damage to the revolver and one unfired cartridge lay on the ground near the gun . . . Because the cylinder locks at both the front and the back it is impossible for this to occur. If the revolver had blown open there would have been severe damage to the cylinder and the frame, rendering the revolver useless; there was no damage to the revolver whatsoever. (Steve Doran, "Confidential Investigative Report," August 16, 2010)

According to forensics experts, when a bullet penetrates the heart, the individual remains conscious and maintains muscle control for about fifteen seconds. With a bullet to the head, the body goes limp immediately. If it's a hammered revolver involved in a suicide shot to the brain, the force of discharge would project the weapon backward, and the hammer would cut or bruise the hand in the process.

The large-caliber bullet entered behind the ear, and the force of the impact removed the rear of Burick's skull and brain. The handgun was lying south of the deceased's feet, instead of at or near the upper torso, as would be expected. The open cylinder was also atypical because, for safety, locking mechanisms should have kept the cylinder securely in place during and after discharge. This means manual intervention would have been required for unlocking, such as unscrewing a holding pin or pressing down forcefully on a release lever.

With large-caliber handguns, two locking mechanisms are often used. Both have to be manipulated simultaneously to initiate release. As for the spent cartridge discovered partially sticking out: this, too, was unusual. Exploding gunpowder projects the bullet and simultaneously expands the casing, lodging it in the cylinder. Manual prodding with a dislodging mechanism is often required to force it out. To validate his concerns, Steve sought the opinion of other experts:

> I made contact with firearms court-certified expert Michael Stamm, and gave him the information on how the firearm was found. Mr. Stamm in turn called this country's foremost Smith & Wesson expert, John Podergois. After discussion, the two came to the conclusion that it is *absolutely impossible for the gun to have been recovered on the ground in the location it was found without human assistance*, and there was no way to recreate this situation in a lab. *FBI expert Dave Williams was also consulted on the matter, and he agreed* with their conclusion [my italics]. (Steve Doran, "Confidential Investigative Report," August 16, 2010)

The next crucial step in the investigation was to obtain a copy of the Office of Medical Investigator (OMI) report. I accompanied Steve to Albuquerque on that day.

> [T]he report indicates that the Medical Investigator found powder residue on Mr. Burick's right hand. It is to be noted, that when a person commits suicide in the alleged

manner of Mr. Burick's suicide, their body instantly relaxes. Because of this, and the large caliber of the handgun used, according to experts there should have been a wound on the top of Mr. Burick's hand from the hammer coming back and striking it. There was no such wound listed in the notes. According to experts the powder residue could have been deposited if Mr. Burick's hands were in the surrender position, or if he moved his hand to defend himself. . . . Based on the medical synopsis report, it also appears that Mr. Burick may have had injuries consistent with being hit or assaulted in some way. (Steve Doran, "Confidential Investigative Report," August 16, 2010)

The OMI evaluation didn't disclose any injury to the hands, but did mention injuries to the torso consistent with a person being assaulted. My attorney had requested a copy of the report from the OMI, along with access to all supporting documentation, including interview notes, photos, and the autopsy analysis. We received only the report.

I obtained a copy of the synopsis of the autopsy and MI investigators' reports. . . . However, when I attempted to get the whole file I was advised that the warehouse where the complete file was being stored had been set on fire, possibly by an arsonist. When the blaze was put out the fire was re-started, and they were unable to access the complete record. (Steve Doran, "Confidential Investigative Report," August 16, 2010)

Had someone intervened on LANL's behalf, or was the OMI only inclined to release the more graphic supporting materials to law enforcement? In any case, if the underlying record no longer existed, nobody could see it.

In January 2003, at the time of Richard Burick's sudden and tragic demise, Los Alamos was hemorrhaging from a string of negative news stories about misplaced secrets, allegations of espionage, missing computers, cost overruns, fraudulent procurements and, most recently, the flubbed terminations of two highly respected and well-proven criminal investigators. But the mysterious death of LANL's second-in-command, and his possible association with Bussolini—the perpetrator of the fraud Glenn and Steve were fired for uncovering—represented an unprecedented political and public relations nightmare. Inviting the FBI to investigate Burick's demise, along with waiting for the OMI autopsy report, would have encouraged speculation. An on-the-spot determination of suicide, on the other hand, could end it. And it did.

Steve and I, standing on the steps of the OMI's front entrance, anxiously examined the death report within seconds after getting it. We read each page carefully, stopping briefly every now and again to draw each other's attention to something of interest. At the very end was what appeared to be the smoking gun:

> [The OMI report] indicated that Mr. Burick may have committed suicide because of his health or *because he was under investigation by the laboratory* [my italics]. (Steve Doran, "Confidential Investigative Report," August 16, 2010)

The revelation that Burick "was under investigation by the laboratory" was damning. Establishing *what* Burick might have done that triggered an internal evaluation was critical, but we didn't have the supporting documentation for the OMI report. We didn't even know if the evidence still existed. If we could locate the medical examiner who wrote the report, perhaps we could find out. It took considerable effort, but Steve was finally able to interview him on July 15, 2010.

> He (the medical examiner) did recall sending a subpoena to the lab's HR office requesting a copy of Mr. Burick's personnel file, and a copy of the report he allegedly was under investigation for, but the lab denied the subpoena request. (Steve Doran, "Confidential Investigative Report," August 16, 2010)

At the time of the interview, several years had lapsed since the OMI assessed Burick's demise. The assessor had since retired, but still remembered the case and rumored laboratory investigation of Burick. It made sense that there'd been an internal investigation, the type of "evaluation" I'd done in the past for Tommy Hook when he was the LANL whistleblower officer. The Internal Evaluation Office (IEO) did them, and I, for a brief stint had been on that team. So I knew how the IEO worked. It was a clandestine operation. Our findings had limited distribution because of the office's secrecy, and when an investigation was completed, regardless of topic or findings, we destroyed all supporting documentation, including report drafts and copies. We essentially wiped away all traces of our work. We'd been instructed to do this, told that our "evaluations" were "preliminary" in nature. The lab's legal office made the final determination as to what, if anything, would be done with our conclusions, which was convenient in the sense that the lab's lead attorney reported to the University of California, and was the sole recipient (allegedly) of our reports. This, in turn, served to buffer the

LANL director from learning of problems that might translate into a liability for the university, given that the prime contract between UC and the Department of Energy indemnified the university if there was no evidence linked to the lab director's action or inaction, and a related loss should occur. It was an insidious concession the DOE had made in the contract, creating the incentive to cover up problems rather than fix them.

Last but not least, our IEO work product was said to be protected under attorney-client privilege. The objective was to prevent everyone other than lab legal from seeing our reports. And by shredding our work papers, evidence that we'd even done the review was eliminated. Institutional lawyers orchestrated the scheme. They became administrative "black holes" that caused reports, which were characterized as "internal evaluations" (as opposed to audits), to disappear and never be seen or heard of again. For an audit professional, it was an appalling process. I left IEO after just a few months.

The whistleblower officer at the time of Burick's demise was the LANL executive director. Wherever there was controversy, he always seemed to be nearby. In 2003, he'd prevented the procurement assessments Tommy Hook and I did from being released, so it didn't seem far-fetched that he'd do the same with respect to an IEO review of Burick's possible connection to Bussolini. He had the authority to do so and, as an attorney by trade, the legal mind-set as well.

It all made sense—that an investigation would have been done by the IEO, that the related report was never made public, and that the day Burick was rumored to have left a laboratory meeting in anger, he'd probably been confronted with the results. The OMI may have gotten wind of the report through someone having direct knowledge of it, or who knew about the meeting with Burick. Perhaps the medical examiner received the heads-up anonymously, or in confidence; hence his inability (or unwillingness) to divulge the source. Regardless, without a reasonable basis for believing Burick was "under investigation," it's doubtful the medical investigator would have mentioned it in the OMI report, or issued a subpoena in an attempt to obtain the "internal evaluation" that was probably done. And if the lab had nothing to hide, it would have at least provided Burick's personnel folder in response to the subpoena. Yet it didn't.

Burick retired from the lab effective January 2002. In the spring of that year, Glenn and Steve learned about the Bussolini fraud; by October Burick had sold his ranch for one dollar and "other valuable consideration." Perhaps someone had given him a heads-up:

> Not until May 2002 did [lab employee John] Jennings go to Walp and make the first vague allegations that something was wrong. Several days later, Jennings said he went to LANL's Audits and Assessments Division [Katherine Brittin] to tell officials there they should look into a blanket purchase agreement that had little oversight or accountability. "Two hours after I went there, Pete [Bussolini] found out that I talked to them, so that started making life get miserable," Jennings said. (Adam Rankin, "Lab Worker Aided FBI in Theft Case," *Albuquerque Journal North*, May 30, 2004)

The lab is a closed community, so a logical hypothesis is that once the beans were spilled regarding Bussolini being investigated, someone from within the laboratory informed Burick. This, in turn, might have spurred him to liquidate his "dream" quickly. Nor is it inconceivable that Bussolini would have been summoned surreptitiously, by lab legal, in connection with the IEO investigation that may have been done. Perhaps he was even offered assurances regarding jail time in exchange for staying low-key about Burick's possible involvement. The laboratory had established similar pacts of silence with others involved in undermining Glenn and Steve's efforts. In the end, Bussolini admitted to stealing over $300,000 in merchandise, and could have received a ten-plus-year prison sentence, but got six *months* instead. LANL didn't receive the same level of scrutiny as others, was largely unaccountable for anything, and in the rare event any punishment was meted out, received a slap on the wrist in comparison with the rest of the country:

> In August 1986, two building inspectors were indicted
> for extorting more than $40,000 in bribes and kickbacks
> .... Both defendants pleaded guilty. One was sentenced
> to five years in prison and a $100,000 fine.... [T]he other
> received a three-year term and a $10,000 fine.[1]

The medical examiner couldn't recall, nor admit to knowing how he'd learned about the lab's internal investigation of Burick. But he did remember sending the laboratory a subpoena requesting a copy of the report, as well as wanting a copy of Burick's personnel folder. LANL ignored the official demand for disclosure, and without law enforcement taking an active interest, nothing came of it. Raising further suspicion was the fact that Burick had been looking forward to retiring:

---

1. Ronald Goldstock, *Corruption and Racketeering in the New York City Construction Industry: The Final Report of the New York State Organized Crime Task Force.* New York: New York University Press, 1990, 111–112.

On Jan. 4, the former deputy laboratory Director of
Operations will officially trade in his duties as a career
engineer and lab manager for new duties as a rancher
managing nearly 160 head of fine Black Angus cattle.
"Being able to shift my focus from a career as an engineer to owning an absolutely beautiful working ranch is
a dream come true," says Burick, who plans to spend as
much time as possible at his Rocking Sigma Ranch, a
sprawling 20,000-acre spread located in Southern New
Mexico. (James Rickman, "From 'Conehead' to Cowboy:
Burick Says 'Don't Fence Me In,'" *Los Alamos Newsletter*
2, no. 25, December 12, 2001)

It seemed odd that a top executive of a nuclear weapons installation—someone who'd been hardened by all the trials and tribu-
lations associated with running a national security facility, and
who'd just retired to pursue his "dream" of becoming a rancher—
all of a sudden decides to end his own life. The Los Alamos police
theorized that a bout with prostate cancer was the reason behind
Burick's presumed suicide, but he'd dealt with the cancer scare
before retiring, and was rumored to have done so successfully.
The article announcing his plans "to spend as much time as possible at his Rocking Sigma Ranch" seemed to prove it.

It was time for Steve Doran to visit Burick's ranch to determine if any merchandise stolen by Bussolini and Alexander
was there. This should have been done years earlier, and likely
would have occurred if Glenn and Steve hadn't been fired in the
middle of their investigation. The evidence trail was stone cold
now, but it was still important to look.

It took Steve three hours to reach the area where the ranch
was, and even more time to find its precise location. The property was located in an isolated region of south central New Mex-

ico. Not only was it remote, but it offered excellent grazing for cattle and prime habitat for wild game—pronghorn, bison, deer, elk, bear, mountain lion, javelina, oryx, turkey, and quail. The lab's article about Burick's retirement plan, titled "Don't Fence Me In," said the ranch bordered a 359,000-acre wilderness area owned by media mogul Ted Turner. Large tracts of acreage had been acquired by Turner, whose aim was to conserve pristine habitat for wildlife. Seeing that his land bordered Turner's, a hunting operation was ideal for Burick, given the abundance of game likely to spill over from Turner's land.

The ranch that Steve found now was an abandoned relic of a dream, with a dilapidated main structure largely devoid of furnishings, a yard overgrown with weeds, and a weather-beaten ATV left deteriorating in the sun. In the distance was a large cylindrical water tank, similar to the one purchased at LANL and later declared missing. If a tracking number was still attached, perhaps it could be traced to a manufacturer or the individual who bought it. The same could be said for metal corrals and fencing materials on the property.

> The ranch has an expensive, white iron fence, and a large Sigma on the gate. I walked up to the house in an attempt to locate the current owner. . . . The ranch house was sparsely furnished, with a bed, table, sleeping bags and other miscellaneous outdoor type gear. The bed and some of the miscellaneous [items] appeared to be of the type purchased at stores like Cabela's. It was noted that some of the furnishings had been removed based on marks left on the floor. . . . I obtained the warranty deed showing that Mr. Burick sold his ranch at less than market value at that time. Included in the sale was his brand, all livestock and ranch equipment. The livestock was listed

individually, but the ranch equipment was not identified. . . . [The Buricks] sold the ranch . . . for one (1) dollar and other valuable consideration. . . . [A] second contract filed . . . showed the Buricks sold the property acting as the bank to [another party] . . . who then sold it to their son . . . The transaction immediately removed Burick's name off the property. The sale occurred at the same time Mr. Burick's former lab employees were under investigation by the FBI. (Steve Doran, "Confidential Investigative Report," August 16, 2010)

Burick's former employees were Peter Bussolini and Scott Alexander, and both pled guilty to using lab procurement processes to acquire large quantities of hunting, camping, and ranching gear for personal use—merchandise normally associated with the type of venture Burick was apparently contemplating for himself and Bussolini. But was it all just a wild coincidence, or had Bussolini been funneling stolen merchandise to Burick's place? And if it was the latter, was Burick aware of it, or an innocent victim of someone else's greed? But then why did he sell his lifelong dream after only a few months, and for just one dollar and other "valuable consideration"? The timing of these events was as important as the plan for Bussolini and Burick to collaborate on a hunting venture. There were many questions that needed answering, but no one seemed inclined to tackle them, except for Glenn Walp:

Convinced there was more to uncover during an investigation from 2002 at Los Alamos National Laboratory, former Office of Security Inquiries (OSI) Leader Glenn A. Walp said he intends to ask the Federal Bureau of

Investigation for help . . . "There are a lot of loose ends that need to be addressed and I will be asking the FBI to reopen the case," Walp said during an interview from Arizona. "Based on serious allegations and unresolved questions uncovered in 2010 during the Chuck Montaño whistleblower suit, it is imperative that these lingering issues of possible criminality be investigated to the full-est. Truly, I have one goal only and that is to have the case reopened to get to the truth . . ." said Walp. (Carol Clark, "Walp Wants Authorities to Reopen Probe," *Los Alamos Monitor*, June 15, 2011)

A search warrant would be needed for a more thorough inspec-tion of the ranch, along with access to related purchase orders and reports of merchandise received, plus subpoenas for wit-nesses to be interviewed under oath. But that was a job for law enforcement.

Glenn Walp points out in his book, *Implosion at Los Alamos*, that lab officials sought to undermine his investigations. After he and Steve Doran discovered widespread fraud occurring at LANL, they were directed by those in charge to hide this reality. They were later terminated for refusing to participate in a related cover-up. A lot of news coverage and a congressional inquiry ensued in the wake of their firings, but significant issues surrounding their terminations were kept hidden—a mysterious death, and a criminal fraud investigation sabotaged on purpose.

The commitment to impose accountability in Los Alamos had always been too shallow, too short-lived, too politically tainted to be effective. Even those engaged in obstructing jus-tice, it now seemed, were immune from consequence.

40

TRUTH, JUSTICE, AND THE AMERICAN WAY

BY THE FALL OF 2010 my whistleblower complaint had languished in judicial proceedings for nearly six years. My attorney, Lynne Bernabei, had skillfully brought up Dick Burick's name for the first time during the June 2010 depositions of UC officials; the reaction we'd gotten from those we deposed had triggered the related investigation done by Steve Doran. The value of Steve's effort, in relation to my case, was its potential to entice institutional leaders to settle. But a resolution was likely only if there was some reason for LANL or the university, or both, to not want Burick and Bussolini brought up at trial.

To derail a criminal investigation was more than a cover-up; it was an obstruction of justice. Murder, as well as covering it up, was a criminal act. Lying under oath, whether in a court of law, to the FBI, or to a congressional committee, had legal ramifications as well. If my attorney could establish a link between Burick, Bussolini, and the firing of Glenn Walp and Steve Doran in the midst of their fraud investigation, that could be a problem for the University of California and the Los Alamos lab. If institutional leadership had nothing to hide we were going to trial.

But if they were nervous about something, perhaps my years of struggle, career stagnation, and professional marginalization might then come to an end.

Steve's investigation was introduced into evidence at the September 2010 deposition of the LANL executive director. Within days following that, the first cracks in the ice began to show, with opposing counsel expressing an interest in pursuing a settlement, at last. My attorney's strategy worked, and by the end of October a framework for resolving my case had been hammered out. And so effective on January 1, 2011—my birthday— my thirty-two-year tenure as a lab employee came to an end. It was not a firing or forced resignation, but a way to conclude a dispute that had dragged on for much too long, had cost taxpayers far too much, and had been stressful to way too many lives, including my own. Plus it provided my family and me a level of vindication and remedy that I could live with. And though I may never be able to divulge specifics about the settlement, suffice it to say that to this day I have no regrets.

Steve's investigation of Burick was my saving grace, plus a revelation for him and Glenn as well. After so many years of trying to make sense of what had happened to them and why, the final piece of the puzzle now seemed to be in place. Or was it?

Our July 12, 2012, meeting with Kenneth J. Gonzales, United States attorney for the District of New Mexico, was our last-ditch appeal to authority. Glenn brought a lifetime of law enforcement achievement to the discussion. I was there to fill in the blanks as needed. The attorney brought a member of his prosecuting team with him, someone intimately familiar with the investigation Glenn and Steve were in the middle of at the time of their discharge. The FBI was the investigative arm of the Department of Justice, and the US Attorney's Office was the prosecuting authority. The challenge Glenn posed was simple— test the condition of the handgun found at the scene of Burick's demise. The FBI crime lab could do this—establish whether the cylinder of the gun could pop open by itself, without human intervention. And if not, then the question remained—was the shot that killed him self-inflicted or not?

At the end of the meeting, Glenn offered a two-inch-thick stack of documents in support of the arguments he'd made. Included was a copy of Steve's investigative report.

"Who should I leave this with?" Glenn asked.

The US attorney extended his arm and said, "I'll take it." He'd given us an hour and a half of his time.

Glenn's presentation was powerful. The discussion it had triggered demonstrated considerable understanding on the part of everyone sitting at the table. The interest seemed genuine, another good sign. We left the meeting feeling hopeful.

All of us—Glenn, Steve, and myself—were absolved. We did the right thing in our respective careers, and because of it the whistleblower label will always be associated with our names. We grew up separated by time and age, distance and backgrounds, our lives intersecting purely by chance while doing battle with the military-industrial giant on the hill. Like foxhole buddies, we were now bonded through struggle, forever connected by workplace experiences none of us wanted, or could have ever imagined possible for a facility as historic and widely known as the Los Alamos National Laboratory—birthplace of the world's first atomic bomb.

41

NATURE OF THINGS

IT'S AN INTERESTING FABLE—THE story about the scorpion and the frog. "Would you carry me across the pond?" asked the scorpion. "I'm not sure I want to do that," responded the frog. "You'll sting me with your venom."

"I promise I won't," said the scorpion.

"How do I know you won't?" asked the frog.

"I just want to get across the pond," responded the scorpion, "and if I sting you we'll both drown."

"True," agreed the frog. "Okay, hop on."

About halfway into their journey, the frog felt a painful jolt on its back. The venom began to take effect immediately. "Why?!" the frog exclaimed as its limbs became numb. "Now we're both going to drown!"

"I know," said the scorpion. "I'm sorry, but I just couldn't help myself."

"Why?!" exclaimed the frog once again.

"Because," responded the scorpion as they descended into their watery grave, "it's in my nature."

The Rocky Flats plutonium plant was established in 1952

near Denver, Colorado. Forty years later, in 1992, widespread Pu contamination associated with the plant's operations led to its doors being closed permanently. But the stage is now set for the sequel—Rocky Flats II—to occur in Los Alamos. Is it our nature, as human beings, to repeat our mistakes?

Since the start of the new millennium, LANL had been positioned to become the next plutonium (Pu) nuclear warhead ("pit") manufacturing site for the DOE complex. Its predecessor, Rocky Flats, no longer exists. Thus, despite LANL's motto—World's Greatest Science Protecting America—basic research hasn't been the lab's primary mission for a while. Pit production, on the other hand, has.

The type of plutonium (Pu) used for bomb making is Pu239. It has 145 neutrons and 94 protons in its nucleus, hence the number 239. It is ideal for bomb making because it's highly unstable, meaning it has a tendency to break apart when struck by a neutron particle traveling at the right velocity. This is called fission, and if enough neutrons are released into a compacted area full of Pu239 atoms, many more neutrons are released at an accelerating rate, causing more and more fissions to occur—a chain reaction.

Controlled reactions are what nuclear power plants achieve to produce heat, which converts liquid into the steam that turns turbines to generate electricity. Uncontrolled events, on the other hand, are associated with accidents and bombs, producing intense flashes of thermal energy (heat) and neutron radiation that can be lethal to anyone not properly shielded. Heat causes atomic linkages forming molecules to break, and atoms to drift apart, resulting in smoke and flames. But to the extent Pu239 atoms remain compacted, in combination with a source of intense neutron exposure, the chain reaction accelerates to the point of releasing an enormous burst of energy in very short order. This, accompanied by the expanding shock wave, fireball, and mushroom cloud, is an atomic detonation, which is precisely what the grapefruit-sized silvery-grey balls of plutonium 239, euphemistically called "pits," are designed to achieve.

> Plutonium metal is difficult to handle and store safely, because it is radioactive and "pyrophoric," meaning it oxidizes and can become very hot when exposed to air. It can ignite nearby flammable materials, causing fires that can result in plutonium exposure of workers and the public. In addition, workers must avoid storing more than a few pounds in close proximity to prevent runaway fission, an uncontrolled nuclear chain reaction. Such a reaction's burst of energy, known as a "criticality event," would not become a nuclear explosion, but could release radiation very dangerous to nearby workers. Such an event can also result in uncontrolled releases of both plutonium and fission products to the environment. (Colorado Department of Public Health and Environment, "Technical Topic Papers: Rocky Flats Public Exposure Studies," September 17, 2011)

Radiation is the process of an unstable atom changing, over time, into something else. This is known as decay, and the time required for half the original quantity of such atoms to mutate is called a "half-life." Natural background radiation—radiation at the surface of the earth coming from cosmic rays, rocks, and naturally radioactive minerals, as well as what's already in the atmosphere, is theoretically achieved after ten half-lives. But outside of an exploding star, Pu239 isn't really "natural" to our planet. We've created it in nuclear detonations, and in a DOE facility in Hanford, Washington, where nuclear-fueled power reactor cores are lined with layers of natural uranium—U238. There, U238 is exposed to intense neutron radiation, with the objective being to get the uranium atom to absorb a neutron and morph into the much more useful bomb-making atom—Pu239. In a nutshell, this is how we've created a new route to death on earth, a pathway capable of destroying cities in the blink of an eye and individuals, one at a time, over the course of many generations.

Pu239 has a half-life of 24,000 years. Rocky Flats was where it was isolated and refined into higher concentrations, processed into metallic form, and machined into precisely formed spheres—the hearts of nuclear weapons. Because of the number of processing steps involved, and quantity of material in production at any point, the volume of related contaminated waste produced each year is significant . . . filters, sludge, rubber gloves, glass, tools, equipment, paper, smocks, shoes, rags, and so on, all of it Pu-tinged and radioactive.

Stabilizing contaminated liquid normally involves solidifying it into concrete or glass. Packaging solids entails filling up fifty-five-gallon metal barrels. Storage means stacking packed containers on-site, often for years and above ground, which exposes the containers to the elements. Virtually every DOE facility across the nation stockpiles waste, but Rocky Flats was among the worst because of the enormous amount of toxic trash generated there each year. Burning combustibles to ash reduced volume but created other problems, including radioactive smoke and gas. The Waste Isolation Pilot Plant (WIPP) in southern New Mexico was supposed to be the solution, though it only guaranteed to keep the Pu239-contaminated material isolated for 10,000 years—less than 5 percent of the needed 240,000-year span. But in 2014, after only fifteen years of operations, something went seriously wrong:

Technicians at the Waste Isolation Pilot Plant were taking surface samples Saturday afternoon after a radiation leak was reported at the nuclear waste repository.
The airborne radiation was detected around 11:30 p.m.
on Friday, according to officials with the Department
of Energy. (Zack Ponce, "Radiation Leak Detected at
WIPP," *Carlsbad Current-Argus*, February 15, 2014)

On February 14, radioactive contamination from the tunnels below escaped into the open air. No one was under-
ground, but at least 17 workers on the surface ingested
some of the radioactive particles. . . . The contamination
drifted across the countryside and 26 miles west, all the
way to the city of Carlsbad itself. (Bob Martin, "WIPP Radiation Leak Still a Mystery," *KRQE News*, March 11, 2014)

I began my career in Los Alamos working for the Special Nuclear
Material (SNM) Safeguards group. I was trained extensively
in the hazards associated with handling SNM; in the process,
I acquired a unique appreciation for the challenge. To empha-
size the danger, the laboratory used an exposed nuclear reactor during our education. It was nicknamed Godiva, a tribute
to the naked (unsheathed) horsewoman, Lady Godiva. As part
of the training, the instructor used an orange-sized sphere of
Pu contained within a thin layer of cladding. He invited us, as
class participants, to hold it for a few seconds. It was heavy, like
a shot put made of lead. The instructor said our palms would
appear sunburned if we held it too long. That's because plutonium atoms, as they mutate, radiate low-energy alpha and beta
atomic particles that barely penetrate the skin. Since they don't
travel far, they primarily affect surrounding tissue, which is
why Pu239 is so dangerous if ingested. A tiny speck of pluto-

nium lodged in lung tissue will, within forty-eight hours, expose over 10,000 healthy cells to radiation. Given enough interactions and time, perhaps a gene mutation will occur. The mutant cells may result in cancer, or in the case of a genetically modified egg or sperm triggering a pregnancy, a deformed fetus.

The instructor placed the small sphere of plutonium into a similarly sized holder shaped like a bowl. Directly above it was the other half. The two parts, when brought together, fitted precisely over the metal ball. Each section was constructed of a material that slowed down and reflected back neutrons spontaneously being released by the Pu atoms within the sphere. As the sections came close together, fission reactions increased exponentially, as detected by a Geiger counter—a piece of equipment designed to measure the amount of radiation being emitted. It was positioned alongside the contraption, while we sat in another room shielded from the experiment, watching the counter's readings appear on a separate monitor. The lesson wasn't difficult to understand—the proper handling and storage of plutonium is, literally, a matter of life and death.

I'd held the heart of a nuclear weapon in my hand, but to believe there is a foolproof way to process Pu is delusional. Handling this material is like charming a king cobra—a momentary distraction, slight hesitation, or misjudgment can result in death. Such is the nature of Pu239, and of those who believe dangerous things can be handled without consequence.

I'd once seen a brand-new, intact, heavy-duty forklift tossed into an unlined dirt trench in Los Alamos because it was contaminated with plutonium. The Waste Isolation Pilot Plant repository is now the preferred site for such mistakes. The facility is licensed to accept low-level transuranic waste—material tainted with radioactive elements having an atomic mass (neutrons plus protons) greater than uranium. These are typically isotopes of the Pu atom and its decay products (other atomic elements).

High-concentration/high-energy power plant reactor waste isn't included, at least not yet. For transporting such material on public highways is likely to irradiate everything coming within close proximity of the truck carrying it, not to mention the unconscionable health risk to those doing the transporting.

WIPP is located near the Texas border, two dozen miles outside of the city of Carlsbad, New Mexico. It consists of large tunnels excavated into salt beds 2,150 feet below ground level, remnants of an ancient inland ocean that has been undisturbed for 225 million years. In the early '90s I was sent there on lab business, and given an electric golf cart tour of the facility. I was told that the tunnels, carved from a salt deposit 3,000 feet thick, remained a comfortable 70 degrees year-round, and because of the saline-laden air and constant temperature employees were resistant to sinus infections and colds. I tasted the salt-infused air on my lips, and wondered if it affected people with high blood pressure, or if human skin might become mummified over time. Maybe the cure for the common cold had finally been discovered. Unfortunately, however, it was in the depths of WIPP, within the bowels of a plutonium-contaminated tomb. But was it worth the risk? For those in financial need—those with limited options or resources, who don't truly appreciate the full extent of the hazard, it always is.

Encased in the salt crystals of WIPP are tiny liquid remnants of an ancient ocean. The salt acts as a natural barrier between the surface and water table below. Walls, ceilings, and floors carved from it are elastic and in a constant state of contraction, meaning they need to be scraped and cleaned periodically to maintain desired tunnel dimensions. Once a section of tunnel is filled to capacity with waste, it's sealed. The salt encroachment is then allowed to proceed unabated, and the material, once encapsulated, is supposed to remain isolated from human contact for 10,000 years—approximately 140 generations. But digging caverns in salt formations that have been stable for millions of years is a destabilizing act in itself. Putting metal containers filled with decomposing waste in those tunnels is disrupting as well. The gases and heat created during decomposition produce enormous pressures over time, and the water encased in the salt only adds to structural deterioration and pressure buildup. Over decades and centuries, these forces may cause fissures and cracks, potentially creating pathways to the surface and into the aquifer below. Last but not least, even though 10,000 years may seem like a long time, the material in question remains dangerous for 240,000 years.

Death isn't something we usually anticipate or want to perceive coming, but pretending doesn't change reality either. We can't see Pu atoms, nor can we smell or taste them, except when plutonium is on fire. In that case we might glimpse the blue flame, or catch a metallic whiff in the air or taste it in our mouths. But that's something you never want to experience, because among those who have, many are no longer with us. And among those who are gone are some who never even knew the danger existed.

Kristen Iverson, who grew up in the shadow of Rocky Flats, wrote a book describing what happens when towns like Los Alamos become a reflection of the military-industrial mind-set nearly every household in such communities is beholden to:

> Silence is an easy habit. But it doesn't come naturally. Silence has to be cultivated, enforced by implication and innuendo, looks and glances, hints of dark consequence. Silence is greedy. It insists upon its own necessity. It transcends generations. (Kristen Iverson, *Full Body Burden*. New York: Crown Publishers, 2012, 300)

When ingested though air, food, or drink, plutonium tends to embed itself in the soft tissue of vital organs, including the lungs, liver, gonads, and kidneys. The radioactive emissions of Pu239 atoms, as they decay, lead to cell mutations—the only question is when. It may take years to suffer the consequences, maybe decades, or the individual may die of natural causes long before anything occurs. But generations down the road, if someone were to be exposed to the remains of the departed—an archaeologist, perhaps, or a construction worker bulldozing through an ancient burial site long forgotten—what then? The plutonium particles ingested by the deceased will remain dangerous for thousands of years.

The Rocky Flats plant was the facility where plutonium warheads (pits) for the nation were manufactured. But recurring accidents and plutonium fires, coupled with improper handling, disposal, and storage of waste products, forced its closure in 1992.

> To his credit, DOE manager Mark Silverman calmly continues to face the press. He knows he's sitting on a time bomb. There's enough radioactive waste on the plant premises to cover a football field to the depth of twenty feet. . . . [T]he DOE projects that it will take at least until 2065 and cost American taxpayers more than $40 billion to marginally clean up the nuclear waste at Rocky Flats.
> (*Full Body Burden*, 243)

The Rocky Flats cleanup, initially projected to take decades and tens of billions of dollars to achieve, was ultimately done in ten years and for $7 billion. The solution was to mitigate, as opposed to remediate. Plus milestones were changed, enabling higher concentrations of Pu to remain in place, a classic DOE move— assuring victory by moving goalposts in the middle of the game.

Presumably the expectation, now, was for surface vegetation in and around Rocky Flats to never again be consumed by fire, regardless of lightning strikes or other recurring flame starters, since contaminated smoke might raise doubts as to the integrity of the cleanup effort. And besides, the vegetation in place is needed to prevent plutonium embedded in topsoil from being picked up in the eighty-mile-an-hour wind gusts common to the region. The vegetation also prevents Pu from being washed away in drenching downpours and spring runoff that replenishes streams, rivers, and lakes, providing water to Denver residents and other downstream users. Similar leaps of faith were needed with respect to animal behavior. Grass eaters—deer, for example—supposedly know better, now, than to eat contaminated vegetation. And if they do eat the vegetation, they also supposedly know how to avoid being shot by unsuspecting humans for consumption.

In deeper layers of the soil, the Energy Department allowed even higher concentrations of plutonium to remain in place, with heavily polluted below-surface facilities, ductwork, and drainage pipes being simply abandoned. Apparently this meant that burrowing critters like gophers, prairie dogs, and ants would no longer be digging up earth in and around Rocky Flats.

It was only a matter of time before Mother Nature would respond:

> Like the rest of the region, the rain started soaking into the ground at Rocky Flats on Monday, Sept. 9. By the following Wednesday night, the ground was fully saturated and the flooding began in earnest, with runoff from the hills, gullies and holding ponds at the site, filling North and South Walnut Creeks as well as Woman Creek beyond their capacities. As the water finally began to recede, the

debris caught in the fences above the usual creek banks bore witness to the unprecedented water levels that had swept through the area between Wednesday night and Saturday morning. (Joel Dryer, "Flood Raises Questions at Rocky Flats," *Boulder Weekly*, October 10, 2013)

Surface areas remaining "hot" (i.e., areas where fifty-five-gallon barrels filled with plutonium waste might have been stored too long and spilled out) were capped with a layer of asphalt or concrete to minimize further disturbance, and to limit the cost associated with a more permanent restoration effort. Finally, to complete the illusion, the Rocky Flats legacy had to be obscured. Labeling the former plutonium pit factory a wildlife refuge would help, with a hiking trail or two serving to bolster official pronouncements proclaiming the place as "safe."

> Everything else is, as the government likes to say, nothing but conjecture. Speculation. Exaggeration. Media hype. They say there is no direct link between Rocky Flats and health effects in the surrounding communities. All contaminants are at levels that have been declared safe by the government. (*Full Body Burden*, 339)

During its years of operation, cancer rates shot up at Rocky Flats, along with inexplicable diseases in children and spouses living nearby. Through it all, real estate developers continued developing, builders kept building, and realtors never stopped selling. Worst of all, much of the populous didn't seem to care, or were unwilling to hear those sounding the alarm. The area was simply too beautiful, the cost of living too affordable, and the economic prosperity and jobs associated with having a nuclear facility in the neighborhood too enticing to walk away from.

We don't talk about plutonium. It's bad for business. It reminds us of what we don't want to acknowledge about ourselves. We built nuclear bombs, and we poisoned our- selves in the process. Where does the fault lie? Atomic secrecy, the cold war culture, bureaucratic indifference, corporate greed, a complacent citizenry, a failed democ- racy? What is a culture but a group of individuals acting on the basis of shared values? (*Full Body Burden*, 339)

Rocky Flats had been at the epicenter of the doomsday produc- tion line, and the Los Alamos National Laboratory had always been the mad scientist behind the scenes, designing the next generation of weapons and delivery systems needed to address new threats and battlefield scenarios being conjured up by those intent on keeping the military-industrial dragon well fed. And while the depths of the WIPP salt beds are, for some, the per- manent solution for low-level transuranic radioactive waste, the truth is there's nothing certain about plutonium—except that it will continue to kill so long as we have it in our midst.

42

LEGACY

MY LIFE AS AN obscure presence in Northern New Mexico ended in 1994, when I realized that my son and daughter were being conditioned by local school officials to view themselves, through the lens of the high school Topper Man mural, as powerless in the face of injustice. The mural is gone now, and the labor dispute triggered by the '95 lab-wide layoff has long since been settled. And yet, despite nearly two decades of recurring controversy and turmoil, there was very little actual change in Los Alamos.

The University of California, in concert with the US Department of Energy, led everyone to believe a military-industrial consortium controlled by the university would improve things. But the corporate and political imperative—maintaining the status quo—was in conflict with that claim. And while I never heard whether US Attorney Gonzales ever responded to the appeal that Glenn Walp and I made in 2012, requesting the condition of the handgun, as found at the Burick death scene, be recreated in the FBI's crime lab, I did hear about Gonzales's lifetime appointment to the federal bench:

The Senate Judiciary Committee this morning approved the nomination of US Attorney Kenneth Gonzales to become the state's next federal district judge . . . (Michael Coelman, "Senate Committee Approves Kenneth Gonzales for Federal District Judge," *Albuquerque Journal,* April 11, 2013)

The mind-set that held all three UC-run federal laboratories exempt from accountability had remained in place. And because of it, the layoff debacle of 1994, which was settled in 1998, repeated itself in 2008 at Lawrence Livermore National Laboratory:

Jurors on Friday awarded the five longtime workers reimbursement for their lost wages after finding that the [Livermore] lab had violated a contractual promise to terminate them only for "reasonable cause." Individual damages ranged from $242,000 to $853,000. A new jury will now consider their claims of age discrimination, which could bring additional damages for emotional distress and punitive damages. . . . [A]nother 125 laid-off employees are awaiting their own trials on similar claims. . . . 130 plaintiffs were among more than 440 employees the lab dismissed in 2008 . . . soon after Bechtel signed on [with UC] as the lab's first private contractor. The plaintiffs averaged 54 years of age and 20 years of experience. . . . [T]he lab had disregarded its own rules that were supposed to protect senior employees. In one case, [plaintiffs attorney Gary] Gwilliam said, the lab laid off a worker with 38 years of experience while keeping a co-worker who had been on the job for 15 months.

(Bob Egelko, "Livermore Lab Jury Awards $2.7 Million,"
San Francisco Chronicle, May 16, 2013)

Among the military-industrial complex's staunchest allies are those we elect to serve us, and the longer they're in office the more susceptible they are to the compromising influence of large campaign donors. For this reason the virtue of public service is so easily overshadowed by the self-serving needs of career politicians, and why these same individuals become corporate lobbyists after leaving office.

Four contractors managing the Energy Department's national laboratories charged the department $450,000 for consulting fees paid to a former GOP congresswoman [Heather Wilson] from New Mexico, but the contractors could not document her work, according to a report by the department's inspector general. . . . Former GOP Senator Pete V. Domenici, whose seat Wilson campaigned to fill in 2008, filmed a campaign ad for her last year, praising her ability to protect New Mexico's national laboratories. (Steven Mufson, "Lockheed, Others Billed Energy Dept. for Undocumented Work by Ex-Rep. Wilson, IG Says," *Washington Post*, June 11, 2013)

[Heather] Wilson failed to provide documentation for the work she did to earn $20,000 a month from Los Alamos and Sandia national labs in New Mexico from January 2009 to March 2011, the [DOE OIG] report said. Officials at the Nevada Test Site and Oak Ridge National Laboratory in Tennessee acknowledged there "were no deliverables" associated with the $30,000 the two labs paid Wilson. Sandia had Wilson lobby for more defense dollars . . . (Jeri Clausing, "IG Faults Payments to Ex-Rep. Wilson," Associated Press, June 11, 2013)

"No deliverables" means a person is being paid for nothing in return, and under federal law giving away taxpayer resources is unallowable, as is lobbying. But in truth, who's inclined to comply when those we elect to pass laws benefit when they're violated? And who'll enforce them . . . the DOE—the toothless guard dog of the taxpayer's resources—or the politicians supported by the moneyed interests that benefit as well? Or is it the judges, who are themselves politicians?

At Los Alamos National Laboratory, a seven-year, $213 million upgrade to the security system that protects the lab's most sensitive nuclear bomb-making facilities doesn't work. Those same facilities, which sit atop a fault line, remain susceptible to collapse and dangerous radiation releases, despite millions more spent on improvement plans. . . . Virtually every major project under the National Nuclear Security Administration's oversight is behind schedule and over budget—the result, watchdogs and government auditors say, of years of lax accountability and nearly automatic annual budget increases for the agency . . . (Jeri Clausing and Matthew Daly, "Nation's Bloated Nuclear Spending Comes Under Fire," Associated Press, September 12, 2013)

The Los Alamos story is, and has always been, tied to the military-industrial complex—the powerful corporate interests that influence elected officials, dominate public policy, distort spending priorities, and skirt accountability. The consequence has been and always will be the undermining of common sense . . . and the adverse impact that this has on people's lives, and on our democracy.

> It is rather for us to be here dedicated to the great task remaining before us—that from these honored dead we take increased devotion to that cause for which they gave the last full measure of devotion—that we here highly resolve that these dead shall not have died in vain—that this nation, under God, shall have a new birth of freedom—and that *government of the people, by the people, for the people* [my italics] shall not perish from the earth. (Abraham Lincoln, Gettysburg Address, November 19, 1863)

Are we still a nation governed by its people, or did the US Supreme Court change that to a government of "corporations and the wealthy" in its 2010 Citizens United decision? And while we can impeach a president for failing to preserve, protect, and defend the constitution of the United States, why not a Supreme Court justice appointed for life, who is supposed to be the final arbiter when it comes to upholding our rights as citizens, but then consistently fails to do so? Indeed, why should we be even fearful of asking the question?

> Overruling two important precedents about the First Amendment rights of corporations, a bitterly divided Supreme Court on Thursday ruled that the government may not ban political spending by corporations in candidate elections. . . . [D]issenters said that allowing

corporate money to flood the political marketplace would corrupt democracy. (Adam Liptak, "Justices, 5–4, Reject Corporate Spending Limit," *New York Times*, January 21, 2010)

Once upon a time the promise of democracy in the United States was real, just as the storied Los Alamos National Laboratory, where the world's first nuclear lab came to life, used to be the crown jewel of cutting-edge research—an incubator for gifted scientists to develop. And the University of California was once a source of inspiration for them and the entire nation. But today it's a different world, one that only the military-industrial complex could ever have wanted to achieve. The future that our long-departed US president, Dwight D. Eisenhower, once warned us about is, now, a frightening reality.

43

IN THE BEGINNING

THE SPANISH SETTLED NEW MEXICO in 1598, but the area has been occupied for thousands of years by Native Americans—the pueblo people, who managed to hang on to much of their ancestral lands despite each succeeding European invasion. They're descendants of the Anasazi—the ancient ones, also known as the original inhabitants.

For more than 200 years the Spanish flag flew over what later became known as the American Southwest. Mexico gained its independence from Spain, and for twenty-five years the New Mexico territory and surrounding regions fell under Mexican rule, but then changed hands again in 1848. Manifest Destiny was the reason, the notion that divine authority ordained the United States to possess the entire landmass between the Atlantic and Pacific Oceans. God's will was codified into policy, resulting in the Mexican-American War of 1846. The war ended two years later with the signing of the Treaty of Guadalupe Hidalgo. A central tenet of that agreement was that the property, customs, and rights of inhabitants—those of Spanish and Native American descent—be preserved. The pueblo communities of New Mexico still exist today because of that treaty; inhabitants of Hispanic descent, however, were subjected to very different treatment.

Historic animosities between the imperial dynasties of Spain and England empowered the disreputable to take advantage of Spain's former subjects, now citizens of the United States. The preferred target for these backroom dealers and snake oil salesmen was Spanish land grants, a system that allocated large swaths of acreage for shared use. The American system, in contrast, encouraged settlement by providing individuals 640-acre segments of land. The more acreage the individual claimed to be in productive use, the more land was granted. Thus, while the Spanish conquest had a communal bent to it, the English legacy was private ownership.

With each passing generation came more divergent interests, and greater disagreement among land-grant heirs regarding rights and responsibilities. Conflict arose, often rooted in the false claims of those seeking to challenge ownership. Among those brokering resolutions and enriching themselves in the process was attorney Thomas Catron.

Catron was a member of the Santa Fe Ring, a cadre of lawyers, politicians, and wealthy individuals organized for the purpose of acquiring countless sections of land from Spanish land grants and Hispanic homesteads and families. They were determined do so by hook or crook; the latter more often being the case. Catron amassed three million acres for himself in the process, and to this day a New Mexico county is named in his honor.

The land grab after the Mexican-American War rendered future generations of Hispanics throughout the American Southwest economically destitute. Few were more disenfranchised than those scraping out a living on the Pajarito Plateau of Northern New Mexico. Against this backdrop, land for the

WWII effort code-named the Manhattan Project was acquired. Professor Peter Bacon Hales talks about it in his book, *Atomic Spaces: Living on the Manhattan Project*:

> This is a story about the birth of America's atomic spaces, their creation by military fiat and necessity, their occupation by people, buildings, and social networks, their consolidation into a new type of cultural environment, penetrating work, leisure, environment, language, and belief, and present even today as a significant, if surreptitious, strain of American culture. (Peter Hales, *Atomic Spaces: Living on the Manhattan Project*. University of Illinois Press, 1997, 1)

Atomic culture, ingrained in big science and military-industrial thinking, became the colonial occupier of the Southwest in the twentieth century, but nowhere was it more enduring and self-preserving than in the isolation of Los Alamos. The strategy, as described in Hales's book, was to acquire land not controlled by powerful interests, and the focus was on those with minimal resources and influence. In 1943, few were as powerless as the thirty-three Hispanic homesteaders of the Pajarito Plateau, a perfect space to ensure secrecy, and for those inclined to dominate.

> Donaciano Gomez received a patent to 160 acres of land. ... The Gomez family lived year round on their property. ... They farmed beans, wheat, corn, squash and alfalfa, owned cows, goats, chickens, oxen and horses and had grazing rights. The wheat was sold and the family subsisted on the other crops ...

Jose Elfego Montoya (and his wife Tibursia Montoya)
owned the west 80 acres. His son owned the east 80 acres.
. . . Each family farmed the typical crops of the plateau:
pinto beans, green beans, peas and corn. They raised
livestock including cows, horses and chickens. They cut
and sold timber and held National Forest grazing rights
. . . (United States District Court Complaint No. CIV01-
588RLP, District of New Mexico. Filed May 22, 2001)

The part of the Manhattan Project established in Northern New
Mexico was code-named Project Y, aka the Los Alamos Project. Land was acquired, but with little regard for those already
inhabiting it. It was as though they didn't exist. The injustice
they experienced would remain hidden for six decades, but
would finally be exposed in 2001 through a lawsuit. The typical
claim went something along these lines: Family members were
busy working their fields when olive-green vehicles approached
on heavily rutted dirt roads, raising dust in their wake. Entire
families were then forced at gunpoint to vacate their land and
possessions by day's end. They were instructed to return in a few
days for more, and told they'd be allowed to reclaim their land
after the war. Homesteads were abandoned and furnished cabins were left behind, along with wells, irrigation ditches dug by
hand, planted crops, established orchards, livestock, equipment,
and mills used to process timber from surrounding forests. The
homesteaders, in that moment, became refugees. When they
tried returning a few days later, soldiers strategically posted on
roadways blocked them. But some of the homesteaders managed
to sneak back in on horseback. What they found was destruction—stoves crushed, clothes torn, orchards cut, crops dug up,
furnishings broken, livestock shot and left bloating in the high
desert sun . . . cabins, sheds, corrals, farm equipment, mills, all

bulldozed to the ground. Not many were ever paid. Those that were received payment for just raw land, and only at a fraction of its real value. Many people waited months, often years, for the government to validate their claims. Few spoke English; fewer still could read it. None had the means to hire an attorney.

> U.S. Army jeeps rolled up to a log cabin on an isolated mesa in Northern New Mexico. Soldiers ordered the owner, a farmer and cattle rancher named José Patricio Montoya, to abandon his home and 80 acres of land: The government needed his land for an important mission. "There wasn't anything to do," says Montoya's 93-year-old widow, Maria Ernestina Montoya. "They said we had to go, so we went." The Montoyas packed up what belongings would fit in a horse-drawn wagon and retreated down the hill. Military personnel then used their abandoned livestock for target practice, and a few years after the eviction, sent the family about $800 for the land. (Barbara Ferry, "Homesteaders Sue Over Ancestral Land," *High Country News*, March 27, 2000)

A painful irony is that the homesteaders, at the time, had family members fighting enemy forces in Europe engaged in similar acts of displacement. The takeover scenario, as described in Professor Hales's book, was executed to perfection in Los Alamos, on the Pajarito Plateau. But there were even more disturbing things to reveal:

> Hispanics removed from their land for the Manhattan Project were subjected to slave-like labor conditions, detainment under armed guards and involuntary medical

experimentation, a lawsuit filed in Santa Fe federal court earlier this week claims. . . . [Gomez's] family was forced by the federal government to leave their ranch in the Los Alamos area. . . . He was also required to clean areas around the project believed to be contaminated by radiation. . . . Every eight days, Gomez was forcibly examined by doctors and required to allow doctors to draw his blood every 15 days. . . . [H]e was forced to drink an unidentified substance before leaving work each day. . . . [A]nother plaintiff, 98-year-old Marcos Gomez, said in the lawsuit that he was forced to swear an oath at gunpoint not to reveal any of the activities he saw while being forced to live in Los Alamos military barracks and dig ditches for the project at $1 a day . . .

Arguably, for some homesteaders the loss of land and property was offset by jobs they didn't have before, but at what price?

. . . Gomez said in the lawsuit that one day while he was digging ditches, he saw the body of a dead Hispanic woman at the side of the ditch. Soldiers standing near him would not do anything about the body, Gomez said. . . . He was forced to use his earnings at the company store for food . . . . [He] was not allowed to leave for two years, he said in the lawsuit. A third plaintiff . . . said her father was forced to work in areas believed to be contaminated with radiation and was subjected to forced medical examination . . . forced to drink an unidentified liquid before leaving work every day. (Wren Propp, "Suit: Nuke Project Harmed Hispanics," *Albuquerque Journal North*, October 12, 2011)

The inertia of political apathy, when it comes to injustice, is appalling. One morning a contingent of homesteaders and I convened at the Santa Fe home of former congressman Tom Udall. Udall had invited us and his predecessor, former DOE secretary Bill Richardson, to meet.

First to enter the Udall residence was a member of the Secret Service. After ensuring the area was secure, he returned outside to guard the entrance. At that point, Richardson appeared. Brief pleasantries were exchanged before sitting down to a meal of breakfast burritos. Then Tom Udall's father arrived, Stuart Udall—former US Secretary of the Interior. We were starstruck by his presence, but mostly thankful for his appeal to the DOE secretary to pursue a fair resolution of the homesteaders' claims. Within days the official agency response came—an offer by Richardson to make available a few acres of rocky ledge along a Los Alamos canyon, for the homesteaders to erect a monument commemorating their sacrifice. In other words, they'd have to proceed without his assistance.

A lawsuit was filed, depositions were taken, and surviving homesteaders were videotaped at or near the end of their lives. But some in Los Alamos remained unsympathetic and unmoved:

> The Hispanic families who lived on the Pajarito Plateau didn't have lawyers on hand in 1942 when government officials showed up at their doors to condemn their land for a secret mission which later became known as the Manhattan Project. But members of 35 families who are seeking the return of land have now hired a prominent local attorney—and they plan to sue the government. . . . The homesteaders—several of whom are in their nineties—and their descendants are seeking the return of about 2,800 acres as well as compensation for lost

grazing, water and timber rights. . . . DOE and Los
Alamos County officials argue that the homesteaders
don't have any legal claim to land in the area . . . (Barbara
Ferry, "Residents to Sue Government for Land Lost to
Manhattan Project," *Santa Fe New Mexican*, November
19, 1999)

Town leaders had LANL affiliations, and institution officials
(or their spouses) were local politicians. The laboratory was
the town, the community was the lab, and neither was inclined
to acknowledge the homesteaders' claims. But in the wake of
the Cerro Grande fire that destroyed so many Los Alamos resi-
dences, all of Northern New Mexico rallied around the community, thus making the town's inability to empathize that much
more difficult to grasp:

Recently I was asked, "Why don't Hispanics just forget
about the land grants since it happened over 100 years
ago and will just cause more divisiveness?" . . . Another
question is "Why should we care about the land grants
since Spain took it from the Indians?" . . . The land-
grant story is more than a black eye in New Mexico's
history or a dirty little family secret. . . . The Los Alamos [Cerro Grande] fire and the plight of the families
affected have dominated the news in New Mexico. Our
hearts and support go out to those who lost their homes,
were evacuated and had their lives disrupted. . . . Perhaps the time is right to ask, "Where is the compas-
sion and justice for Hispanos who have been waiting to
return to *their* homes?" (Daniel Ulibari, PhD commen-
tary—educational psychologist, researcher, and author

of *Devil's Hatband.* "Land-Grant Story Stays with Us All," *Santa Fe New Mexican,* May 28, 2000)

After years of litigation, a remedy was finally obtained. It was a fraction of what the homesteaders deserved, but infinitely better than the small patch of boulder-encrusted cliff the DOE secretary had offered in his halfhearted tribute.

Congress has approved $10 million to compensate Hispanic homesteaders whose land on the Pajarito Plateau was taken for a top-secret government project that grew into Los Alamos National Laboratory. All but a handful of the homesteaders have died since the World War II Manhattan Project that used their land, but their heirs have battled the federal government for years. . . . "I feel good about it, but it's still going to be a long process," said Peter Gomez, 59, of El Rancho, whose grandfather, Elfego Gomez, farmed and raised cattle on the plateau until the government took the land in the 1940s. "They were so brokenhearted that they never spoke about it after it happened," Peter Gomez said of his grandparents. Sens. Jeff Bingaman, D-N.M., and Pete Domenici, R-N.M., who pushed for a compensation program, have said Los Alamos Ranch School, a prep school on the plateau, received $367,000 for its land—the bulk of $414,000 appropriated in the 1940s to buy property for the lab. The school received $225 per acre; Hispanic homesteaders got $7 to $15 an acre, the senators said. (Staff Report, "$10 Million OK'd to Compensate Los Alamos Hispanic Homesteaders," *Albuquerque Journal,* November 23, 2004)

Virtually none of the original homesteaders lived to receive any part of the remedy, carrying their burden of sacrifice with them into eternity. Their children and grandchildren understood their torment, but the relatively modest amount of compensation suggested only marginal appreciation for their loss. It was, nonetheless, acknowledgement of the injustice.

> Some 65 years ago the government took over the land we today call Los Alamos to begin Project Y, the building of the first atomic weapon. Few doubt the acquisition was necessary given the times we lived in. But 65 years to pay those whose land was taken is shameful beyond words. And those payments have really not even started—they are still in the works. There are times when our government does not do us proud and this is one of those times. . . . While the settlement is too small and too late, at least it is something. We find ourselves agreeing with Chuck Montaño . . . who said the settlement is "long overdue." To say the least. (Editorial, "Landowner Payments Way Too Late," *Los Alamos Monitor*, March 8, 2007)

One of our nation's darkest secrets, the uncompensated forced displacement of the homesteaders of the Pajarito Plateau, is now out in the open. From this seed sprang the Los Alamos mindset—rooted in military-industrial ethos and dominance—and this book.

EPILOGUE

IN A HEALTHY REPRESENTATIVE democracy, stakeholders don't treat politicians as though they're infallible, or expect them to be immune to the influence of money. We should, therefore, confront them publically with key questions: Do they endorse term limits for themselves and all other elected offices? If so, what are they doing to make this happen? Do they support public financing for elections and, likewise, what steps are they taking in this regard? Last, do they agree that US Supreme Court justices should be subject to impeachment, or removal by voter referendum for behavior contrary to the proposition that our republic is beholden to "We the People" and not corporations? If responses to these questions are noncommittal, it's likely the person is motivated by campaign contributions, not the public interest; more focused on being a career politician than a servant of the people. And then it is incumbent upon us, the intended beneficiaries of our form of government, to vote accordingly, regardless of political bent.

My objective in writing this book was to make connections between people and events, money and power, roles and responsibilities, corporate thinking and public policy, and to expose related truths impacting people's lives. I also wanted to compile a historical record of significant events that might otherwise be forgotten; a reference for historians perhaps, but of equal value to those concerned about the corrosive effect unlimited campaign spending has on democracy. I reference news stories, sworn depositions, witness statements, agency audits, and reports for perspective, support, and to enhance understanding. Quotes are intended to be verbatim, but based on notes and memory. Last but not least, I wanted to provide a sense of acknowledgement, purpose, and appreciation for citizens of conscience working to make the world a better place, especially whistleblowers, and for those who value their sacrifices. This is my tribute to them. *CM*

About the Author

CHUCK MONTAÑO HAS MORE than forty years of audit and investigations experience, including a two-year assignment (2007– 2009) as the director of fraud and special audits for the New Mexico State Auditor. He began his professional career in 1972 with the US Comptroller of the Currency, auditing federal banks in Wyoming, Colorado, and New Mexico. He then worked for one of the world's largest public accounting firms. In 1978 he joined the Los Alamos National Laboratory, beginning in the Special Nuclear Materials Safeguards group, then assuming a variety of other roles during his thirty-two-year lab tenure. He earned a master's degree in 1989 from the University of New Mexico, and four profession subject-matter designations—Certified Management Accountant, Certified Fraud Examiner, Certified Internal Auditor, and Certified Information Systems Auditor—over the course of his career. Chuck was born and raised in Santa Fe, New Mexico, twenty-five minutes from the outskirts of Los Alamos. He's taught college courses as an adjunct professor in two state universities, and is today semiretired, working part-time as the chief financial officer and controller in his wife's medical practice.

INDEX

A

Abraham, Spencer, 233

ACFE (Association of Certified Fraud Examiners), 146

Act 3161, 45-52

age discrimination, 332

Agnew, Harold, 73

Alexander, Scott, 283-284, 290-295, 310-312. *See also* procurement fraud

American GI Forum, 17, 39

Anastasio, Michael, 165, 243-245, 281

Aragon, Manny, 80

Area G, 14-15, 123-124

Arthur Anderson, 144, 209, 253

Assange, Julian, 92

Association of Certified Fraud Examiners (ACFE), 146

Atkinson, Richard, 108

Atomic Spaces: Living on the Manhattan Project (Hales), 339

at-risk notices, explained, 42

Attkisson, Sharyl, 210-212

Atwater, Henry, 59

audits and internal control, 28-31, 35, 99-104, 143-152, 171-176, 180-183. *See also* procurement fraud

award fee, 109, 228-230, 240, 242

B

Babcock & Wilcox Technology (BWXT), 240-242

Bakke, Allan, 8

Ballistic Missile Defense System, 93-94

Barber, Laura, 116

Bechtel, 240, 242-243, 332

Bennett, Gloria, 116

Bennett, Merit, 182

Bernabei, Lynne

executive director's deposition regarding contract, 174

and the FMIS audit, 28-31

and Hook's beating, 214

and the investigation of Burick's death, 301

and Montaño's assignment, 205

photo, 167

and the procurement fraud, 265-275, 290-297

representing Walp and Doran, 249-250

and retaliation claims, 278-280, 315-316

and the retribution against Hook and Montaño, 257-262

beryllium disease, 95

best qualified doctrine, 149, 151

Bingaman, Jeff, 45, 47, 62-63, 345

Bodman, Samuel, 242

Bohnhoff, 29, 268-272

Brittin, Katherine, 175-178, 267, 286-288, 308

Brown, Vern, 261-262

Browne, John, 1, 163, 178, 266, 274, 281

Burick, Richard "Dick," 166, 267-268, 270-273, 292-298, 301-312, 315-317, 331

Burnaham, David, 136

Busboom, Stanley, 178-180, 267

Bussolini, Peter, 253, 283-297, 305-315. *See also* procurement fraud

BWXT (Babcock & Wilcox Technology), 240-242

C

California Higher Education Employer-Employee Relations Act (HEERA), 82-83

California legislature, 81-83

California-New Mexico legislative forum, 80-83

cancer, 13-14, 95, 121, 123-124, 310, 324, 329

Carruthers, Garrey, 207

Catron, Thomas, 338

CCNS (Concerned Citizens for Nuclear Safety), 231-232

Centers for Disease Control and Prevention (CDC), 122-123

Cerro Grande fire, 344

Chandler, Chris, 117, 260-262

Checkpoint Surveys, 282

China, secrets allegedly divulged to, 67-77, 86, 91-92

chronic pain, 95

Citizens for LANL Employee Rights (CLER)

congressional delegation meeting, 61-65, 162

DOE meeting, 63-65

establishment of, 1-2, 39-43, 53-54

gaining public support, 57-60

Citizens United decision, 335-336

Clark, Cathy and Bob, 69-70, 72-73

classified data handling, 33-35,
67-77, 86, 91-92, 119, 285-286

Clean Air Act compliance, 125,
137, 139, 231-233

CLER. *See* Citizens for LANL
Employee Rights (CLER)

Clinton, William Jefferson, 59-60,
93

Cochiti Lake, 95

collective bargaining rights, 82

Committee on Energy and Commerce, 153-159

competitive bidding for LANL
management, 233-236

Concerned Citizens for Nuclear
Safety (CCNS), 231-232

conflicts of interest, 158, 201, 243

Connaughton, Theresa, 61

contamination. *See* environmental contamination

contract between UC and DOE,
63, 113, 119, 171-175, 233-236,
307

contracts and procurement proposals. *See* vendor contracts

cover-ups. *See specific issues and
events*

cubicle detention, 187-190

Curtis, Charles, 63-64

D

Darling, Bruce, 86-87, 180-181,
234, 247-248, 265-268, 271-273

Davis, Gray, 82

death threats, 135, 137

defense contracts, 203

DeGrasse, Robert, 49, 61

Denver Steel, 5

Department of Energy (DOE).
See also Office of the Inspector
General (OIG)

allowed exceptions to FAR, 35-36

compliance enforcement, 222-230

contract with UC. *See* contract
between UC and DOE

downsizing mandate, 45-52

and the homesteaders, 343-345

and human radiation experiments, 132-133

and nuclear waste, 327-328

and the procurement fraud investigation, 225-230, 285-289

and radiation leaks, 323

and Topper Man, 25-26

and wasteful spending, 238-239

Department of Labor (DOL), 55,
124. *See also* Office of Federal
Contract Compliance Programs
(OFCCP)

Dickson, Frank, 244, 247-255,
266

discrimination, 17-19, 39-43,
54-56, 244-245, 332, 337-346

discriminatory employment practices, 17-19, 39-43. *See also* layoffs in 1995

diseases. *See* medical ailments

DOE. *See* Department of Energy
(DOE)

DOL. *See* Department of Labor
(DOL)

Domenici, Pete

and air emissions, 125

and the Clean Air Act case, 231-233

and compensation for the homesteaders, 345

endorsed Wilson for Senator, 333

expressed regret for lab's defiance of accountability, 197

and financial control at LANL, 100

and funding at LANL, 45, 47-51

and Judge Herrera's appointment, 250

LANL Foundation start-up funds, 88

and the layoffs, 62-64

photos, 161, 164

and Salgado, 281

and UC's relationship with LANL, 235-236

Doran, Steve

firing of, 153-159, 176-181, 244, 247-255

photos, 164, 167

as private investigator of Burick's death, 275, 301-306, 311-312, 316-317

procurement fraud investigation, 145-147, 219, 283-297, 308-310

settlement with UC, 211

DP West site, 126-127

Ducheny, Denise, 82

Dynes, Robert "Bob," 107-108, 202

E

Eisenhower, Dwight D., 237, 336

Employee Advisory Council (EAC), 239

employee organization. See Citizens for LANL Employee Rights (CLER)

employee surveys, 282

Energy Department. See Department of Energy (DOE)

Enron, 144, 209-211, 253

environmental contamination, 14-15, 95, 121-128, 137-140, 231-233, 323, 326-330

equal pay, 115-118

Erickson, Ralph, 288-289

Eshoo, Anna G., 157

espionage, 67-77, 86, 91-92

Executive Director of LANL

and Burick's death, 307

connection with the DOE, 241, 244, 278-281

employee abuse allegations, 279-281

and the firing of Doran and Walp, 266

and Hook's and Montaño's reassignments, 170-174, 205, 207, 262

and the internal controls assessment, 186-189, 225-228, 286-288, 290-292

F

FBI. See Federal Bureau of Investigation (FBI)

Federal Acquisition Regulations (FAR), 35-36, 88-90, 186

Federal Bureau of Investigation (FBI)

and the beating of Tommy Hook, 217-218

and the investigation of Burick's death, 303, 316-317

and LANL investigations, 298

plant raid, 127-128

procurement fraud investigation, 145-146, 247-255, 284, 312-313

and Wen Ho Lee, 72-75

Federal Equal Pay Act, 116-118

Feinstein, Dianne, 111-112

financial control. *See* audits and internal control

Financial Management Information System (FMIS) audit, 28-31, 99-100

fraud. *See* procurement fraud

Friedman, Gregory, 285-286

Frost, Hal, 59

Full Body Burden (Iverson), 326-330

G

gag orders, 175-184, 236

Gallagher, Bob, 206-207

Garcia, Larkin, 59

General Accounting Office (GAO), 172-173, 242

Gibbons, Larry, 59

Gomez, Donaciano, 339, 342

Gomez, Elfego, 345

Gomez, Marcos, 342

Gomez, Peter, 345

Gonzales, Kenneth J., 316, 331-332

Granich, Tom, 61

Greenwood, James C., 153

Groves, Leslie, 160

Guillen, Reynal, 90

Gustafson, John, 57-58, 226

Gutierrez, Joe, 125, 137-138, 231-233, 292-294

Gwilliam, Gary, 332

H

Hales, Peter Bacon , 339

Hall, Jim, 51-52

Hall, Lee Scott, 298-299

harassment of whistleblowers, 132, 138

hazardous waste. *See* environmental contamination

health risks, 323-330. *See also* medical ailments; safety concerns

Hecker, Siegfried "Sig," 19-20, 48-49, 79, 133, 161, 236

HEERA (California Higher Education Employer-Employee Relations Act), 82-83

Herrera, Judith, 250, 277

high school mascot. *See* Los Alamos High School mascot

Hirahara, Jim, 257-258, 278-281

Hispanics, 54-56, 87, 91

homesteaders, 338-346

homicide, possible. *See* Burick,

Richard "Dick"

Hook, Susie, 212-214, 217, 220

Hook, Tommy

beaten, 165, 212-223

going public with information, 211-212

and internal auditing, 149-152, 177-178

and internal controls assessment, 186-187, 225-230, 287

and litigation, 190

reassignment of, 169-171, 261-262

stroke, 150-151, 190, 208, 222

human radiation experiments, 132-133

hunting operation, 292-297, 311-312

I

IEO (Internal Evaluation Office), 149-152, 306-309

Iglesias, David, 50

illnesses. See medical ailments

Implosion at Los Alamos (Walp), 248, 251-252, 313

internal complaint resolution process, 193-195

internal controls of business operations. See audits and internal control

Internal Evaluation Office (IEO), 149-152, 306-309

isolation, 187-190

Iverson, Kristen, 326

J

Jennings, John, 146, 253-255

Johnson, Ken, 235

Johnston, Jay, 206

Joint California/New Mexico Legislative Committee on LANL Oversight, 106-108, 112-113

just in time (JIT) acquisitions, 185

K

Kerr-McGee, 134-136

Koska, Lea, 95

Kuckuck, Bob, 239

L

Labor Department. See Department of Labor (DOL)

labor protection laws, 81-83

LAHDRA (Los Alamos Historical Document Retrieval and Assessment) Project, 126-127

land grants, 338, 344-345

LANL. See Los Alamos National Lab (LANL)

LANS (Los Alamos National Security LLC), 159, 240-245

Lawrence, Ernest O., 93, 199

Lawrence Livermore National Laboratory (LLNL), 110-112, 244-245, 298-299, 332-333

layoffs in 1995

effects of, 79-80

and extension of insurance benefits, 49-50

and funding, 46-47

implementation of, 48-52, 54-59

injunction, 51-52

intimidation during, 54

investigation by DOL, 55

investigation by OFCCP, 151

photo of those targeted, 161

planning and implementation of, 40-43

settlement, 1-2, 83

Lee, Alberta, 90-91

Lee, Wen Ho, 67-77, 86, 91-92, 163

Leyba, Jerry, 59

limited liability (LLC) status, 242-243

Lincoln, Abraham, 335

LLNL. *See* Lawrence Livermore National Laboratory (LLNL)

local vendor agreements, 185

Lockheed Martin Corporation, 242

Longmire, Veronica, 116-118

Los Alamos High School mascot, 21-26

Los Alamos Historical Document Retrieval and Assessment (LAH-DRA) Project, 126-127

Los Alamos National Lab (LANL). *See also* Manhattan Project

employment practices, 17-20

exempt from labor protection laws, 81-83

exempt from usual vendor rules in the FAR, 35-36

expressed values *vs.* real values, 281-282

financial control problems, 99-104

interference with investigations, 39-40, 55-56, 145-148, 156-159, 184, 283-299

and the internal controls assessment, 149-152, 306-309

intimidation, 54, 69

as plutonium warhead production site, 93-96

political influence, 43, 101, 139, 141, 156-157, 241, 313

protest limits, 58-59

security system, 334

Los Alamos National Lab Foundation, 87-90

Los Alamos National Security LLC (LANS), 159, 240-245

loyalty pledges, 152, 176, 180-183, 228

Lujan, Ben, 124

Lujan, Eddie, 123-124

lung cancer, 124

M

Madoff, Bernie, 144-145

Maestas, Alex, 95

Maestas, Eloy, 59

Mahar, Marlayne, 138

management fee, 109, 228-230, 240, 242

Manhattan Project, 7-8, 160, 237, 339-345, 339-346

Markey, Edward, 251

Martinez, Eric, 254-255

Martinez, Lyda, 61

Material Unaccounted For (MUF), 9-10

McDonald, Jaret, 137, 145

McLeod, Frances, 124

McNeal, Rhonda, 133

Mead, Margaret, 54

Mechels, Chris, 70, 82

medical ailments, 13-14, 95, 121-124, 310, 324, 329

Medical Investigator report, 303-308

mercury poisoning, 95

Mexican-American War, 337-338

Mike, 4-11, 207-208

military expenditures, 46, 129, 202-203

military-industrial complex. *See* Department of Energy (DOE); Los Alamos National Lab (LANL); University of California

minority workers. *See* discrimination

Montaño, Charles "Chuck"

anxiety attack, 207-208

and the classified data handling audit, 33-35

and college roommate, 4-8, 10-11

cubicle isolation, 187-190, 258, 261-262

family background, 2-3

and the financial control problems at LANL, 35-36, 99-104, 150-152, 170-171, 186-187, 225-230

going public, 209-211, 217-220

honored by community, 105-106

MBA program lobbying, 206-207

NMHU temporary position, 97-99

photos, 162-163, 166-167

political influence, 56-57

promotions rejected, 18-19

recruiting for LANL, 205-206

retaliation against, 27-31, 99, 140-141, 277-282, 315-316

Montaño, Elaine, 85, 121, 212-214

Montoya, Jose Elfego, 340

Montoya, José Patricio, 341

Montoya, Maria Ernestina, 341

Montoya, Tibursia, 340

Mortandad Canyon, 127

MUF (Material Unaccounted For), 9-10

multiple myeloma, 123

Munson "Whitey," 8-10, 13-14

N

Nanos, Pete, 106, 108, 112-113, 118-119, 164, 233, 236, 281

Narang, Deesh, 191-197

National Defense Authorization Act, 45-52

National Ignition Facility (NIF), 110-112, 245

The National Labs: Science in an American System, 1947-1974 (Westwick), 199-200

Native Americans, 337-346. *See also* discrimination; stereotyping

Nevada Test Site, 333-334

New Mexico, history, 337-346

New Mexico Highlands University (NMHU), 97-99

New Mexico Human Rights Act, 116-118

New Mexico State University (NMSU), 206-207

NIF (National Ignition Facility), 110-112, 245

Northrup Grumman Corporation, 242

nuclear material. *See* Special Nuclear Material (SNM) Safeguards Group

nuclear waste, 232, 319-330. *See also* environmental contamination

O

Oak Ridge National Laboratory, 333-334

oath of allegiance, 183. *See also* loyalty pledges

Office of Federal Contract Compliance Programs (OFCCP), 17-19, 39-40, 64, 151

Office of Medical Investigator (OMI). *See* Medical Investigator report

Office of the Inspector General (OIG), 88, 99, 172-176, 227-230, 242, 250, 253, 277, 285-287, 333

Olberman, Keith, 216-220

O'Leary, Hazel, 61, 63, 132-133, 138

OMI (Office of Medical Investigator). *See* Medical Investigator report

Oppenheimer, Carol, 51

Oppenheimer, Robert, 160

organization of employees. *See* Citizens for LANL Employee Rights (CLER)

Orion Technical Resources LLC, 158-159

Ortiz, Darlene, 95

Ortiz, Robert "Bob," 294-297

overhead rate, 88-90, 103, 150

P

Pajarito Plateau, 14-15, 160, 338-346

pancreatitis, 95

Parker, James, 74, 92

Parras, Bill, 59

patents, 109, 240

pay equity, 115-118

P-cards, 185

Peña, Federico, 59

plutonium contamination, 95, 122-128, 320-322

plutonium warhead production, 94-96, 128

Podergois, John, 303

POGO (Project on Government Oversight), 134, 209-210, 287

Polanco, Richard, 80

politics, 39-40, 45-52, 65-71, 110, 145, 194, 333-336, 343-347. *See also specific topics and names* pollution. *See* environmental contamination

prime contract. *See* contract between UC and DOE

procurement fraud. *See also* Doran, Steve; Walp, Glenn

assessments never given to DOE, 225-230

depositions, 265-275, 290-297

DOE and the investigation, 225-230, 285-289

FAR violation, 186

FBI investigation, 145-148, 247-255, 284, 312-313

and the internal controls assessment, 170-174, 185-187, 209-211, 229-230

merchandise acquired through procurement process, 284

missing equipment, 285-286

retaliation, 278-282

Project on Government Oversight (POGO), 134, 209-210, 287

Project Y, 340, 346. *See also* Manhattan Project

Przybylek, Tyler, 241

Public Affairs Office, 35-36

public's right to know, 242-243

R

radiation experiments, 132-133

radiation releases, 122-127, 323

radioactive waste. *See* environmental contamination

Rankin, Adam, 75, 112, 177-181, 222, 254, 286-288, 308

Reagan, Ronald, 93

retaliation. *See specific issues and names*

Richardson, Bill, 61-63, 70-72, 75-77, 162, 239, 293, 343

Robinson, Paul, 73

Rocky Flats, 94, 127-128, 184, 319-322, 327-330

Rodas, Harry, 158-159

Rodriguez, Ronald, 182

Rollins, Gayle, 251-252

Rothstein, Robert "Bob," 214

Rove, Karl, 50

royalties, 109, 235, 240

Roybal, Arleen, 254-255

Rudman, Warren, 238

Ruminer, John, 295-296

Ryman, Lowell Edward, 123

S

safety concerns, 124-127, 133, 137, 319-330, 334. *See also* environmental contamination

salary disparity, 115-118

Salgado, Joseph "Joe," 98-99, 244, 247-249, 266, 274, 277, 281

Sandia national labs, 333-334

Santa Fe, 128

Santa Fe Ring, 338

SDI (Strategic Defense Initiative), 93-94

secret data on missing computer disks, 119

security concerns, 33-35, 67-77, 86, 91-92, 119, 285-286, 334

Silkwood, Karen, 134-136

Silverman, Mark, 327

Simon, Morty, 51

Snodgrass, Roger, 229

soil-sampling, 122

Spanish heritage, 337-346

Special Nuclear Material (SNM) Safeguards Group, 9-10, 14-15, 323

Stamm, Michael, 303

status, importance of, 5-6

Steele, Christopher, 133

stereotyping, 5-6, 10-11, 85-87, 91

Stevens, Rose, 59

Stewart, James, 137, 145

stockpile stewardship program, 46-47, 94, 110, 245

Stockton, Pete, 134, 136, 287

stolen merchandise cache, 145-148, 284-287, 293, 297, 309-313

Stone, Jim, 184

Strategic Defense Initiative (SDI), 93-94

suicide, 10-11, 137. *See also* Burick, Richard "Dick"

Supreme Court, 335-336

T

television exposé, 209-211

Teller, Edward, 93

thyroid cancer, 121

Topper Man, 21-23, 25-26, 167

transaction testing, 171

tritium release, 137, 232

Trujillo, Manny, 107-108, 112

Tucker, Gene, 178-179

U

UCOP (University of California Office of the President), 33, 148-152, 257, 267

Udall, Stuart, 343

Udall, Tom, 343

unassigned workers, 187-190, 196-197

University of California

competitive bidding for LANL management, 233-236

contract with DOE. *See* contract between UC and DOE

and the Hook and Doran firings, 178, 257-263

LANL oversight, 80-83, 106-108, 108-109, 112-113, 234-235

and the layoff dispute, 49, 83

management award fee, 109, 228-230, 235, 240, 242

patents, 109, 240

political influence, 109-110, 202

and the procurement fraud investigation, 290-292

protected from financial penalties, 139

relationship with LANL, 199-203

royalties received, 109, 235, 240

and suspicious deaths, 298-299

University of California Office of the President (UCOP), 33, 148-152, 257, 267

University Professional and Technical Employee (UPTE) Local 1663, 107

V

Van Ness, Robert (Bob), 28-31, 99-100, 267-275, 281

Van Riper, Ken, 59

VanBuskirk, Dick, 95

Velarde, Archie, 59

vendor contracts, 35-36, 149-152, 185. *See also* procurement fraud

Villarreal, Jake, 41

W

Wallace, 267

Walp, Glenn

firing authorized by Salgado, 244

firing of, 153-159, 176-181, 247-255

photos, 164, 166-167

procurement fraud investigation, 145-147, 219, 283-297, 308-310, 312-313, 316-317

and retaliation, 136-137

settlement with UC, 211

as a whistleblower, 134

Warwick, Dora, 26

Washington, Dennis, 241

Washington Group, 240-242

Waste Isolation Pilot Plant (WIPP), 322-326, 330

water contamination, 139-140. *See also* environmental contamination

Watkins, James D., 122

Welch Study, 115-116, 259

Westwick, Peter, 199-200

Wetherell, Barbara, 49

whistleblowers. *See specific topics and names*

white power, 21-26. *See also* discrimination

White Rock, 3-4, 14-15

Williams, Dave, 303

Williams, Dewayne, 297-298

Wilson, Heather, 165, 333-334

WIPP (Waste Isolation Pilot Plant), 322-326, 330

witness tampering, 263

women, 54-56, 86, 115-118, 244-245

workforce restructuring initiative, 48, 61

workpapers for procurement assessment, 229-230